Praise for *Write to Influence!*

I am humbled by the multiple awards and accolades this book and my workshops receive from wide-ranging audiences: professional reviewers; corporations; academic staff *and* students; the military; and, of course, individuals. What follows is a sample that propels me ever forward.

Winner of 11 national-level awards:

- 2022 Goody Business Book Awards – Winner: Marketing – Communications and PR
- 2022 Goody Business Book Awards – Winner: Marketing/ Sales – General
- 2022 Goody Business Book Awards – Finalist: Business – Career Success
- 2020 eLit Book Awards – Gold Medal: Education/Academic/ Teaching
- 2020 Best Book Award – Finalist: Business: Communications/ Public Relations
- 2020 Best Book Award – Finalist: Business: Marketing & Advertising
- 2020 Reader's Favorite Award – Honorable Mention: Marketing
- 2018 eLit Book Awards – Bronze Medal: Business/Careers/Sales
- 2017 Next Generation Indie Book Awards – Finalist: Careers
- 2017 Best Book Award – Finalist: Careers
- 2017 Reader's Favorite Award – Honorable Mention: Occupation

Testimonials

"By developing your *'Write to Influence!'* training, **you succeeded in improving the writing of many supervisors, which led to increased professional advancement opportunities for countless numbers of service members.**"

—Lt Gen Dana T. Atkins, USAF (Ret), President and CEO, Military Officers of America Association (MOAA)

"Write to Influence! **is sorely needed in this competitive world;
it opens doors to opportunity!"**

—Alain Chetrit, YPO Gold (Young Presidents' Organization)
Former International Chairman

"Write to Influence! **is a gem!** Anyone interested in powerful, super-
charged writing will appreciate this **clear discussion of how to produce
attention-grabbing pieces** ... **where standout writing means the
difference between success and failure."**

—D. Donovan, Senior Reviewer,
Midwest Book Review

"**This helped me pass my college classes!** *Write to Influence!* **is an
amazing source if you're looking to improve your writing to earn
higher grades. I like this MUCH better than a standard textbook. 10/10
recommend!"**

—Emily, Amazon Reviewer

"**FTI Consulting partnered with Carla for good reason.** Here's what our
employees say:

- **Carla's an exceptional writer and a great presenter!**

- **Phenomenal 2-day class!** Wish I had this sooner!

- **Informative, educational, awesome. Pace and teaching
  methods were perfect!**

- **Powerful, interactive workshop;** definitely enhanced my
  writing skills. Highly related to daily work.

- **Her workshop and book are invaluable—Spot on!"**

—Beth Krause, Director, Learning Solutions,
FTI Consulting

Praise for Write to Influence!

"This book is fantastic! It should be the required textbook for all incoming college freshman, high school students, and military officers, and used as a refresher at most companies. I don't know of anyone who would not benefit from this book!"

—Dan Cornford,
NetGalley Reviewer

"I recommend this book enthusiastically! It teaches students and adults how to edit their writing to achieve purposes with clarity, directness, and grace. I am a writing teacher with 30+ years of experience teaching middle and high schools."

—H. Lyman, PhD

"If effective writing is your goal, put this book in your tool kit!"

—Dr. Lani Kass, Senior Vice President
Corporate Strategic Advisor, CACI

"*Write to Influence!* is a book to study diligently and reread regularly. Carla makes it easy to acquire the skills to write accurate, clear, concise and focused copy that drives your readers to deliver your most wanted response ... every single time."

—Lorraine Cobcroft, *Readers' Favorite Book Reviews and Award Contest*

"*Write to Influence!* should be in every professional's library."

—Baba Zipkin, Former Senior Counsel, IBM

"In a 2-hour workshop, **Carla added thousands of dollars to the bottom-line of organizations in Loudoun County**. Using her techniques, the public and private sector leaders who participated can write to win."

—Leadership Loudoun

"Not only is Bass charming and entertaining, **the tips and writing strategies she provides are brilliant.** Today, more than ever, standout writing means the difference between success and failure. **Succeed with** *Write to Influence!*"

—Susan McCorkindale, Editor,
SHE! magazine

"Carla's book and workshops are invaluable for students, faculty, and staff (military and civilian). She ably and passionately equips them to succeed in any environment, academic or operational, by learning to *Write to Influence!"*

—Dr. William C. Spracher, Colonel, U.S. Army, (Ret),
Contracted Professor and Director of the Writing Center,
National Intelligence University

"Write to Influence! **will rejuvenate the lost art of clear, concise, professional writing.** Moreover, corporate CEOs will rejoice at no longer being encumbered by reports difficult to read and frustrating to unravel!"

—Judith A. Sprieser, Non-Executive Director Allstate Corp.,
InterContinental Exchange Inc., and Reckitt Benckiser PLC

"Write to Influence! **is an essential guide for anyone seeking to inform or influence others with the written word."**

—Mark Amtower, Managing Partner, Amtower & Company

"Write to Influence! **will be my go-to-guide for many years to come. It is now a must-read for all of my employees."**

—Rick Mix, President and CEO, Cleared Solutions Inc.

Contents

Praise for *Write to Influence!* iii

Acknowledgments ix

New to This Edition xi

The Journey Begins 1

Part 1: Strategies to Influence **5**

1. Solid Framework: Critical for a Home . . . and Writing 7

2. Know Your Audience: Psychology of the Catch 11

3. Set the Hook.. 15

4. Make the Case... 23

5. Clinch the Deal 31

Part 2: Word Sculpting Tools **41**

6. Useless Words: Find, Chisel, Discard 43

7. Shorter Is Better: Don't Hog Space................................. 51

8. Redundancy: Once Will Suffice 61

9. Lead with the Basics: Horse before the Cart 71

10. Verbs Are Your Friends: Rely on Them 81

11. Avoid Gibberish: It's Confusing 89

12. Tethers: In Sentences and Otherwise............................ 107

13. Be Clear: Who-Does-What-to-Whom?........................... 117

14. Keep the Focus: Shut the Gates 125

15. Final Steps: Revise, Edit, and Proofread 135

Part 3: *Write to Influence!* Applied Daily **147**

16. The College Application: Essays That Open Doors 149

17. Your Resume: Stand Out from the Crowd 153

My parents provided the foundation for my every success. When I was commissioned, my father, Colonel Ralph A. Bass, offered this novice second lieutenant three pieces of advice: 1) Focus on the mission (i.e., don't participate in office drama or politics); 2) Keep your sense of humor (spoken with a twinkle in his eyes); and 3) Always, always … take care of your people. My mother was an author, artist, newspaper columnist, radio talk show host, couturier dress designer, and military wife. Flair and creativity—she had them! Parents—none better.

Profound thanks yet again to Robert D. Warrington—himself, an author—for his indispensable assistance and ever-valued "second set of eyes" with the manuscripts of both editions.

My sister, Claudia, and children (young adults but always one's children)—Sarah and Eric—are enthusiastic cheerleaders.

Finally, I couldn't have written this book without the support of my husband, Lynn Reeves, whose encouragement in this—and all my other endeavors—remains consistently unflagging.

New to This Edition

Second edition, already?!? This book is chock-full of **new material (items bolded below),** developed as a result of the many workshops I've taught and articles I've composed. "Can you teach a workshop on essays for college applications? On writing grants? How about helping teenagers write their first resumes and prepare for job interviews? Submitting input for one's own performance appraisal—any hints? Can you teach a 2-day workshop for corporate professionals?" These are only a few of the queries I received. My response to each was immediate and definitive: "Certainly!"

In my workshops, I teach writing as a two-step process. First, strategize your message to make your case. Then, apply *Word Sculpting Tools* to hone your draft so it is clear, concise, and compelling. If I present material in that sequence, the book should be similarly organized. Well, it is now!

Part 1 offers "Strategies to Influence" and consists of *five* chapters:

1. **"Solid Framework: Critical for a Home . . . and Writing"** delineates steps to frame any influential communication.

2. **"Know Your Audience: Psychology of the Catch"** explains how to accomplish that first and most critical step in writing.

3. "Set the Hook" is examined from the perspective of various products and addresses the importance of titles and opening sentences.

4. "Make the Case" provides techniques to help an author assemble substantiating data that will make a product "pop": gathering information, digging for details, employing statistics, putting the story in context, and identifying information to exclude.

5. "Clinch the Deal" addresses writing proportionally (allocating appropriate time and space); framing the discussion; showcasing the leading fact; the importance of objectivity;

sequencing the message; and highlighting the conclusion, proposal, decision, outcome, etc.

Part 2 presents ten *Word Sculpting Tools,* each addressed in its own chapter and reinforced by ten examples and corresponding exercises. **I expanded the last tool, adding the critical steps of revision and editing; these steps precede proofreading.**

- Chapter 6—Useless Words: Find, Chisel, Discard
- Chapter 7—Shorter Is Better: Don't Hog Space
- Chapter 8—Redundancy: Once Will Suffice
- Chapter 9—Lead with the Basics: Horse before the Cart
- Chapter 10—Verbs Are Your Friends: Rely on Them
- Chapter 11—Avoid Gibberish: It's Confusing
- Chapter 12—Tethers: In Sentences and Otherwise
- Chapter 13—Be Clear: Who-Does-What-to-Whom?
- Chapter 14—Keep the Focus: Shut the Gates
- Chapter 15—Final Steps: **Revise, Edit,** and Proofread

Part 3 is *"Write to Influence!* Applied Daily." See how the writing strategies and tools from Parts 1 and 2 are applied to resumes, email, and presentations. **New here are three chapters: the essay for college applications, grant submissions, and the elevator speech**. Please note, the chapter on grants is not intended as a full-fledged tutorial on that topic; it *does* offer valuable insights about strategies and *Word Sculpting Tools* to compose potent submissions.

Part 4 provides 100 additional exercises and answers. "Exercises: Test Your Skills" includes a "Graduation Exercise" with a solution. Answers for this exercise and others found in this book are not the only correct responses. They serve as a foil for the teaching points at hand.

Please note: Many exercises and examples are based on items in resumes. At first glance, these appear to be sentence fragments (sentences lacking a subject or verb), generally a grammatical foul.

However, resume bullets have the implied subject, *I*. Therefore, they are correct without the subject, given the context.

Part 5 consists of appendices. You'll find new material here, too. **Appendix B, "The Dirty Dozen: Most Common Errors in Professional Writing,"** is expanded in number and content from its predecessor in the first edition. **Appendix C** introduces you to my **"Baker's Dozen"** collection, products that provide 13 tips each on writing resumes, input for your own appraisal, reports, email, and grant submissions.

A. Answers to the Chapters 6–15 exercises

B. **The Dirty Dozen: Most Common Errors in Professional Writing**

C. **Baker's Dozen Collection**

D. Grammar highlights address proper use of commas, semicolons, and capitalization

E. Challenges in editing someone else's work

F. A single-page summary, *"Write to Influence!* in a Nutshell"

G. A list of references

I wrote *Write to Influence!* for four reasons:

First—Powerful writing changes lives. Why? It correlates directly to success, personal and professional, by opening doors to opportunity that would otherwise remain closed. People, businesses, and organizations often fail, hindered by their inability to positively influence the audience.

Second—Powerful writing is the lifeblood of effective operations for private businesses, corporations, nongovernmental organizations (NGOs), government agencies, and especially for the military. It is fundamental to justify additional resources, defend existing budgets, build public support for an issue, attract talented job applicants, publicize an upcoming conference, and sell products and services. In each case, a well-crafted, persuasive message often tips the scale in your favor.

The Journey Begins

I begin by acknowledging the varying writing styles and cognitive frameworks people use when composing. My own technique is the "gut dump." I write all thoughts without interruption, then revise, edit, and proofread. Others prefer to write and polish sequentially as they move from paragraph to paragraph. That is OK, too! No single writing style can claim to be "the best fit."

This book is not intended to destroy a writing style in order to save it. Rather, the strategies and *Word Sculpting Tools* I present can be incorporated into your own approach to improve the resulting product. Bottom line, don't stop what you are doing . . . improve it!

It's important to observe writing as subjective. I present examples and exercises in the format: **Before, After,** and **Analysis**. These are foils to demonstrate strategies and tools presented here. The revision for each (i.e., the **After**) is not necessarily the only way to improve upon the **Before** version.

Write to Influence! is based on five principles:

1. Each writer is constrained by two factors: time and space ... the reader's time (and patience) and physical space in which to convey the message. Make each word count and every second of the reader's time play to *your* advantage. I repeat this point throughout the book—like a persistent drum beat—because it is critical to influential writing.

2. Empathize with the audience. Make your product easy to read, understandable, and unambiguous, and tailor it to their needs.

3. Include detail to make your case. Ensure the product conveys the "so what."

4. Avoid jargon inappropriate to the audience. Don't presume the reader understands your terms, acronyms, or references, and don't burden the audience with extraneous information.

5. Revise, edit, and proofread. Each is a distinct step; each is necessary. Outstanding performance here is essential.

In addition to helping the individual who wants to get ahead, these writing skills are particularly relevant for those who:

- Rely on influential communication to grow business

- Employ a large staff, especially one geographically dispersed

- Deal with abstract ideas (e.g., analysis of social, economic, and political trends)

- Account to the public, to other institutions (e.g., Congress), and to history, and must explain and record their activities accordingly

- Face the possibility that an error caused by poor writing could be damaging either financially or to important national matters (Goldstein 1989)

Again, reflecting a sense of humor, I offer a new perspective on writing that might prove helpful. I quote Mary Poppins! "In every job that must be done, there is an element of fun. You find that fun and *SNAP*, the job's a game!" Writing is:

- **A scavenger hunt** – Apply *Word Sculpting Tools* to find and discard useless words, words that hog space, redundancies, etc.

- **Painting** – Add detail to infuse your message with contour, depth, and dimension that provide the reader a mental yardstick to better understand your message.

- **Photography** – Bring a fuzzy concept into focus by conveying a clear message.

- **Poker** – Examine the message from the reader's perspective and write to those needs. If competing for funds or proposing an alternative position, contrast yours with the competition. Present the benefits of *your* approach and explain how it is the better option (Hint: do so factually and professionally).

Genesis of *Write to Influence!* – Inspiration for this book occurred when, as a lieutenant colonel, I commanded a unit of 480 people. There, I witnessed the critical correlation between the influence of the written word and career progression—or lack thereof.

Many supervisors were ineffective writers, unable to convey the significance and impact of individuals' accomplishments in performance appraisals and award nominations. As a result, this unintentionally impeded the career progression of deserving and talented people. Why? They lost to the competition—whose packages *were* well written—for awards, early promotion, and other significant recognition.

That problem exists today in the military and civilian arenas. People, businesses, and organizations want and deserve to succeed, but fail. Why? Again, the inability to write effectively and make their case to the audience holds them back.

I resolved this problem for my Air Force unit by composing a handbook that—in today's vernacular—went viral, reaching Air Force units worldwide. Here is a testimonial from Charles Allen, who, as a young officer, served with me at that time:

> **"I learned how to "Write to Influence" when working for Lt Col Carla Bass in 1994**. She composed and disseminated a handbook on powerful writing to everyone in her squadron. The unit suddenly began to regularly sweep the All-Air Force Hawaii awards. Our awesome airmen hadn't suddenly become more talented or dedicated, **but our writing and how we presented their accomplishments improved dramatically. THAT made all the difference. All, thanks to Carla . . . her ability to write is legendary."**
>
> —Charles Allen, Lt Col, USAF (Ret)

I subsequently taught my writing techniques and strategies to thousands of Air Force members for the next fifteen years, not as an assigned duty, but as a voluntary labor of love. Response? Rave reviews and testimonials on how powerful writing actually changed lives.

Write to Influence! fills that same need for the contemporary audience. By employing strategies and tools in *Write to Influence!,* your writing will be focused, organized, dynamic, polished, and persuasive and will leave the reader wanting more! To achieve your goals, personal and professional, make *Write to Influence!* your tool of choice when persuasive writing is paramount.

Part 1

Strategies to Influence

Game's on! You might be required to:

- Compose letters to solicit business
- Market your product on a website
- Advertise to attract talented employees
- Write a grant submission
- Author a bid for a contract
- Compete a project for funds
- Give a business presentation

What do these have in common? To succeed, you must influence. How? Employ strategies presented in Part 1 to frame your message, understand your audience, assemble supporting information, and organize it into that captivating case to clinch the deal. Strategizing is the first of a two-step process in writing to influence. The second step, addressed in Part 2, is to hone your draft using *Word Sculpting Tools*.

These steps are synergistic; neither is singularly effective. Ask yourself, "How persuasive is a product that, while well-organized and substantive, consists of thirty lengthy, rambling, vague, and confusing sentences?" Conversely, "How effective are thirty individually sculpted sentences without strategies to deliver the right message to the right audience?"

Finally, remember that writing is constrained by two factors: time and space. The audience's **time** and attention are fleeting—sometimes measured in seconds. Physical **space** can also be limited. The author who best leverages time and space often wins.

That said, let's discuss strategies!

1. Solid Framework: Critical for a Home . . . and Writing

An annual report, contract bid, submission for a grant, academic paper, essentially any major communication . . . just like a home . . . requires a solid framework. To create that framework, begin with a sound outline, the counterpart to an architectural drawing. Use this tool to focus, structure, and strategize your message. It's the first step in leveraging readers' time to *your* advantage.

You're probably wondering, "Must I outline? Why can't I just *write*?" Consider this:

- A family taking an extended road trip navigates with a *roadmap* (digital or paper).
- A football coach preparing his team for the big game generates a *playbook*.
- A general leading forces into battle employs a *campaign strategy*.
- The astute writer uses an *outline*.

Here's a riddle to reinforce this point. What do these have in common: a marathon runner, mom or dad who manages the family's monthly budget, and a writer?

Answer: Each balances conflicting interests. The runner balances time and distance against available energy and stamina. The mom or dad prioritizes the family's needs against available funds. The author's writing is constrained by the reader's time and allocated space.

The outline equates to the runner's stopwatch or the family's budget. Using this valuable tool, the writer can:

- **Structure** and present a well-conceived message
- **Avoid** tangents that waste his or her time and dilute or confuse the message
- **Establish** the thesis, key points, and propositions
- **Answer** questions foundational to the message
- **Identify** contrary points, uncertainties, ambiguities, and other items that impact the argument
- **Size** the issue proportionately to space constraints

And, that's not all! Upon completion of the first draft, writers can use the outline to:

- **Confirm** the draft addresses all intended points
- **Identify** propositions that need to be amplified
- **Determine** if information *not* reflected in the outline supports the thesis
- **Find and purge** tangential information that slipped into the draft
- **Ensure** the opening and key points lead to and correlate with the conclusion

Following your outline, apply strategies in Part 1 to compose the initial draft. Just like the builder constructing a house, the writer should strive for the following:

Solid infrastructure – *Goals and objectives of the message are clearly identified, as is the audience, including its background and needs. Key assertions, arguments, and main points support the thesis. Counter arguments or other alternatives are thoroughly and equitably addressed.*

Quality building materials – *Information is logical, cogent, non-emotional, substantiated, balanced, and based on solid research. Persuade the reader by presenting fact, after fact, after fact—boom, boom, boom.*

Good floor plan – *Information flows smoothly. Topic sentences build upon each other and flow logically to advance the story. Sentences within each paragraph flow from and support the topic sentence. The conclusion circles back and ties neatly to the thesis.*

Well-proportioned rooms – *The author elaborates on each key element in detail sufficient to make the point; the discussion is neither too sketchy nor disproportionately excessive. The paper contains no information irrelevant to the thesis or purpose, regardless of how interesting the author finds it.*

Character – *A paper can—and should—have character. Lively expression capitalizes on the rich nuances of the English language and invigorates writing. Your message will convey with an engaging robustness, rhythm, and movement that captivates the reader. Antiseptic, depersonalized, bureaucratic blather robs your product of sparkle, making it flat, limp, shapeless, boring, and often impossible to understand.*

Congratulations! You now have an initial draft. Next, apply the 10 *Word Sculpting Tools*. Through this process, you make each word count and every second of the reader's time play to *your* advantage.

- Ch. 6–Useless Words: Find, Chisel, Discard
- Ch. 7–Shorter Is Better: Don't Hog Space
- Ch. 8–Redundancy: Once Will Suffice
- Ch. 9–Lead with the Basics: Horse before the Cart
- Ch. 10–Verbs Are Your Friends: Rely on Them
- Ch. 11–Avoid Gibberish: It's Confusing
- Ch. 12–Tethers: In Sentences and Otherwise
- Ch. 13–Be Clear: Who-Does-What-to-Whom?
- Ch. 14–Keep the Focus: Shut the Gates
- Ch. 15–Final Steps: Revise, Edit, and Proofread

By applying the strategies and *Word Sculpting Tools,* you will achieve a solidly constructed, intellectually well-grounded, and influential product.

2. Know Your Audience: Psychology of the Catch

The most fundamental step in powerful writing correlates directly to fishing. What!? Consider the psychology of the catch. Both the fisherman and the author must know the audience. The former must know the habits of that discerning, evasive fish such as where and when to find it, impact of weather on feeding patterns, and bait the fish finds most *alluring* (couldn't resist that pun).

Similarly, the author must know the audience. What is its familiarity with the subject—expert, novice, or somewhere in between? What do recipients need or expect from your message? What are their business values, goals, and objectives? Who are *their* customers? How do recipients define success in the context of their own mission? Are they working under a time constraint and, if so, what?

When applying for a grant, for example, the author should research the grantmaker's mission, vision, and objectives; similar projects it previously funded; partner organizations; and so on. Provide required information in the specified format and on time. Your goal is to deliver a product that is crisp, readily understood, easily applied, and tailored to reflect the grantmaker's needs.

With these insights, the fisherman and the author can develop and execute a strategy to reach the targeted audience. With every cast of the line and each communication, the fisherman and author engage in a battle of wits with the persnickety fish—or the elusive audience. Five tips presented below are central to the psychology of the catch:

1. **"Knock, Knock" . . . "Who's There?" – Wrong Response!** The challenge, as you well know, is that people are busy. Today, the reply to "Knock, knock" is often *not* "Who's there?" but, "What do you want!?!" Respect the audience's time. Make your case pithy. Imagine a cartoon man struggling uphill, burdened by large stones piled on his back. This represents a convoluted message, loaded with extraneous words that encumber the message and disinterest the reader.

2. **Focus on the Audience.** Write from the audience's perspective. Don't focus the communication on yourself or your product or service; concentrate, instead, on the audience. Whether competing for a grant or a contract, defending against budget cuts, applying for a job, submitting a college application, or marketing a product, highlight the advantages for the recipient. To do so, you must "know the audience."

3. **"You're Speaking My Language!"** Strive to elicit this reaction. How? Tailor your message to the audience using terms pertinent to the context. If pitching a business investment, use financially oriented words such as *market research, investment opportunity,* and *return on investment.* If addressing scientific, technical, or other specialized experts, job-related jargon is appropriate, even preferable. Complex

or abbreviated dialect conveys considerable information and streamlines the communication. Military linguists, for example, immediately understand *+3/-3 on the Chinese DLPT*. Elaboration or simplification in such circumstances is counterproductive. Alternatively, and equally detrimental, is presenting material in job-related jargon an audience cannot implicitly understand. We examine this latter situation in Chapter 11, *"Avoid Gibberish: It's Confusing."*

4. **Play the "Match Game."** Once you've researched the audience, pair your talents and resources to the missions, goals, values, objectives, and needs of the audience. Identify, elaborate on, and emphasize these areas. For example, when the interviewer states, "Tell me something about yourself," draw as many parallels as possible between your experiences, skills, training, and interests with what the company seeks. Projects competing for funds should correlate proffered capabilities to identified mission deficiencies. In short, you entice the fish—the audience—to bite on your hook.

5. **Place the Horse before the Cart.** This relates to *Word Sculpting Tool* #4, Chapter 9. Open with the most important part of the message. Don't waste the audience's time with extensive, lead-in, preparatory information. This is a common and unfortunate malady in contemporary, professional writing. Remember #1 above, KNOCK! KNOCK! . . . Get to the point, *then* elaborate with substantiating or explanatory information.

Question: When submitting for a grant, competing for a contract, being interviewed for a job, or composing the essay for a college application, are you the fisherman or the fish?

Answer: Played correctly, you are the *fisherman*. Why? You researched the audience and are employing the psychology of the catch!

3. Set the Hook

A curious fish cautiously examines the baited hook, deciding to bite . . . or not. Similarly, the reader approaches your product with an open mind—for a few seconds. You have a fleeting opportunity to hook the reader with your opening words.

Continuing the analogy, just as hooks are designed for specific fish, written products are crafted for particular audiences. After all, the opening line for a corporate report, a subordinate's annual appraisal, or a letter to Congress would not read the same as the opening line of a novel.

The hook for a corporate report or article is an effectively written opening line that flows seamlessly into the rest of the paragraph. Here are some examples:

- *The character of war is changing. Our adversaries have shifted their strategy to engage our nation asymmetrically, exploiting seams of our democracy, authorities, and even our social differences. They respond often in misattributed ways through blended operations occurring in supply chains and the cyber domain.* (Reprinted with permission from MITRE, *Deliver Uncompromised: A Strategy for Supply Chain Security and Resilience in Response to the Changing Character of War, Aug 2018*)

- *Is space exploration really desirable at a time when so much needs done on Earth? It is an often-asked and serious question that requires a serious answer.* (From *Why We Explore: First in a Series of Essays* by NASA's Chief Historian, Steven J. Dick

  https://www.nasa.gov/missions/solarsystem/Why_ We_01pt1.html)

The hook for an effective personnel appraisal or award nomination is also unique. You seize the reader's attention within the first few seconds. Here are some examples:

- *Never settling for the status quo, she led an effort that . . .*

- *Tireless efforts this past year resulted in the successful completion of . . .*

- *The top three of her many significant achievements this year are:*

- *Not only the best engineer on my staff of twenty, he is also the most gifted briefer I've ever encountered!*

The opening hook must be immediately reinforced by solid, potent facts that delineate the individual's accomplishments. Think of the boxer in a gym punching the bag: right, left, right, left— fact, impact, fact, impact—with no pauses, no diversions. When finished, the reader should be as breathless as the boxer following the workout and should definitely be impressed! By the way, don't forget the integrity test. The objective is to write forcefully about solid accomplishments, not to exaggerate mediocre ones.

- *Acting as team lead for ten days, she orchestrated the team's multiple tasks while keeping pace with her own workload.*

She effectively altered priorities and production schedules and delivered a quality product that met the deliverable deadline. (More detailed accomplishments could follow these entries as space allowed.)

- *Superiors characterize her writing skills as "gifted." She is often called in to pinch hit because, as one supervisor expressed, "Jane's the best writer on the staff!" She reached, wrote, and flawlessly presented six briefings on core topics to the CEO and his senior staff, clearly identifying issues and proposing ways ahead.*

- *A wealth of insight and initiative! Recently besting her own steep learning curve, she developed a primer to orient other new team members, highlighting the organization's structure, mission, operating procedures, products, and primary clients. She enhanced productivity by making this information immediately available and in a format tailored to new employees.*

Resumes also have hooks. While formats vary, the writer must still grab the reader's attention. To be effective, the composition must be tight and the message inducing. Here are examples of **weak** opening hooks (including original mistakes):

- *Job objective is to fully utilize my office and security management experience in a business-oriented environment.* (aka: "I want to work.")

- *Apply technical and leadership skills in a fast-paced professional environment, while continuing to develop a passion for state-of-the-art tools and technology.*

- *Has over six years experience (should be "six years' experience" or "six years of experience") supporting five federal agencies.* (This line opens the garden gate! The reader immediately wonders, "Why did you move so often, essentially one agency per year?")

- *Senior-level consultant providing leadership and management expertise in IT program and project management, policy and governance development, and OMB reporting across a wide spectrum of federal information sharing initiatives, controlled data access, information discovery, process re-engineering, quality assurance, contingency planning, systems integration, strategic planning, technology systems life-cycle management and coordinating the research, planning, dissemination, staffing, and collaboration of unified community efforts.*

Wow, that last example is quite a mouthful! Test its effectiveness and read it again at regular speed, not as though you are actually studying it. Now, without looking, I challenge you to recite three concrete facts.

Here are some examples of good, solid openings:

- *Twenty-three years of senior leadership and management experience in defense and international S&T projects. In-depth expertise in policy, planning, operations, and security at the following organizations: A, B, C, D, E, and F. Outstanding executive skills including interagency coordination, executive correspondence, decision making, staff management and team building.* (This was followed by six precise and significant examples of specific agency-level accomplishments.)

- *Extensive experience with strategy, communications, program analysis and budget forecasting. Liaised with senior leadership at four federal agencies regarding security management, strategic communications, process improvement methodologies, and portfolio management.*

- *Most recently a manager with Company X, Ms. Smith has more than twenty years of professional experience in various corporate industries and government agencies, including Agencies A, B, and C. She has experience writing policy, speeches, talking points, articles, and briefings for senior-level executives. She won the highly competitive APEX Award for Publication Excellence.*

The literary hook is completely different. It is teasing, almost daring the reader to continue. This technique is also appropriate for essays or themed pieces such as, "Explain what the 4th of July means to you in 500 words or less." Hook the reader in the opening line, then deliver your story, making every word count. Below are examples of great openings.

- *Stand in front of a bright window. Close your eyes! Squeeze them together. You see black! While still closed, relax them. You might see gray or red. Now open them wide and a world of color is before you.* (From *Quilting & Appliqué with Southwest Indian Designs* by Charlotte Christiansen Bass.)

- *It is February 20, 1991 and Colin Powell is irritated.* (From *Sacred Honor: Colon Powell, The Inside Account of His Life and Triumphs* by David Roth.)

- *It was a bright cold day in April, and the clocks were striking thirteen.* (From *1984* by George Orwell)

Perhaps the most important hook a young adult will compose is for the college application essay. So much rides on this solitary sentence. Why? This document could open the first significant door to opportunity. The opening line must simultaneously tantalize and intrigue, while hinting as to insights soon to be revealed about the author. Remember the mandate, "know your audience"? Well, this audience—the reviewer— wants to know about the applicant. Here are some great examples:

- I change my name each time I place an order at Starbucks.
- I have old hands.
- I almost didn't live through September 11, 2001.
- I had never seen anyone get so excited about mitochondria.

  (From https://www.cbsnews.com/news/10-great-opening-lines-from-stanford-admissions-essays/

For many analytical products and studies, a work's title functions as the hook to catch the reader's attention. From a substantive perspective, the title should identify a story's center of interest and precipitant development and should lie midway between subject and plot. A reader, by virtue of knowing only the title, should have a valid expectation of the message to follow. As you read these next examples, recall Goldilocks and her evaluation of the bears' porridge (too hot, too cold, ahhh—just right).

- **Bulgarian Economic Development.** This title is nebulous; it identifies a subject but reveals nothing about the story. The reader knows that the item addresses Bulgaria's economy but gains no insight as to the direction of the author's message. Without a better understanding of the content, the reader might emulate the elusive fish, sniff the hook, and swim to more lucrative waters. The title lost your audience.

- **Ballooning Imports and Stagnating Exports Make Bulgaria's Trade Deficit Soar.** This title is poor for the opposite reason. It is too extensive, outlining the plot of the story instead of offering only a promise of what's to come. The reader might presume to have grasped the message through the title without reading the article. The hook was too large; the fish swims away. Again, the title lost your audience.

- **Bulgaria's Trade Deficit Soars.** This is a good title. It conveys the article's center of interest (Bulgaria's trade deficit) and the precipitant development (soars). *Soars* is an especially descriptive verb, far richer in dimension than more neutral words like *increases* or *grows* that might have been used. Why? The latter words express an unremarkable trend, whereas *soars* conveys not only the trend but the additional sense of magnitude, speed over relative time, and a noteworthy event. Congratulations. Your title hooked the fish!

In these products, the opening sentence complements the title and draws the reader further into the author's journey. The opening sentence is appropriately called the "first impression sentence." A good opening sentence functions as the bellwether, signaling the direction a story will take and setting the stage with details that give texture to the story. Much is expected of this literary tool. A finely crafted opening sentence should do the following:

- Flow naturally from and build upon the title

- Solidify the reader's interest in the story

- Enlighten the reader regarding the author's chief purpose in writing the piece

- Indicate how the story will develop

- Accomplish these goals with rich, yet economical text

Consider the following three examples of an opening sentence. Each correlates to this title, "ABC Party Leaves Coalition: Latvian Government's Fate Uncertain."

- *The ABC Party on June 10 withdrew from the ruling coalition, raising the prospects of the Latvian Government's collapse.* This is a poor opening sentence because it reiterates information contained in the title and fails to indicate how the story will develop.

- *John Doe, Prime Minister and leader of DEF, on 10 June met in Riga with senior party officials to discuss courses of action in the wake of ABC's withdrawal from the coalition, which include holding elections to form a new government or attempting to reconstitute the coalition by seeking to find a moderate party—most likely QRS or XYZ— to replace ABC, but it is unclear if the leaders of those parties—Ben Millen and John Smith, respectively—would be willing to affiliate with the scandal-ridden DEF by joining the government.* What a mouthful! In addition to being diffusely worded, the sentence is overloaded with substantive and repetitive details. Apply the *Word Sculpting Tool,* avoid gibberish. Identifying the city in which DEF officials met and names of the leaders of QRS and XYZ and repeating that ABC has withdrawn from the coalition clutters the opening sentence beyond all effectiveness. That is not to say that these details are not important. However, they might be placed later in the piece as context and background for the primary message.

- *Prime Minister Doe of DEF will likely reach out to moderate opposition parties of QRS and XYZ to keep the government afloat, but they might decline to affiliate with his scandal-ridden party, leaving Doe virtually no choice but to call new elections.* This opening sentence has substantive punch and builds effectively on the title, elucidating the chief purpose of the article: assessing efforts to reconstitute the coalition and outcomes associated with those efforts. It also provides markers for the story's development: 1) Examining the most likely course of action the party remaining in the coalition (DEF) will take to remain in power (reach out to the opposition); 2) Factors affecting DEF's situation as it seeks to save the coalition (party is scandal-ridden); 3) Perspectives of parties on joining the coalition (concerns over affiliating with the DEF); and 4) Consequences if DEF is unable to reconstitute the coalition (new elections a virtual certainty).

4. Make the Case

What do these three scenarios have in common? First, you stand before the glowering judge, who demands to know, "What did you do?!" Second, your stressed boss peers at you from behind an imposing desk and tersely exclaims, "I'm busy! What do you want?" Third, you stand rigidly before your father's withering interrogation, "How exactly did you wreck my car?" In each instance, you better have a solid, logical, fact-based response. This chapter provides five strategies to do just that.

1. Gather information. This is the critical first strategy in making your case to a discerning and demanding audience. Like the fairy tale figure, Rumpelstiltskin, one must have straw from which to spin gold. Similarly, you must have hard-hitting facts to make your case. To preclude cuts in your organization's staff or budget, or to justify increases, you must demonstrate the operational value with concrete, indisputable, and quantifiable facts. If applying for a college scholarship or an internship, showcase your scholastic and community-related activities—especially leadership roles—throughout high school. How do you accomplish this? In a word, research.

Let Rudyard Kipling help. His poem, "I Keep Six Honest Serving Men," gained *who, what, where, when, why*, and *how* worldwide recognition. This technique to elicit detail has been taught to children for generations.

> I keep six honest serving-men
> (They taught me all I knew);
> Their names are What and Why and When
> And How and Where and Who.
>
> (From "The Elephant's Child"
> in Rudyard Kipling's *Just So Stories*)

Collectively, these can define a problem, whom it affects, the impacts, and the path to a solution. Organizations leverage Kipling's "serving men" in the fields of journalism, science, engineering, education, psychotherapy, and more. Professionals use the "serving men" to direct research, investigate crimes, develop business proposals, and a host of other applications. Use the "serving men" to document events as they occur and keep notes on your personal accomplishments.

Preserve letters of appreciation and laudatory quotes from instructors, supervisors, senior executives, government clients (for contractors), or other figures of authority. Maintain these, along with the date and originator's official title. Establish an email file to retain accolades. If your organization uses Weekly Activity Reports, contribute regularly with precise, detailed submissions. Retain this information as a reference for periodic performance appraisals and reports.

Gathering information applies to individuals and organizations. To compose an annual report, it is far easier to organize facts already collected than to sift through one year's data, desperately panning for significant accomplishments and doing so under strict time constraints. For example, a congressional subcommittee requested a federal agency to report at the close of the fiscal year on progress made on its top ten priority projects. Because the agency regularly collected and organized supporting data throughout the year, it quickly responded with a fact-filled, efficacious report that ensured continued funding.

2. Dig for details to uncover key information. If the initial story is vague, the author must often assume the role of an investigative reporter. Here is an example generated by a well-intentioned boss; however, it falls flat, lacking solid facts. *Provides great behind-the-scenes support. His contributions were invaluable to the team.* Don't make this mistake.

Ask questions—sometimes of the individual—and you'll learn the full story. For example, *Kent was selected as the Program Manager of the Year.* Yep, there's a pony in that stall somewhere or he wouldn't have won the award. Digging deeper, you'll learn that *Kent was selected as the Program Manager of the Year from 350 peers in the 10,000-person company.* The story becomes more impressive as you delineate specifics of the accomplishment that justified the award. Consider these questions to flush out details:

- What exactly did the individual do?
- What was the level of responsibility?
- Did the individual supervise anyone? If so, how many people?
- What was the monetary value of equipment or systems for which the individual was responsible?
- How did the individual's efforts further the mission?
- Did the individual resolve a significant issue or a serious problem?
- Did the individual complete projects early and/or under budget? If so, specify.
- Did the individual save resources? If so, specify.
- Did superiors or customers compliment the individual? Include quotes, as appropriate.
- What was the duration of the highlighted achievement, expanse of its impact, etc.?
- Did the individual demonstrate initiative?

Consider this statement: *She was honored with multiple awards for her excellent performance as Team Lead.* We can refine it to, *She was named "Employee of the Quarter" for her achievements as Team Lead and received a Letter of Appreciation from the Deputy Director for Operations and a financial performance award.* Better, but this only partially tells the story. Here's the final version, *She was named "Employee of the Quarter" for her achievements as Team Lead, selected from 250 colleagues, and received a Letter of Appreciation from the Deputy Director for Operations and a financial performance award. She was responsible for a three-month investigation that identified fifteen anomalies in the financial recordkeeping system that resulted in a savings of $178,000.*

3. Employ statistics to hone the message, as demonstrated above. Just as spices add a nuanced flavor to a meal, statistics add depth, dimension, and contour to the story. They set the context and equip the reader with a mental yardstick. Watch this evolution below as the real story comes into focus.

- Mary expeditiously processed **many** job applications. (So what? How many?)

- Mary expeditiously processed **fifty-four** job applications. (Is that a lot?)

- Mary expeditiously processed fifty-four job applications **this month alone**. (This sounds significant, but we're not sure why.)

- Mary expeditiously processed fifty-four job applications this month alone, **twice the office average**. (Oh my, that's impressive!)

- Mary expeditiously processed fifty-four job applications this month alone, twice the office average and **three times that of her peers**. (Wow! Raise her salary!)

Set the context by describing how big, what duration, number of hours invested, number of participants, how many, what percentage, etc. You could improve, *My best supervisor* by placing that fact in context, *My best of fifteen supervisors.* Here is an opening hook that quantifies the context. Does this leave you wanting to know more? *For the first time in the five years the report has been produced . . . .*

These examples of statistics make a story "pop":

- Drafted the justification and oversaw the project that increased staffing from three to twenty-five people in eleven months.

- Rated as the second of eighteen senior staff officers. Led the corporation's fourth largest unit with a $10-million budget. Saved $120,000 through an energy recovery project in the site's power plant. Turned $5,000 deficit in recreation funds into $20,000 profit in nine months. Reduced negative unit moral factors from sixty percent to ten percent.

- Directed and managed daily operations of a selectively staffed branch of 33 personnel. Responsible for an R&D lab and its $25-million operation. Guided $500,000 upgrades to test new analytic tools. Drove a study to procure $1.5 million in digital analysis hardware and software, the implementation of which increased analytical production by 700 percent.

Beware! Improperly used statistics can backfire. Like spices, too many can be overpowering; used improperly, they can distract. Ineffective statistics waste space and fail to convey the message. They can also open the garden gate (See Chapter 14, *Keep the Focus: Shut the Gates*), causing the reader to stray from your message wondering, "XX out of how many?" For example, *improved distribution by ten percent* doesn't state much because the writer doesn't complete the thought. Try this: *Improved distribution of 6,500 pieces of mail by 10 percent.* Even better is, *Single-handedly improved distribution of 6,500 pieces of mail by 10 percent in the first 3 months on the job.*

Here are additional examples: *Organized and led dozens of White House briefings for elected officials on a variety of issues, including international exchange rates, foreign trade, and exports/imports.* How many is *dozens*? Tell the reader! *Her program resulted in a ten-*

fold increase. What does that mean? *More than sixty percent of the users who participated in the survey were either extremely satisfied or satisfied.* How many people participated, and what was the +/- error rate?

4. Put the story in context. Identify the level of responsibility or the level at which the accomplishment occurred. This could add considerable significance to the storyline. Take, for example, *He was selected from three nominees to be Executive Assistant to the Secretary of Defense.* This may not seem so impressive from a statistical perspective—one from three—big deal! However, this is a significant statement for what it says—and doesn't say. The unspoken statistic is *the Secretary of Defense* because the pool of candidates from which the Secretary of Defense can select is substantial.

Here is another example: *One of four advisors selected to prepare the Secretary of the Interior for testimony to Congress.* The same principle applies; it speaks to the number of candidates from whom the individual was selected. Here is another example: *The division chief specifically asked for her to participate in the study.* That sounds good as far as it goes but add the fact that the division chief is an SES-2 and the sentence gains gravitas. That assumes the audience understands that SES-2 is a senior-level government employee. If not, avoid the problem of jargon and explain what it means—Senior Executive Service.

Here is a variant of this same principle that emphasizes setting the context: *Selected through an agency-wide competitive process for a one-year internship at the White House.* This rings bells for three reasons. First, it involves the words *selected* and *competitive;* both indicate a stand-out individual. Second, *agency-wide* performs the same scoping function as did *Secretary of Defense,* referenced above. Both subtly depict the magnitude of the competition. The third bell ringer is, *internship at the White House,* another clearly important discriminator. That particular bullet in the resume continued, *Successful candidates for these positions were identified by their respective career services as potential executives.* In the vernacular, *This person is going places!*

5. Finally, recognize what *not* to include. Reflecting the theory of survival of the fittest, prioritize your stories according to the "wow" factor and sort them from "most" to "least." As with a budget, items will fall above and below the cut line. Some stories must be cut short or simply go untold due to space constraints. You'll find below an example comprised of two strong items, but only one can be submitted. Can you determine which one and why?

Background: John is composing input for his performance appraisal; the form allows three inches for this information. He excelled this past year on a corporation's strategic communication staff. During the first six months, he authored articles published in the organization's monthly magazine that reached 20,000 employees. He also wrote a majority of, edited other inputs for, and published a highly acclaimed monthly newsletter for 5,000 employees at the corporate headquarters. He regularly received and documented accolades from supervisors and readers. The corporation eliminated both products in June due to budget cuts. John generated two inputs for the appraisal:

Newsletter: Produced six editions (data calls, research/writing articles, tech editing others' submissions, coordination, and dissemination). Newsletter circulated throughout the 5,000-person corporate headquarters. Each edition drew high praise from his supervisors: "As usual, John did a great job pulling this together!" "Another excellent edition!" "Love the articles! Great job as always!" The division chief explained, "John, thank you very much for all your hard work and creativity; very much appreciated! Discontinuing this product was a difficult decision!"

Corporate Magazine: Researched and composed six articles highlighting significant corporate accomplishments published in this highly visible product, reaching not only the corporate headquarters but also 20,000 readers worldwide. Each article was lauded by several senior-level executives. "Outstanding, thank you for sharing!" "Very good article!" "This is great—approved!" "Thanks for being such a proactive spokesman on our behalf!"

John faced a dilemma. Despite the great material, each is a downer. Placed sequentially, they constitute a double downer—discontinued . . . discontinued, imparting a disagreeable sense of "has been." Perhaps the author should not mention that these products were discontinued. However, failure to do so opens a garden gate and leaves the reader wondering, "Why only six articles in a monthly magazine over the course of a year?" and "Why only six monthly newsletters? What did he do for the remaining six months?"

John submitted the item about the magazine, because that product enjoyed the greatest circulation and customer impact. Given the business climate, he hoped the reader would understand one instance of *discontinued* with no prejudice against his overall annual performance. He relegated the write-up on the newsletter to his scrapbook.

5. Clinch the Deal

Congratulations! You've gathered potent facts to make your case and sway the reader to your position by following the five strategies presented in Chapter 4. The next step is to develop an outline or a roadmap that leads the reader to the desired conclusion.

Identify the key points in your message, ensuring it has a beginning, a middle, and the all-important conclusion. Then, augment that roughed-in structure with your facts, arranging them to construct a message that will clinch the deal. The eleven tips below will guide you.

1. Determine the goal of your communication. The problem statement is an effective tool here. It can also constitute the heart of your document and guide its development. A well-written problem statement consists of three parts: the problem, the resolution, and the vision of success.

Describe each part in only a few sentences. Define the present, untenable situation. Who is affected? Does the problem have ancillary impacts beyond the first tier? Support your claims with evidence;

two or three facts will suffice. Next, describe the proposed resolution, why you recommend it, and the projected impact. Conclude the problem statement by briefly describing the envisioned end state.

2. Tailor the product to questions it should answer. Anticipate the reader's possible follow-up questions and include this information as well. For example, the query letter an aspiring author submits to a publisher should address the following:

- What is the genesis of the book's concept?
- What does the author envision as the primary market?
- What experience does the author bring to the project?
- Has the author been previously published?
- How does this proposed book vary from others available in its genre?

Review your initial draft. Did you address all questions? Does the text flow logically? Does it emphasize the proper points?

3. Examine the situation from the reader's perspective. If you were *selecting* instead of writing a submission to a government-issued Request for Proposal (RFP) what information would *you* expect it to contain? Consider these questions as a possible outline for your product.

- What specific skills can the company offer to meet the requirements in this contract?
- What are some previous accomplishments in this field?
- How can your company out-perform its leading competitor?
- What insights can your company offer related to the contracted tasks?
- How can the customer benefit from your company's familiarity with the customer's style, mission, organization, personalities, etc.?

Sometimes you must look beyond the RFP to completely understand the operational need being addressed. Perhaps the RFP incorrectly defined the problem or failed to reflect all aspects. Ensure you respond to requirements stated in the RFP, but amplifying—clearly defining the problem or the needed service or capability—can set your submission apart from the competition.

As the CEO who must reduce the company's staff or budget, what information would *you* need to make the wisest decisions? Because it is really *your* office in jeopardy, responses to the questions below will help craft a vigorous defense.

- Has the workload increased quantifiably over a defined period of time?

- Has the office already taken resource cuts? If so, how recently and to what extent?

- How does your office further the overall mission of the organization?

- How will reductions in resources impact those contributions? Specify without exaggerating and don't write with emotion. Strong facts result in a robust message.

- Can you cite complimentary feedback from customers on your products or services?

4. Review the draft and ensure information flows logically from the thesis through topic sentences and subordinate paragraphs to the conclusion. To validate the sequencing, apply the technique I characterize as "sorting laundry," one pile each for colors, darks, and whites. From a literary perspective, this refers to grouping like thoughts rather than inadvertently mixing them, which gives the reader a bad case of mental whiplash. To "sort laundry" at the sentence level, for example, ensure each sentence logically relates to its topic sentence.

This also applies at the paragraph level. Imagine reading a paragraph on apples, followed by one on oranges, followed by another on apples, followed by . . . you see the pattern. Arrange paragraphs to first discuss apples and then oranges.

Modify if the thoughts are disjointed; add, delete, or adjust information as needed. You might rearrange thoughts by increments of a few words, sentences, or entire paragraphs. Even experienced writers modify the initial draft, sometimes extensively.

The following story demonstrates this technique. An individual sent a letter soliciting investors with a business opportunity. The writer discussed both esthetic benefits of the proposed location and financial particulars of the deal, but repeatedly mingled these disparate thoughts—one sentence discussing the location and the next, finances and so on throughout the document. This confused the reader. The proposal, as written, was completely ineffective. The revised letter addressed benefits of the location in one paragraph and financial details in another. Bottom line, investors rallied and the business now prospers!

5. Use signposts to guide the reader. I'm referring to number words and/or numerals such as *first, second, third* or *next, then*, and *the following* as I've applied throughout this book. These signposts communicate to the reader, "OK, we're turning to a different point. Please change gears." This is an effective technique, especially when conveying either a lengthy or complex message.

6. Depending on your product, open with your strongest fact and conclude with your second strongest. Why? You want to end on a strong note, rather than—in theater parlance—fading to black with less gripping information. Analogous to this is beginning a fine meal with an enticing appetizer, correlating to the opening punch in your product that grabs the reader's attention. The meal should conclude with an epicurean offering, leaving the guest with an enjoyable and memorable taste. This correlates to your final thought. Bottom line – conclude on a strong note.

7. Showcase your leading fact. I highlight this because authors often inadvertently bury the most important fact—the golden nugget—in the center of a paragraph, smothered by a mass of less important information. When this occurs, you lose the reader before presenting your best point. Think like a parent at a restaurant—the analogy is instructing the child not to fill up on bread and butter or a drink before the main course. Too much of the former and interest is lost in the main feature, which is your star point or that expensive entrée! Here is a prime example of the author inadvertently burying the leading line:

> *Best analyst on my staff of fifteen, working on experimental technology for energy production. Conducted long-term S&T research on six projects. Due to her excellent briefing skills, was specifically requested to update the division director weekly on project developments. Selected from seventy-five candidates to fill one of five positions in the White House Internship Program. Regularly interacts with counterparts in the seventeen Department of Energy national laboratories, testing theories and developing new concepts for environmentally friendly technologies. Excels at applying insights from other laboratories into ongoing projects here.*

Did you detect the buried golden nugget? It is the information about the White House Internship Program. That should have been the leading line.

8. Write proportionately, based on allocated space. To exemplify, space in an annual performance appraisal (let's call it four inches for this discussion) equates to a twelve-month period. Obvious statement, I know, but with a purpose. Visualize the space in quarters, each representing three months. This will help preclude describing a single accomplishment in such detail that a one-week effort consumes six months of competitive writing space. This temptation is difficult to resist, even for the most skilled writers, and especially if that task was complex, all consuming, and yielded tremendous results. But, you can bet reviewers will notice disproportionate use of space and wonder, to your detriment, what you did for the rest of the year.

9. Be shrewd in placing your key facts. Spread them throughout the product rather than frontloading them into a single category. Some competitive forms are divided into categories such as Operational, Teamwork, Self-Improvement, Community Support, Leadership, etc. Authors instinctively frontload the Operational and Leadership categories with the strongest facts. Consequently, scores for these categories are often tied. The winner is, therefore, often selected based on the seemingly "lesser" categories such as Self-Improvement and Community Support. Hint: Consider the individual's accomplishments in the context of these other criteria and place golden nuggets strategically throughout to effectively compete in all of the categories.

10. Write objectively. This is an essential element of analysis and composition. It means treating a subject thoroughly, honestly, consistently, and accurately while diligently avoiding bias and self-interest in presenting the material. In the parlance of Hollywood, it means equitably addressing "The Good, the Bad, and the Ugly." Objectivity is an attitude toward material rather than a special manner of writing. Mistaking the meaning of objectivity as it applies to writing can promulgate two errors that detract from a paper's credibility and usefulness: Being too detached or being too skewed in presenting the information.

Being objective does not mean detaching yourself so completely from the material that writing becomes antiseptic and depersonalized. Colorless, sterile prose does not imbue your writing with a sense of professionalism. It does not amplify its aura of objectivity or authority. It does, however, rob your product of sparkle, making it flat, limp, shapeless, and boring. Need a visual here? Imagine a shampoo commercial: detached writing equates to the model *before* the shampoo is applied. By contrast, lively expression that capitalizes on the rich nuances of the English language invigorates writing. Your message will convey with an engaging robustness, rhythm, and movement that will captivate the reader. To complete our visual, writing with a touch of sparkle equates to the model *after* the shampoo is applied!

Interpreting material with the goal of persuading the reader to your viewpoint is acceptable as long as your presentation is forthright and unprejudiced. Evaluations and judgments aimed at supporting the interpretation should derive from careful reflection on the material. Although accurate explanation sometimes entails suppression of personal inclinations and attitudes, interpretation adds value to a paper without degrading its objectivity. Conviction and belief, moreover, give writing a feeling and thrust absent in an informative paper.

11. The final tip is to determine the paper's organization. Three main considerations should influence the general plan for a paper: the material itself, the method of story development, and the expected audience. In some cases, the material and the method of development dictate the structure of a paper, or at least the order of parts comprising most of its content. Indeed, most authors draft a paper according to the natural order suggested by the material, which appears to leave few choices or difficulties in how to proceed. An author does, in fact, have options in organizing a paper. Making an effort to identify the order and make the right decision is time well spent.

Devising an organizational scheme for a paper depends heavily on the extent to which it is an explanation paper (expository) versus a persuasion paper (persuasive).

The explanation paper is intended to increase the reader's understanding of a subject. Some authors open the paper by setting the context, orienting the reader to the subject and then proceeding with the discussion, point by point. Others start by noting a particular event, then building toward some comprehensive generalization or point and amplifying with specific details. Both approaches are commonly employed in this type of paper.

The persuasion paper is intended to influence the reader's convictions, beliefs, or actions. It consists of two essential elements: the thesis and the proof. A thesis, or main proposition, gives focus to the paper—a center to the discussion. The proof is the evidence advanced to support the thesis. Material is presented fairly and impartially but with the author clearly revealing the intent is to affect the reader's opinion as much as it is to inform.

In a persuasion paper, the author strives to sway the reader's opinion via accurate observation and sound reasoning. The author must determine what combination of evidence and argumentation will dispose the reader to the desired point of view. In organizing this type of paper, the author must first size the issue, logically identifying both the thesis and proof. The next step is to establish a chain of propositions that lead the reader to the thesis and determine which of those propositions can stand alone and which need to be supported with amplifying facts. The more vulnerable a proposition, the more attention must be paid to it, requiring more effort to demonstrate it is sound.

The author must also acknowledge and address conflicting data, gaps in information, uncertainties, ambiguities, disagreements, and other elements that impact the argument. The author should address evidential weaknesses in arguments presented and alternative propositions borne of those same data shortfalls. Not only does this bolster the strength of the author's position, it also adds to the author's credibility. Making a good argument involves dealing with contrary evidence and reasoning as much as it does gathering evidence to support the chosen point of view. A paper must be structured to facilitate both.

Concluding this final item, consider these questions in deciding the organization of the paper:

- What major options are available in developing an organizational scheme?
- How will explanation and persuasion be introduced, developed, and blended in the paper?
- How will evidence and logical relationships be used to support the arguments that are presented?

- How will the existence of contrary evidence, absence of data, or alternative explanations be introduced and examined?

- Which general plan is most likely to catch the attention and exploit the knowledge of the intended audience?

- Which organizational scheme is most likely to induce an audience to agree with the paper's main proposition and accept the evidence and rationale advanced to support it?

Part 2

Word Sculpting Tools

**"Choosing each word to concisely convey maximum meaning.
Powerful writing . . . Precision writing."**

Poof! You are a sculptor dressed in a smock, hammer and chisel in hand, sitting in a sun-drenched studio, facing an eight-foot block of marble. You know the image you want to convey through this medium and the response you wish to elicit from the viewer. Your challenge—transfer that concept from your imagination onto the marble by carefully chipping and discarding extraneous bits, allowing the envisioned image to emerge.

Word Sculpting parallels this, except you work with words instead of marble. As the author, you know the message to convey and the desired result. All that remains is transcribing your thoughts.

I tell my students that the first step in this process—especially for apprentice sculptors—is to do a gut dump onto a blank page. Don't worry about perfection, just write. When complete, you essentially have your equivalent to the sculptor's block of marble. You then apply *Word Sculpting Tools* to chisel excess words and hone your story. The more effectively you sculpt, the more impressive your final product. Take heart—these techniques are so simple and effective, even apprentices will see dramatic results when contrasting the initial draft with the sculpted version!

"Employing *Word Sculpting Tools* is the second major step in composing powerful, influential products."

6. Useless Words: Find, Chisel, Discard

We begin with the most fundamental of the ten *Word Sculpting Tools:* find, chisel, and discard useless words. Methodically review your draft, word by word and sentence by sentence, to eliminate words that contribute little or no substance to your product. As a general rule, candidates for discard include: *a, an, the, can*, forms of the verb *to be, have/has, that, these, in order* [to], [provide] *with, enable, efforts, process,* [first]-*ever,* and *there is/there are.* We address the last instance in greater detail in Chapter 10 on verbs. *There is/there are* often mask the actual subject and verb. With a little thought you can find them hidden in the sentence.

Consider these simple examples:

- Before: *A key premise to* Word Sculpting *is eliminating words **that are** unnecessary.*

  After: *A key premise to* Word Sculpting *is eliminating unnecessary words.*

- Before: *Each **of these** packages was submitted in time.*

  After: *Each package was submitted in time.*

- Before: *She discussed the symposium **that is** scheduled **to run** from **May** 12 to May 18.*

  After: *She discussed the symposium scheduled from May 12–18.*

- Before: *This subject **matter** is outside **of** his **area of** expertise.*

  After: *This subject is outside his expertise.*

- Before: *The development **process** of this document began in 2011.*

  After: *Development of this document began in 2011.*

- Before: *Exercise planning **efforts** continued through**out** the year.*

  After: *Exercise planning continued through the year.*

- Before: *These enhancements further **enable** system integration **objectives.***

  After: *These enhancements further system integration.*

- Before: *We will **be** schedul**ing** another meeting.*

  After: *We will schedule another meeting.*

- Before: ***In the** initial **efforts**, applicants were sorted into three categories.*

  After: *Applicants were initially sorted into three categories.*

- Before: ***There are** many students who study hard and do well at this school.*

  After: *Many students study hard and do well at this school.*

We often unconsciously transfer sloppy, colloquial language into professionally written products and fail to revise the draft to expunge it. *He took time to write up the report.* What does *up* contribute? In another example, a formal email says, *Read over this report and provide comments in three days.* Why not simply state *read* and drop the *over?* Sloppy language also includes clichés such as *hit the ground running, out of the box, get on the same page,* and *with flying colors.* Avoid them! My proscription—don't write as you speak. This problem is so widespread, it made my list, "The Dirty Dozen: Most Common Errors in Professional Writing" (See Appendix B).

Purge words that inappropriately editorialize or convey emotions. For example, *Establishing a department policy is a lengthy process but well worth the energy.* In this example, it is not the author's place to opine that this action is "well worth the energy." Here's another example: *An excellent tool to understand the office's accomplishments is presented in the timeline below.* The author declares the "timeline" is "excellent" but never substantiates that determination. Instead, the author should state the fact without injecting an opinion, as in, *The timeline depicts the organization's accomplishments.* Let the reader decide if it does so excellently or not. *She is a vital member of the staff.* By whose determination and based on what criteria is she deemed "vital"?

Applied consistently, this technique of identifying and discarding useless words cumulatively yields two significant benefits. It generates crisp, cogent text that grabs the reader's attention, adding to your product's impact. It also creates more space—and opportunity—to further elaborate on and strengthen your case. Even the most skilled authors review their drafts and discard useless words. Rarely can anyone generate a perfectly sculpted product in the first draft. Take heart; like any new skill, this will become instinctive with practice.

EXAMPLES

The following *Before* and *After* examples demonstrate this tool. Bolded words are useless and marked for deletion.

Example #1

Before: I purchased a hybrid car **in order** to save money **on** gas.

After: I purchased a hybrid car to save gas money.

Analysis: You can always discard *in order* and cut straight to the *to*. *Money on gas* can be shortened to *gas money*.

Example #2

Before: His test **is** tomorrow, and **that is where his** focus **needs to be**.

After: He should focus on tomorrow's test.

Analysis: *He* is the subject. *Should* replaces *needs to be,* and you can discard *and that is where his*.

Example #3

Before: Additional work remains **to be done** to implement **the review** decisions and **to** resolve other issues **relating to** the conference.

After: Additional work remains to implement decisions and resolve other issues concerning the conference.

Analysis: Eliminate the useless words. Replace the two-word *relating to* with a single word, *concerning*. Also, ask yourself, "What is a 'review' decision?" *Review* makes no sense—delete it.

Example #4

Before: After **approximately** three months, **of searching, for the right candidate**, the company hired a developer **whom we** thought had **usable** knowledge in the specified systems.

After: After searching about three months, the company hired a developer thought to have requisite knowledge in the specified systems.

Analysis: The initial key thought is "searching." The word *approximately* can be replaced with *about. For the right candidate* is understood and, therefore, unnecessary. After all, the company would not search for the wrong candidate, would it? Also discard *whom we* and replace *useable* with *requisite,* a more professional descriptor. Note the comma errors in the *Before* example.

Example #5

Before: He explained how technology can help the company **in its** information shar**ing** and collaborat**ion efforts** with key business associates.

After: He explained how technology can help the company share information and collaborate with key business associates.

Analysis: Answer the question, "Help the company do what?" The answer is, "share and collaborate." You can discard the *in its* and *-ing* from each verb. The word *effort* is sorely overused; avoid it.

Example #6

Before: The writing was so poor**, it lost the reader, making it difficult for** the reader to **grasp the key message intended by the author**.

After: The document was so poorly written, the reader couldn't understand it.

Analysis: The focus is *the document*, not *the writing*. Replace, *it lost the reader, making it difficult for,* with *the reader couldn't*. Replace *grasp the key message* with *understand it*. Delete *intended by the author* as unnecessary.

Example #7

Before: She grabbed **hold of** the doorknob, flung open the door, and fled **out of** the room.

After: She grabbed the doorknob, flung open the door, and fled the room.

Analysis: *Grabbed hold of* is sloppy, spoken language applied to the written page. Beware of this tendency because it is not professional. Also note the useless words *out of.*

Example #8

Before: The topic for the next meeting **is one that** affects the entire school.

After: The topic for the next meeting affects the entire school.

Analysis: Discard *is one that* because it contributes nothing to the sentence.

Example #9

Before: **It is** vital to provide contact information **that is** current.

After: Providing current contact information is vital.

Analysis: In this case, *It is* are useless words and should be discarded. The sentence now needs a subject, so *Providing* will do nicely! The complete subject (gerund phrase) is *Providing current contact information.* Similarly useless in this example is the phrase *That is*.

Example #10

Before: The **purpose of** the rehearsal **is to** identify flaws in the performance.

After: The rehearsal will identify flaws in the performance.

Analysis: *The purpose of* and *is to* are wasted words. What will the rehearsal do? The more specific verb *will identify* clarifies.

CHAPTER 6 EXERCISES—Now You Try!

Exercise #1

Before: Scientific research is continuing the process of documenting the recovery of endangered species.

After: _____

Exercise #2

Before: The agency decided not to continue the service contract in light of the continual cost overruns.

After: _____

Exercise #3

Before: This critical step is necessary to preclude cost overruns.

After: _____

Exercise #4

Before: The intent of the article is to educate the reader on the stock market.

After: _____

Exercise #5

Before: The purpose of the regulation is to ensure the hiring process is the same across the corporation.

After: _____

Exercise #6

Before: There are many people that have vacationed at the beach this summer because it provided them with an opportunity to relax.

After: _____

Exercise #7

Before: We are continuing the process of printing, copying, and sorting applications for the vacant job positions.

After: _____

Exercise #8

Before: We will have to check the records to ensure they are accurate.

After: _____

Exercise #9

Before: I examined four books but didn't buy any of them.

After: _____

Exercise #10

Before: Thank you for your participation. We will be soliciting your comments in the near future.

After: _____

Now, check your answers in Appendix A.

7. Shorter Is Better: Don't Hog Space

This is the most precise of the *Word Sculpting Tools,* analogous to that used for the most intricate and delicate sculpting. Apply this level of refinement when space is limited and, therefore, very valuable or for an especially impactful and focused message. Products requiring this degree of sculpting include executive correspondence (often limited to a single page); formatted applications and personnel evaluations; letters of introduction; query letters; briefing slides; competitive writing including business proposals, applications for grants, congressional fellowships, college scholarships, quarterly and annual organizational recognition, or other merit-based awards; and text on web pages.

Avoid hogging space in three ways. First, select the shortest word to most effectively convey your thought. A thesaurus is an excellent aid for this task. When writing at this level, I often count letters and spaces to determine the briefest word. Because space is paramount, it trumps the esthetics of how a word sounds. For example, I like the sound and flow of the word *numerous.* When applying this tool, however, I state *many.* See the examples below in which the preferred word is bracketed:

- Budget reductions force us to *choose* [pick] *an alternative* [another] course of action.

- We must carefully *contemplate* [consider] other options.

- The boss *appreciated* [liked] Mary's *suggestion* [idea]; she *provided* [gave] a new *perspective* [insight] into the *complicated* [complex] *predicament* [issue].

- The project manager had to decide *whether or not* [if] her *suggestion* [proposal] was *a good idea* [advisable].

- Our *mission stakeholders* [partners] *believe* [think] the *modification* [change] is *on target* [viable].

- The company *triumphed over* [overcame] *numerous* [many] *impediments* [obstacles] and achieved its goal.

- *According to* [Per] company policy, Mary earned a *substantial* [large] bonus.

- This gave her the *opportunity* [chance] to *purchase* [buy] that new *automobile* [car].

- Mary was excited and *made an error* [erred] while driving; *specifically* [i.e.,], she ran a stop sign!

- The officer was *magnanimous* [kind] and only gave her a warning.

- Mary was *exceedingly* [very] *fortunate* [lucky]!

Second, precision is another way to save space. Condense your text by using the fewest possible words. With some thought, you can often identify one word replacing what otherwise would be stated in two or more. In addition to saving space, this results in a snappier product. Please note, sometimes one word might be longer than the few words it replaces. However, this is still preferable because the reader more quickly digests a single word than a combination of several. Consider the following:

- *come up with = develop* or *identify*
- *a number of = several*
- *day-to-day = daily*
- *in accordance with = per*
- *in the meantime = meanwhile*
- *at the present time = presently*
- *those who attended = attendees*
- *doesn't have = lacks*
- *as a result = consequently*
- *negatively impacts = hampers* or *impedes*
- *on a national basis = nationally*
- *that resides within = resident in* or *lives in*
- *with regards to = regarding*
- *a very limited number of = few*
- *point of view = perspective*
- *in addition = also*
- *we were talking about = we discussed*
- *take you up on = accept*
- *prior to that = previously*

The author can also save space by judiciously using adjectives and adverbs. When used excessively, they bog down text and desensitize readers to distinctions highlighted by their use. As with the examples above, these can also be combined into single, more precise words. For example:

- *habitually talkative = garrulous* or *loquacious*
- *mostly harmless = innocuous*
- *very disapproving = censorious* or *reproachful*

Finally, write in the active, not the passive voice. Simply state who or what (the subject) does what (the action) to or for whom (the object). This saves precious space, is more direct, and generates a clearer, more interesting product. Consider these examples:

- *A formal report **will be submitted** to Mary **by** John* is revised to *John will submit a formal report to Mary.* This modification saves ten spaces that could be critical in competitive writing.

- *The division chiefs **were tasked by** the director to attend the conference.* This is revised to *The director tasked the division chiefs to attend the conference.*

Unfortunately, the passive voice permeates government and corporate writing. Here is a typical example:

*Decision-making processes that support integrated planning, implementation, and monitoring of the network operations **will be established**. Innovative approaches that modernize the network while identifying or eliminating duplication and unwarranted redundancies **will be instituted**.*

Authors use the passive voice due to poor writing skills, to avoid making authoritative statements, or to dodge attribution by "seeking safety in the fog," as Mortimer Goldstein states in his book, *Disciplined Writing and Career Development*. [I should note that the passive voice is appropriate in certain forms of writing, such as that found in the scientific community.]

EXAMPLES

Example #1

Before: Managers should **make certain** that **personnel under their purview** understand company policies.

After: Managers should ensure employees understand company policies.

Analysis: *Make certain* is replaced by *ensure. Personnel under their purview* is replaced with *employees.* The word *that* is discarded as a useless word. Total savings—thirty-one spaces!

Example #2

Before: Cutting manpower will **generate** future **cost savings in the out years**.

After: Cutting manpower will save money.

Analysis: This example mentions the future three times—*will, future,* and *in the out years.* We can state this simply with one word, *will.* We also saved words by reducing *generate cost savings* to *save money.* If it is important to convey the thought of saving money many years in the future, retain *in the out years.*

Example #3

Before: **I want to express my appreciation for** your **contribution,** which contributed **in large measure** to the success of our charity drive.

After: Thank you for the donation to our charity drive; you contributed greatly to its success.

Analysis: Two words, *thank you,* replace *I want to express my appreciation for.* To avoid the dual use of *contribution,* we use *donation.* Finally, *in large measure* is replaced by *greatly.*

Example #4

Before: The company is updating its computer system to **take advantage of** technological advances.

After: The company is updating its computer system to leverage technological advances.

Analysis: *Take advantage of* equates to a single verb, *leverage.*

Example #5

Before: **The reason that I'm writing** this sentence **is to provide you with an exercise in which it is possible for you** to identify and **throw out each and every** word that hogs space.

After: This sentence demonstrates how to identify and discard words that hog space.

Analysis: Delete the unnecessary words *the reason that I'm writing* and *is to provide you with an exercise in which it is possible for you*. Replace *throw out* with *discard*. Delete as useless *each and every*.

Example #6

Before: We **have the opportunity to realize financial savings** without **losing unique** mission **capabilities**.

After: We can save money with no mission degradation.

Analysis: *Have the opportunity to realize financial savings* equates to *can save money*. *Losing unique capabilities* equals *degradation*. Using *with no* instead of *without*, conveys the idea more clearly and definitively. In case you are counting, this revision saved fifty spaces.

Example #7

Before: Amy tried to **figure out** the next steps in the process.

After: Amy tried to identify the next steps in the process.

Analysis: Replace *figure out* with *identify*, which is shorter and more professional. The rule of thumb—one word is better than two.

Example #8

Before: Provide this office the following information one week prior to arrival: make, model, and license number of your car. We will submit a parking request **upon receiving this information**.

After: Provide this office the following information one week prior to arrival: make, model, and license number of your car. We will **then** submit a parking request.

Analysis: A little creative thinking enables you to swap one word for four.

Example #9

Before: Insulated sleeping bags **made it possible for** them to sleep in more extreme climates.

After: Insulated sleeping bags enabled them to sleep in more extreme climates.

Analysis: *Made it possible for* equates to *enabled* and saves a lot of space.

Example #10

Before: Gang violence in our neighborhood is **becoming more acute—** we **need to** devise security measures **that are above those already in place**.

After: Gang violence in our neighborhood is intensifying—we must devise more stringent security measures.

Analysis: *Becoming more acute* equates to *intensifying. Need to* can be condensed to *must. That are above those already in place* is replaced with *more stringent.*

CHAPTER 7 EXERCISES—Now You Try!

Exercise #1

Before: She inquired as to whether she could bring a colleague to the meeting.

After: _____

Exercise #2

Before: Jim keeps track of incoming requirements.

After: _____

Exercise #3

Before: After lengthy study of the plan, they are moving directly to the implementation phase.

After: _____

Exercise #4

Before: They were grateful for the demonstration of support.

After: _____

Exercise #5

Before: He responded back to the inquiry in a timely manner.

After: _____

Exercise #6

Before: It is essential that submissions meet the deadline.

After: _____

Exercise #7

Before: This old alarm system could provide a gateway that may allow for an unauthorized individual to access the facility.

After: _____

Exercise #8

Before: I maintained all documents in accordance with the Administrative Instruction in accordance with the office policy for all correspondence and maintained the office library for all reference materials.

After: _____

Exercise #9

Before: We know for a fact that this design is similar to one we reviewed last week.

After: _____

Exercise #10

Before: This reorganization will ultimately help to drive down costs while delivering improved mission services.

After: _____

Now, check your answers in Appendix A.

8. Redundancy: Once Will Suffice

Redundancy refers to hidden, extraneous words that surreptitiously sneak into your text. Did you find the redundancy in that sentence? Such occurrences are often subtle; you must search carefully to find and eliminate them. Poor writing manifests itself in four types of redundancy.

First, look for words inferred within the context of the sentence. For example:

- *He might travel to Spain at some point in the future. At some point in the future* falls within the concept of *might,* which, itself, alludes to the future. Revised, the sentence reads *He might travel to Spain.*

- *Knowing your audience is critical to the effective presentation of a briefing.* The redundancy is with *presentation* and *briefing.* We resolve it as *Knowing your audience is critical to an effective briefing.* Better yet . . . *Know your audience to brief effectively.*

- *A lack of cooperation currently exists between labor and management.* The word *currently* is reflected in the verb *exists.* The result is *A lack of cooperation exists between labor and management.*

- *She was recognized for excellence in her performance as Team Lead and was honored with multiple awards.* The fact that she was *honored with multiple awards* makes *recognized for excellence* redundant. Here is the revision: *She was honored with multiple awards for her performance as Team Lead.* (Remember this example? We discussed it in Chapter 4, "Make the Case." We will revisit it in Chapter 14, "Keep the Focus: Shut the Gates.")

- *This paper could be a potential submission for the project design.* The redundancy lies with *could be* and *potential* because both imply possibility. It is resolved as *This paper could be a submission for the project design.*

- *Recommendations contained in the report are exceptional.* The redundancy lies with *contained* and *in.* The sentence can be sculpted to *Recommendations in the report are exceptional.*

- *As it stands now, the office is staffed at 90 percent.* The redundancy lies with *As it stands now* and *is.* The revision reads *The office is staffed at 90 percent.*

Another type of redundancy is repetition found in lists. See this excerpt from a brochure about Maryland.

Did you know that in the state of Maryland:

- *There are 12,407 square miles*
- *There are 24 counties*
- *There are 53 state parks*

A more effective presentation is seen below. In addition to deleting three instances of *There are,* we also deleted *in the state of* because the reader knows that Maryland is a state. We also tightened the text by deleting *that.*

Did you know Maryland has:

- *12,407 square miles*
- *24 counties*
- *53 state parks*

Sometimes, however, an author will intentionally employ redundancy for effect, emphasizing the message like a purposeful, persistent drumbeat. Read aloud and listen.

Word Sculpting for Success

- *Success in winning awards*
- *Success in defending budgets*
- *Success in justifying additional resources*
- *Success in obtaining employment*
- *Success in presenting your case*

The third type of redundancy is the "patently obvious" or in the vernacular, "no-duh!" This occurs when the author wastes space on— well, the obvious! Consider these examples:

- *Antivirus programs protect your computer from malicious IT attacks.* This sentence contains two redundancies: 1) Since the topic is *computers*, *IT* is redundant and 2) What *attack* is not *malicious*?
- *Phase 1 of the Transportation Plan is only the beginning.* Of course, it is only the *beginning* because it is *Phase 1*!
- *The restructure will result in more effective and efficient operations.* Yes, *effective* and *efficient* have different meanings; however, in this context—unless the author is

really splitting hairs—are *effective* and *efficient* not sufficiently synonymous and, therefore, redundant?

Another variation of the patently obvious is found in resumes in which each bullet of the text begins with *I did* such and such. Personal pronouns should not appear in resumes. Because the resume is autobiographical, bullets obviously pertain to the author. In a five-page resume, an author used the word *I* forty-nine times!

The final type of redundancy is the "double tap," occurring with nouns and verbs. These bullets exemplify "double tap" nouns:

- *Ensure your staff is aware of the new policy and follows it.* The redundancy lies with *policy* and *it.* We revise to *Ensure your staff is aware of and follows the new policy*.

- *Now that you drafted the message, hone it into an elevator speech.* The redundancy lies with *message* and *it.* We revise to *Now, hone the drafted message into an elevator speech*.

Authors often cite a minor action that precedes the more meaningful action—this is the "double tap" verb. A quick example is *They met to plan the event.* Generally, the fact that they had *met* is irrelevant to the main action *plan.*

- *He reviewed and provided comments on the draft report.* The redundancy lies with *reviewed and commented on* because a professional would not comment on a document without first reviewing it. The revision is *He commented on the draft report.*

- *She contacted Jim and reminded him about the meeting.* The verb *contacted* is redundant because it presumably precedes the focal action of the sentence, *reminded.* The result is *She reminded Jim about the meeting.*

EXAMPLES

Example #1

Before: My office **attended** the conference **and** demonstrated information technology capabilities **for the audience**.

After: My office demonstrated information technology capabilities at the conference.

Analysis: Start with the most important verb, *demonstrated.* Discard *attended* because it's redundant. Why? *My office* could not have *demonstrated* if it had not *attended* the conference. So, you need only one action, not two. Additionally, *at the conference* equates to *for the audience,* also redundant.

Example #2

Before: He suggested to the **assembled** audience areas for closer involvement and collaboration **in the future.**

After: He suggested to the audience areas for closer involvement and collaboration.

Analysis: The audience, by definition, is *assembled*; *suggested* implies *in the future.* Discard these last three words.

Example #3

Before: The city council identified the member **within its organization that** will chair the fundraiser.

After: The city council identified its member who will chair the fundraiser.

Analysis: *Within* and *organization* are redundant. Note also a common mistake of referring to a person as *that* instead of using the correct pronoun, *who.*

Example #4

Before: Europeans often vacation **during the month of** August.

After: Europeans often vacation in August.

Analysis: We all know that August is a month. Don't waste text identifying it as such. The shorter word *in* replaces *during*.

Example #5

Before: The project required extensive research **on her part** because Mary **had never previously encountered** this material.

After: Mary had to research the project extensively because she was unfamiliar with the material.

Analysis: Let's begin with the real subject, *Mary.* We then ask, "What did she do?" She "had to research." Discard *on her part* because it refers to *Mary* and is redundant. We replace *had never previously encountered* with *was unfamiliar with*.

Example #6

Before: Much work is **currently ongoing** to coordinate fund drives.

After: People are working hard to coordinate fund drives.

Analysis: *Currently* is redundant with *ongoing.* Unravel this mess by next identifying the true, but unspoken subject of this thought, *People are working hard.*

Example #7

Before: She has **in her possession** a museum-quality painting.

After: She has a museum-quality painting.

or

She owns a museum-quality painting.

Analysis: This exemplifies both redundancy and ineffective use of verbs. *She has* and *in her possession* are redundant. Now, the shortest verb is *has.* However, that is boring and ubiquitous. So, if factually accurate, we would state *owns.*

Example #8

Before: She accomplished the task on her own, **without any assistance**.

After: She accomplished the task independently.

Analysis: *Without any assistance* is redundant to *on her own* and can be eliminated . . . unless you are intentionally restating this for added emphasis. *On her own* can be further reduced to *independently.*

Example #9

Before: She **acts as** the company's **liaison** and **representative** to the local Chamber of Commerce.

After: She is the company's liaison to the local Chamber of Commerce.

Analysis: Two points. First, *liaison* and *representative* are redundant; pick one. Second, we generally avoid using forms of the verb *to be,* preferring verbs with more color. However, in this case we replaced *acts as* with *is.* If space is not a consideration, the verb *serves* also works.

Example #10

Before: A **future** meeting will be planned.

After: They will plan a meeting.

Analysis: Avoid the passive voice by identifying who will plan the meeting. The word *future* is redundant since *will plan* is the future tense.

CHAPTER 8 EXERCISES—Now You Try!

Exercise #1

Before: This is an updated version of the draft previously sent on Jan. 5.

After: _____

Exercise #2

Before: Two reports are due: one on Sept. 30 and the other on Dec. 31.

After: _____

Exercise #3

Before: The annual report titled *The County Financial Report for 2019* covered the 2019 calendar year. This was another highlight from 2019.

After: _____

Exercise #4

Before: The director approved the script for use in support of the movie.

After: _____

Exercise #5

Before: There are thirty individuals currently employed by our company.

After _____

Exercise #6

Before: The event demonstrated that businesses could collectively come together and respond to a community need.

After: _____

Exercise #7

Before: The Marketing Director is the single management official who will be the focal point for ensuring the success of the outreach campaign.

After: _____

Exercise #8

Before: Special attention has been paid in the design of the floor plan to avoid the occurrence of stairs.

After: _____

Exercise #9

Before: The maintenance shop is aware of the broken air conditioner and is working towards a resolution.

After: _____

Exercise #10

Before: The conference is over following the keynote speaker's address.

After: _____

Now, check your answers in Appendix A.

9. Lead with the Basics: Horse before the Cart

Professional products are often rife with sentences that place the cart before the horse. Let me demonstrate:

> You must wade through a lot of lengthy, often convoluted, ancillary preamble and seemingly endless information that will drive you nuts, your patience evaporating by the second *before finally reaching the main point.*

This type of writing confronts the reader with excessive information (aka, "the cart") *before finally reaching the main point* of the sentence (aka, "the horse"). It confuses the intended message; minimizes the product's effectiveness; and irritates the reader, especially if this sloppy writing permeates the entire product. Reading this is laborious, like wading through knee-deep mud.

Authors often use the periodic sentence, which places its main clause (i.e., the subject and verb) at the end, producing a suspenseful effect. If used judiciously, this construction is legitimate and effective. You'll soon see, however, that contemporary authors abuse this form. Similarly, other instances involve placing key elements of information at the end of the sentence that would have been better situated earlier in the thought. Here are a few examples:

- *Innovative solutions that encourage community cooperation and understanding must be promoted.*

- *Because responsibility for updating the web page had not been assigned, data had become stale.*

- *The report should highlight future events, conditions, or projected expenditures that could affect the corporate finances for the coming fiscal year in the opening paragraph.*

The final teaching point for this chapter is opening with the most important information by placing the bottom line up front (BLUF). Ask yourself, "If I had only five minutes, what information *must* I convey?" Determine the sequence of the information based on its criticality to the audience, then follow with more detailed or background information. To further clarify the product, the author can delineate the information using designations of "BLUF" and "Background." This is especially helpful in complex emails, enabling the reader to quickly grasp the most pertinent facts. Pun intended, authors *can* BLUF their way to success!

That said, applying this is situational; BLUF is not always the best approach. If your message is controversial or one the audience is likely to resist, beginning with the bottom line risks alienating them before you've made your case.

Imagine, for example, you must persuade a corporate board to cut costs by streamlining its organization. Open with that stark statement and the audience is immediately on guard. Board members stop listening or, worse yet, mentally counter your every point. They fear cost-cutting measures might eliminate their own jobs or reduce their spheres of influence. You struck out, regardless of the validity of your judgments, conclusions, and recommendations. In this case, the better approach is to explain the problem, identify contributing factors, suggest and assess alternative solutions, and conclude with your recommendation. Unpalatable perhaps but substantiated. And, the audience listened.

I conclude this tutorial with a question: "When is it acceptable to intentionally and slowly feed an audience information, keep them hanging and hanging and hanging as you incrementally add details and then—WHAM!—hit them with the punch line?" OK, I gave it away. The answer: "When telling a joke." There is a scintillating gratification in drawing out the suspense that precedes delivery of the quintessential punch line. Hint: Do not write that way unless you are composing jokes!

After the ten examples below, you'll find exercises that begin with individual sentences. Then the exercises become more complex, demonstrating that authors must sometimes rearrange sentences within a paragraph to properly sequence the message, placing that horse before the cart.

EXAMPLES

Example #1

Before: **To affect more** efficient **computer security measures implementation within this domain, customer education** is essential.

After: Customer education is essential to implementing effective computer security.

Analysis: How can so short a sentence need so many modifications? Begin with the subject, *Customer education,* to put the horse before the cart. Next, don't use nouns as adjectives and separate *computer security measures* from *implementation.* Finally, *to affect more* and *measures* are discarded as useless words. These modifications yielded a crisper sentence and reduced the original length by half.

Example #2

Before: **So corporate executives can make informed decisions on managing resources,** they should stay current on operations.

After: Corporate executives should stay current on operations to effectively manage resources.

Analysis: We replace *can make informed decisions* with *effectively* and save much space. We place the horse before the cart, beginning with the subject, *corporate executives* and discard everything else!

Example #3

Before: Add **to your calendar the following** events and training opportunities **coming soon**.

After: Add these upcoming events and training activities to your calendar.

Analysis: First, determine if something is out of sequence. Is the horse behind the cart and if so, where? In this example, it is *coming soon*. We reduce *the following* to *these* and *coming soon* to *upcoming*. Now ask, *Future what?* This example also contains another less egregious example of horse and cart; in this case, the cart is *to your calendar*. Can you find the horse? It is *future events and training opportunities.* The simplified structure for this sentence should be *Add this to your calendar.*

Example #4

Before: Because the manuscript does not **contain more than** 60,000 words, **which serves as the** minimum length **for whether or not it will be considered for** publication, there is little likelihood **that** it will be published.

After: The manuscript is unlikely to be published because it does not meet the requisite minimum length of 60,000 words.

Analysis: Here is an extreme example of cart before the horse! The core thought is *The manuscript is unlikely to be published.* Addition of the word *requisite* replaces fifteen words and saves ninety-six spaces.

Example #5

Before: **If your presentation solicits an Information Resources Committee decision,** complete and return the form.

After: Complete and return the form if your presentation solicits a decision from the Information Resources Committee.

Analysis: Put the horse before the cart. Begin with the instruction *complete and return.* Then solve the issue of nouns used as adjectives by separating *Information Resources Committee* from *decision.*

Example #6

Before: **As part of our communication outreach effort to the community,** we **have** held a series of group discussions with the director during the past few months.

After: We held a series of group discussions with the director during the past few months as part of our community outreach.

Analysis: This also has a lengthy lead-in before getting to the point. The word *communication* can be deleted; it is redundant to *outreach. Effort* is a useless word. We also simplify the verb by discarding *have.*

Example #7

Before: By organizing a committee, developing goals, objectives, and milestones, regularly communicating with participants, reserving conference rooms and other facilities, and determining transportation needs, **the chairman demonstrated excellent planning skills**.

After: The chairman demonstrated excellent planning skills by organizing a committee; developing goals, objectives, and milestones; communicating regularly with participants; reserving conference rooms and other facilities; and determining transportation needs.

Analysis: Now this is a lengthy lead-in! Open with the subject, *the chairman* and correct the punctuation by adding semicolons. We also relocate the adverb *regularly* to follow the verb *communicating,* thus preserving the established pattern of beginning the subordinate thoughts with a gerund *(organizing, developing, communicating, reserving, and determining).*

Example #8

Before: Ensure **that** all logistics requirements for the move **have been** addressed by **attending planning meetings.**

After: Attend planning meetings to ensure all logistic requirements for the move are addressed.

Analysis: The horse here is *attend.* Discard *that* as useless. Reduce *have been* to *are.*

Example #9

Before: If an extended absence **is scheduled, provide notification to** your supervisor.

After: Notify your supervisor about projected, extended absences.

Analysis: Start with the verb *notify.* Don't use words that hog space; replace *is scheduled* with *projected.*

Example #10

Before: A plan to continually review infrastructure requirements to ensure the company meets **customer** expectations **will be implemented**.

After: The company will implement a plan to continually review infrastructure requirements. The goal is to ensure the company meets customers' expectations.

Analysis: The horse is *will be implemented.* However, by using the active voice we can delete *will be.* Begin with the presumed subject *the company.* We also modify *customer* to *customers'* so that it is not used as an adjective. It is perfectly acceptable to break a convoluted sentence into two for clarity.

CHAPTER 9 EXERCISES—Now You Try!

Exercise #1

Before: To quantify the costs and expected benefits of transitioning end-to-end IT services, and to help IT leaders build the business case, we created a detailed economic model.

After: _____

Exercise #2

Before: Where possible, (i.e., they can be predetermined by the FY calendar or program plans) these functions and critical interfaces should be captured in Appendix H.

After: _____

Exercise #3

Before: A principal member from each of the twelve counties, designated by the head of each Board of Supervisors, comprise the Transportation Commission.

After: _____

Exercise #4

Before: As the Hospital Liaison Program evolves and the director makes decisions that affect operational requirements and existing policy, updated versions of the Fact Sheet containing this new information, will be available online. In addition, any new questions that are raised based on community feedback, will be included in updated Fact Sheets.

After: _____

Exercise #5

Before: A strategic shift from multiple decentralized commercial outlets spread throughout the state to a centralized location near the capital that employs unified business strategies, common business practices, and standardized IT protocols has begun.

After: _____

Exercise #6

Before: In early 2019, while supporting the American Federation of Organic Horticulturalists and the Virginia Organization of Master Gardeners, he wrote a feature article on gardening.

After: _____

Exercise #7:

Before: Ensured all official documents meet the quality standards (grammar, completeness, timeliness, technical accuracy) to best represent the corporation to all of its clients through superior writing and editorial skills.

After: _____

Exercise #8

Before: While assigned to the Metropolitan Bureau of Community Development and liaison to the Future Highway Architecture program Office, Mr. Jones drafted a benchmark concept paper.

After: _____

Exercise #9

Before: For a corporate management team tasked with deciding among a number of possible options on fielding a major system worth 5 million dollars to manage product dissemination across the U.S., facilitated a team to a decision in four half-day sessions using FacilitateSystems to solicit opinions about the options; DPX, a marginal benefit-cost decision tool to combine probabilities; DPK, a decision analysis tool combining influence diagrams and decision trees for building technology area roadmaps; and SoundDecisions to evaluate options and present results of the discussion.

After: _____

Exercise #10

Before: Network Operation Center (NOC) Expands Operational Capability. As part of the organization's leadership in strengthening existing and building new partnerships with state and local government entities, and with assisting private sector enterprise in protecting critical elements of our infrastructure, the NOC has moved to improve its ability to rapidly communicate, analyze, and respond to network threats. The NOC was able to increase existing staff to enable extending its hours to 24 hours/day, 7 days/week. The NOC also has been providing training, conducting micro exercises as staff began to increase to ensure newly assigned personnel were completely proficient in their assigned tasks.

After: _____

Now, check your answers in Appendix A.

10. Verbs Are Your Friends: Rely on Them

Verbs make your product sparkle. They add pizzazz, depth, color, and excitement. Verbs mesmerize, delight, horrify, and amuse. Like stunt professionals and special effects in the movies, verbs make it happen. Use them and have fun. But, we often don't.

Instead, many authors shy from committing to a simple verb, preferring instead to encapsulate it in bureaucratic "wuz wuz." Imagine a 6-foot tall, hard-boiled egg . . . seriously, imagine one. Now, focus on the yolk—*that* is the verb. The white surrounding the yolk equates to blather in which authors encase the verb, thinking this makes products more professional. Hint: It doesn't.

Potential verbs are often hidden in bureaucratic language:

- *She **served in a liaison capacity** with six associated companies.* With a little thought, the verb *liaised* can surface in *She liaised with six associated companies.*

- *I **sent her a request to** attend the meeting.* Try *I asked her to attend the meeting.*

- *Each student needs a pass card **to gain entry into** the dormitory.* Revised: *Each student needs a pass card to enter the dormitory.*

- *She attended the political rally **to show support for** her candidate.* Try, *She attended the political rally to support her candidate.*

- *She was tasked to **make recommended** solutions.* Try, *She was tasked to recommend solutions.*

- *Tonight **is the inaugural performance** of the play.* We revise to *The play debuts tonight. The inaugural performance of* equates to the verb *debut* and saves twenty-four spaces!

Take a look at—WHOOPS—**Look** at these examples. (See how easily we slip into the mire of imprecise writing!) The trick is to review and expunge for a much crisper message.

- *Extend an invitation = invite*
- *Conduct an inspection = inspect*
- *Provide an estimate = estimate*
- *Execute reviews = review*
- *Submit suggestions = suggest*
- *Make progress = progress*
- *Have a discussion = discuss*
- *Make contact with = contact*
- *Take place = occur*

- *Come to agreement = agree*
- *Pay a visit = visit*
- *Come back = return*
- *Take it down = remove*
- *Give the ability to = enable*
- *Make certain = ensure*
- *Is dependent upon = depends on*
- *Make reservations = reserve*
- *Doesn't have = lacks*
- *Create a draft = draft*

Be cognizant of your word choice. Some words send a subtle but negative message. The words *keeps abreast* come to mind. In a foot race, *keeps abreast* does **not** separate the individual from the crowd. *She put in a solid performance.* Hmmm, sounds like a B or C evaluation to me.

Be attentive when selecting verbs describing someone's accomplishments. Verbs such as *provide, contribute to, support,* and *assist* are overused. Moreover, they add no value to the sentence and bore the reader—not the desired effect when writing to influence! Their inherent vagueness also obfuscates any significant achievement. These verbs, on the other hand, command attention: *surpass, mastermind, lead, direct, implement, organize, orchestrate, eliminate, conceive, instruct, isolate and correct*, and *initiate*.

One last item to address is *there is/there are,* initially mentioned in Chapter 6 as useless words. *There is/there are* almost invariably hide a more accurate and meaningful subject and verb. *There are many opportunities to succeed offered within this career field* can be modified to *This career field offers many opportunities to succeed.*

EXAMPLES

Example #1

Before: Please **provide answers to** the questions below.

After: Please answer the questions below.

Analysis: Use the simple verb *answer.*

Example #2

Before: Many proposals **contained assumptions that** manpower **would be** available.

After: Many proposals assumed available manpower.

Analysis: The verb is *assumed.* Delete useless words *that* and *would be.*

Example #3

Before: **The focus of** this group **is to** identify best practices in guidance counseling **employed by** other high schools.

After: This group identifies other high schools' best practices in guidance counseling.

Analysis: Answer, "Who does what?" "The group identifies what?" This formula also highlights several useless words.

Example #4

Before: The bill, if **signed by the president**, could **have** significant impacts **on** the tax structure.

After: If enacted, the bill could significantly impact the tax structure.

Analysis: *Enacted* is a delightful verb—crisp, to the point, and equates to "signed by the president." Note the conversion of *significant* to *significantly,* which allows you to modify the rest of the sentence by changing *have impacts on* to *impact.* Also note, this is an ambiguous statement because *impact* can be either positive or negative; this sentence does not specify outcome.

Example #5

Before: He volunteered **to be the master of ceremonies** for the upcoming award ceremony.

After: He volunteered to emcee the upcoming award ceremony.

Analysis: Simple. Switch *master of ceremonies* for the verb *emcee.* You can now also discard *to be.*

Example #6

Before: State and local **representation** on the panel **was provided by** Bob and Harry.

After: Bob and Harry represented state and local offices on the panel.

Analysis: Start with the subject *Bob and Harry.* In this instance, *represented* is the hidden verb and eliminates four words *representation was provided by.* And, the revised sentence is in active voice, as opposed to the *Before* sentence's passive voice. Beware using the passive *was* + (verb)-*ed* + *by* such as *was provided by* in this case.

Example #7

Before: More than 200 people **were in** attendance at the symposium.

After: More than 200 people attended the symposium.

Analysis: This includes another hidden verb. Using the actual verb *attended* not only clarifies the sentence, but also eliminates useless words.

Example #8

Before: An agency-**wide** review **process is underway** for the final draft.

After: The entire agency is reviewing the final draft.

Analysis: Identify the subject *agency* and replace *wide* with *entire.* Use the core verb *is reviewing* and discard *process is underway.*

Example #9

Before: Matt is tasked to **perform** the weekly **review** of the grocery **store** inventory.

After: Matt is tasked to review the grocery store inventory weekly.

Analysis: Delete the word *perform* and simply state *review.*

Example #10

Before: Harry **volunteered** to work a second shift.

After: Harry voluntarily worked a second shift so his colleague could attend her son's graduation.

Analysis: Harry may have volunteered for extra work, but did he actually work that extra shift? In the *Before* version, *volunteer* means only that he offered his services, but it doesn't specify that he actually delivered. The issue is clarified in the *After* version. Note: *Voluntarily* is an impactful adverb. The *After* version is longer. Why? To clarify the action and inform the reader about the "so what."

CHAPTER 10 EXERCISES—Now You Try!

Exercise # 1

Before: Harry provided demonstrations of the new software at the convention.

After: _____

Exercise #2

Before: Mary had a meeting with her partners to ensure the schedule was coordinated.

After: _____

Exercise #3

Before: The boss was agreeable to changing the date of the meeting.

After: _____

Exercise #4

Before: Reporters were provided with training on the process by which to conduct interviews with dignitaries.

After: _____

Exercise #5

Before: The Memorandum of Agreement establishes clearly defined responsibilities for managing the program.

After: _____

Exercise #6

Before: She demonstrated the ability to work well under pressure.

After: _____

Exercise #7

Before: The court's interpretation of the law runs counter to its intended purpose.

After: _____

Exercise #8

Before: He generated a draft briefing on the county's quarterly budget.

After: _____

Exercise #9

Before: The corporate representative was in attendance at the meeting and will report results back to the division chief.

After: _____

Exercise #10

Before: Our office is the lead for this effort.

After: _____

Now, check your answers in Appendix A.

11. Avoid Gibberish:
It's Confusing

Warning . . . warning . . . avoid gibberish! This unfortunate commodity exists in four forms:

- Job-related jargon inappropriate for the layman audience
- Unnecessary, detailed information
- Nouns upon nouns upon nouns . . . used as adjectives
- Communication that requires the reader to dig for the intended message

This type of writing is also known as *gobbledygook*, defined in Goldstein's *Disciplined Writing and Career Development* as, "A common form of official writing: an indigestible coagulated concoction of circumlocution and pomposity, pretentious words, and the passive voice, generously seasoned with needless jargon and esoteric acronyms, drained of human juices and packed in overstuffed sentences." Let's look at the four types of gibberish.

1. We begin with job-related jargon. As addressed in Chapter 2, "Know Your Audience—Psychology of the Catch," jargon *is* appropriate, and even preferred, in the correct context. For example, "striking out the side" is idiomatic language appropriate for baseball *aficionados.* However, beyond specific situations, authors often fail to communicate in terms transparent to the larger audience. This is particularly relevant to those in technical, scientific, and other specialized fields, who are challenged when communicating to a cross-functional committee that will determine funding, performance bonuses, awards, and promotions.

To compose a product easily understood, address two aspects: 1) the terminology and 2) the message, itself. To exemplify, when asking Congress to fund a multi-million-dollar IT system, don't speak in technical terms and highlight the improved computing rate or storage capacity. Explain, instead, how the proposed program will enhance your mission and the lives of American citizens. How will these funds benefit the taxpayer? This will contribute to a persuasive presentation.

Below is an example based on a line from a personnel appraisal. We translate it to explain what really happened and conclude with a detailed analysis.

Before: Repaired EWBS computer system after isolating failure to defective voltage regulator; returned the system back to fully operational status, preventing loss of mission-critical data.

After:

- Single-handedly prevented loss of critical data; identified subtle yet critical technical problem.
- Repaired complex weather monitoring system; worked 17 non-stop hours until he made the fix, long after others quit.

Avoid Gibberish

Analysis: This is a great example of pure gibberish! The reader has no idea regarding the significance of the operational impact or the heroic effort of the employee. The *EWBS* is the Emergency Weather Broadcasting System (fictional for the purpose of this book), but the author does not inform the reader. Just as well because the length of the name consumes valuable space. Next, what is a *defective voltage regulator* and does the reader need that level of detail? *Returned the system back* could have been shortened to *returned,* but we delete it in the revision. Wearing the hat of the investigative reporter, we ask the individual to describe his actions. As the fictional detective "Monk" so frequently states, "What really happened . . . " is conveyed in the *After* version. The golden bullet, by the way, is not that the individual fixed the computer system, but he *prevented loss of critical data* and did it *single-handedly*!

Acronyms are a major source of job-related gibberish, especially those known to you but meaningless to an audience outside your specific field or even outside your immediate department. Not only does improper use obscure your message, it can also hinder career progression. Here's how.

A headquarters convenes an annual awards board with voting members and nominees reflecting components throughout the organization (i.e., administration, logistics, human resources, finance, planning, and IT). To be competitive, nominations must be written in terms clear to all board members. How effective is the submission below?

> *I am pleased to nominate Joe for this annual Excellence Award. He handles a complex portfolio that consists of TYQ, SFF, IP Enterprise, NFIM, TSIB, and architecture patterns.*

In the example above, acronyms were all IT-related (modified for purposes of this book) and were neither spelled out nor explained in the nomination package. This gibberish frustrated the board members and torpedoed Joe's nomination.

Here is a military example; for most of you, this is a foreign language.

I went TDY to EUCOM but because of my AFSC, AFPC changed my orders. After MPF processed them, I PCS'd to EUCOM instead, ASAP! TMO performed brilliantly, and the ETA for my HHG was exactly as projected. Finally, MMC!

Deciding what acronyms to spell out is subjective and can be tricky. First, identify acronyms known by the intended reader—and do not spell them out. Why? First, each name spelled out consumes space. Second, the lengthy version slows the reader, who can more rapidly grasp, for example, *FBI* contrasted with the *Federal Bureau of Investigation.* This last point and the reader's frustration are compounded if a paragraph contains several of these examples.

Spell out uncommon acronyms and present the abbreviated form at its first introduction; use the acronym thereafter. Often, authors mistakenly repeat the full spelling and introduce the acronym at its second or third use. Mistakenly, the author also spells out the acronym after having already introduced the short form. These are common errors in professional writing. Bottom line, if you use an acronym, do so correctly and consistently.

You must sometimes differentiate between primary and secondary audiences, giving preference, of course, to the primary. I once regularly authored a Weekly Activity Report for a very senior-level executive, my primary audience. Accordingly, I spelled out some but not all acronyms because he knew them. A colleague suggested that I spell out all acronyms for the convenience of subordinate staff members who also received the report. I declined to do so; benefitting the subordinate staff did not justify inconveniencing the primary audience. If a reader was unfamiliar with an acronym, he or she could look it up. Tough, yes, but I maintained the proper focus.

An alternative to using the acronym is to explain in general terms what the item is. I demonstrated this in the EWBS example above. This approach also applies to the names of operations and exercises (usually military), such as Operation Enduring Freedom. Unfamiliar with that name? It refers to military operations in Afghanistan that began in late 2001. Using such monikers in resumes or other products without explanation will lose and frustrate the reader. Here are some examples:

Before: Harvey was ecstatic after purchasing the **STG44, Sturmgewehr 1944** at the gun show.

After: Harvey was ecstatic after purchasing the antique German rifle at the gun show.

Before: Angela excelled in learning **PESOS (Prepare, Explain, Show, Observe, Supervise).**

After: Angela excelled in learning the new training method.

Before: The new medicine contained soy-derived **phosphatidylserine (S-PS).**

After: The new medicine contained a nutritional supplement that claims to enhance cognition.

Before: They used **CONEX (Container Express, ISO inter-modal shipping and cargo containers)** to transfer the machine parts overseas.

After: They used large, steel shipping boxes to transfer the machine parts overseas.

However you deal with acronyms, be careful. When an author refers to *NDU* does he refer to the *National Defense University, North Dakota University,* or something else? *T&E* equates to *test and evaluation,* and *threatened and endangered. A&E* equates to *accident and emergency, architecture and engineering,* and *Arts and Entertainment. FBI* stands for *Full Blooded Indian; Faith-based Initiatives; From the Big Island* (i.e., Hawaii); *Fungi, Bacteria, Invertebrate;* and the *Federal Bureau of Investigation. CIA* stands for *Celestial Intervention Agency, Culinary Institute of America, Cleveland Institute of Art,* and the *Community Improvement Award.* Let's not forget the *Central Intelligence Agency!*

Granted, one can sometimes determine the intended meaning from context, but why burden the reader? *He was injured by the IED.* Does *IED* stand for *improvised explosive device* or *Intermittent Explosive Disorder? Contact Mr. Smith at the HL if you need assistance.* Does *HL* refer to *help line, hot line,* or *House of Lords? The budget stimulus prompted long-anticipated enhancements to the HUD.* Does this refer to *Heads-up Display* or *Housing and Urban Development?*

2. The second type of gibberish is unnecessary, excessive detail. As background to the example below, an individual is applying for a job as a reference librarian. Can you identify the gibberish in this extract from her resume?

Before: As reference librarian, my duties included obtaining books and articles, reference material, and other publications as needed or requested, restacking books, and performing Internet searches for customers on a daily basis.

After: Current position — Senior of three reference librarians at Virginia's largest public library that contains 400,000 books and supports 35,000 visitors monthly.

Analysis: Most employers seeking to hire a reference librarian are cognizant of the core duties. Therefore, the author doesn't need to delineate them. The space is better used by scoping the magnitude of his or her responsibilities and accomplishments.

Can you detect the excessive detail in this next example?

Before: I managed the security program for the Office of Project and Fixed Asset Management, Defense Programs Office of Maintenance Facilities, and the Office of Environmental Oversight and Management in agency ABCD.

After: Managed the security program supporting 1,400 people in three divisions of agency ABCD. This entailed all aspects of physical, personnel, and computer network security.

Analysis: This is based on a resume. Therefore, the author does not need to specify *I*. The titles of the offices are gibberish. The author should more effectively use this space to explain the organizational level at which she works (we identify it as *division*) and quantify the scope of her accomplishments.

How does one strike the proper balance between too much or too little detail? The answer is simple—empathy. Know your audience. This mantra cuts to the core principle of effective communication. Is the intended reader a fellow subject matter expert or does that individual work at a higher level in the organization? If the latter, the reader's familiarity might be at a wider corporate level and less functionally deep than yours.

Are you writing items for senior-level executives in the corporate or government arenas or for members of evaluation boards, all of whom are pressed for time? These are cut-to-the-chase people, so tailor your products and provide only necessary information. Perhaps your audience is completely unfamiliar with your field. A team of journalists addressed several troops of Girl Scouts at a museum in Washington, D.C. Did they speak in professional acronyms or use scores of statistics to tell their story? Certainly not.

3. This next type of bureaucratic blather is so egregious, it made my list, "The Dirty Dozen: Most Common Errors in Professional Writing." Authors tend to pile noun upon noun as modifiers of yet another noun. This is ubiquitous in professional writing and smothers the author's intended meaning.

Let me demonstrate. A pair of nouns (the first used as an adjective) is simple—grocery store, desk top, kitchen counter, and computer security. However, watch what happens when the author excessively piles on the nouns:

- computer security
- computer security risk
- computer security risk management

- computer security risk management policy
- computer security risk management policy objectives
- computer security risk management policy objectives implementation plan

A reader is thus inflicted with the sentence below:

The corporation will use a computer security risk management policy objectives implementation plan to enable strategic, data-driven decisions regarding partners and partnerships.

4. The final type of gibberish is information that only partially communicates the message and forces the reader to extrapolate the intended message based on incomplete information. Be kind, and don't make her work to understand your communication.

For example, this memo was sent on November 24 to the director of a company that manufactures textbooks, alerting her to a potential production problem:

Before: To meet the contractual deadline of Nov. 29, we must produce 2,500 textbooks. However, many of our employees will be on vacation.

After: We have three working days to meet the Nov. 29 deadline of producing 2,500 textbooks. Twelve employees will be out for Thanksgiving, leaving nine to accomplish the task. We can make the deadline by working extended shifts.

Analysis: The *Before* example seems sufficiently clear. However, the director is forced to determine exactly how much time and resources remain to meet the deadline. The author should provide this information in the alerting email. As an ancillary teaching point, if you highlight a problem to the boss, also recommend a solution.

EXAMPLES

Example #1

Before: **Tracks and** ensures all deadlines are kept for the corporate Chief Executive Officer's **take ins and due outs**.

After: Ensures the CEO meets all deadlines.

Analysis: So many items to discuss in this short sentence. Does the reader care about *tracks* or is this just a subset of the action, *ensures*? Does one not automatically *track* to *ensure*? Next, the reader must intuit the meaning of *take ins and due outs,* presuming that these are items requiring action. This lack of clarity can distract a busy reader— such as a possible employer. The writer can assume that *CEO* is a familiar acronym and shouldn't be spelled out. Finally, we revise to place this in the active, not passive voice.

Example #2

Background: This example is based on a submission to the Weekly Activity Report, a product by which the staff informs corporate senior leadership about significant events or accomplishments.

Before: The Director, Business Development Group **and six staff members attended a meeting on July 6 from 9:00 a.m. until 11:00 a.m. in room 546 of the Roosevelt Building,** chaired by Jane Nesbitt, Director of the Financial Division, on the **impact** of recently increased interest rates.

After: The Director, Business Development Group and the Director, Financial Division discussed the impact of recently increased interest rates. They devised an approach that protects the corporation's assets while soliciting new business opportunities.

Analysis: As originally written, this is unworthy for senior-level readers. What does it say? People A met People B to discuss topic C. *Impact* is an unspecific noun—it can be good or bad; the author fails to clarify. Next, would the boss really care how many people attended; the exact location, date, and time of the meeting; or that these individuals actually met? Probably not. Would the boss care who chaired the meeting? Perhaps, depending on the context. Note also the absence of a "so what." What actually happened as a result of the discussion? We added that in a concluding sentence.

Example #3

Before: He advised the **Manager** on key issues and project milestones **as they occur as they relate** to **Project Hot Enchilada**.

After: He advised the manager on key issues and project milestones relating to opening a new chain of Mexican restaurants.

Analysis: Avoid unnecessary use of a project name by explaining what it is. *Manager* should not be capitalized. The sentence contains several useless words, *as they occur* and *as they.*

Example #4

Before: Communicates technical and complex information **easily and concisely** prepares effective proposals, reports, and presentation **utilizing charts and graphs**.

After: Concisely communicates technical and complex information. Prepares effective proposals, reports, and presentations.

Analysis: This is also based on a resume. Delete *utilizing charts and graphs* as excessive detail. The potential employer doesn't need to know the prospective employee uses charts and graphs in presentations. The line is vague, leaving the reader wondering to what *concisely* refers: *communicates technical and complex information* or *prepares effective proposals.* We chose the former, reducing *easily and concisely* to simply *concisely.* We also break the line into two sentences. But, this still begs the question, "What constitutes *effective*?"

Example #5

Before: **Skillfully utilized the listed computer system daily Automated Message Handling System (AMHS), Aircraft and Personnel Automated Clearance System (APACS), Common Access Card (CAC), Joint Personnel Adjudication System (JPAS), visitor Badge System (VBS), Synchronized Pre-deployment and Operational Tracker (SPOT), G-Forge and E-Trip,** to obtain **Combatant Command** and U.S. Embassy approvals to travel **in the various Areas of Responsibility.**

After: Proficient in using a wide variety of software systems and databases to obtain permission from the military and U.S. embassies for personnel to travel and operate overseas. In one year, processed 146 requests, 30 percent more than her peers.

Analysis: This, too, is based on a resume. The author should not inflict the reader with this litany of complex names and can save space—and spare the reader some torment—by instead referring to them as *a wide variety of software systems and databases.* If these names are important, list them at the end of the resume under "Technical Skills" or "IT Proficiency." The author includes the acronyms for each system but does not refer to them again anywhere in the resume, wasting valuable space.

Mistakes: Did you catch *listed computer system,* which should have been plural? The author fails to capitalize *visitor* in the proper name *Visitor Badge System.* A comma is mistakenly added following *E-Trip.* Remembering that the reading audience could be civilian, we replace military jargon and streamline wording: *Combatant Command* equates to *military,* and *in the various Areas of Responsibility* translates to one word, *overseas.* We also expound on the purpose of the travel by adding *to travel and operate overseas* because the point of these trips is not *to travel* but *to operate.* The *Before* version also misses the opportunity to complete the story with a "so what" line. We craft this one to exemplify how the reader can add just a bit more to provide a more consequential message.

Example #6

Before: Successfully automated inventory control **through implementation of Mobility Inventory Control Access System (MICAS), Property Book Unit Supply Enhanced (P-BUSE), Property Accountability Support System (PASS), Integrated Logistics System (ILS), and Joint Acquisition Chemical System (JACKS).**

After: Successfully automated inventory control by leveraging four fundamental software systems critical to this functional area.

Analysis: This, too, is based on a resume. The reader does not need all these complex names but can save space by referring to them as *software systems critical to this functional area.* If these names are important, list them at the end of the resume under "Technical Skills" or "IT Proficiency."

Example #7

Before: The **DCM** advised the country team that a **CODEL** would arrive in country next week. He tasked the **RSO** to coordinate security arrangements of the visit with the host nation. Following their scheduled courtesy call with the **COM**, the **CODEL** wanted to meet the **DATT, OPSCO, ARMA, AIRA,** and other personnel in the **DAO**. Prior to returning to **CONUS**, the delegation also requested time with the **FLO** to determine how families of embassy staff were coping with life overseas. Upon conclusion of the visit, the **DCM** would include an outbrief in the **DAR.**

After: The Deputy Chief of Mission (DCM) told the country team that a congressional delegation would arrive in country next week. He tasked the Regional Security Officer to coordinate security arrangements of the visit with the host nation. Following a scheduled courtesy call with the ambassador, the delegation wanted to meet with the Defense Attaché and other personnel in the Defense Attaché Office. Prior to returning to the U.S., the delegation also requested time with the Family Liaison Officer to determine how families of embassy staff were coping with life overseas. Upon conclusion of the visit, the DCM would include an item in the Daily Activity Report.

Analysis: In essence, we translate this into English, removing all gibberish. First, spell out acronyms when first used, as they might not be familiar to the reader. *CONUS,* for example, stands for *the continental United States,* which when shorten to *the U.S. COM,* also equates to the *Chief of Mission,* also known as *the ambassador.* Second, determine if the acronym lends any benefit—if not, don't use it. Third, if the acronym will not be repeated then don't use it. Fourth, is it necessary to specify the other members of the Defense Attaché Office, such as Operations Coordinator (OPSCO), Army Attaché (ARMA), and Air Attaché (AIRA)? If so, the author should spell out each of these acronyms, but it's cumbersome reading, to be sure. If not, *other personnel in the Defense Attaché Office* can describe the group.

Example #8

Note: Previous examples use the format of *Before, After,* and *Analysis.* However, this example challenges you to decide what information your reader needs based on the scenario.

Scenario: You recently organized and executed a meeting with senior leaders across corporate headquarters. You need to provide a one-paragraph summary of this event to the Senior Vice President for Production. What do you convey? Here is the information you **could** include. Decide what makes and doesn't make the cut. How much information is enough? What does the boss really **need to know**?

1. Specific date, time, location (to include building and room number of the meeting)

2. Names and duty titles of all attendees

3. Names of organizations represented

4. Logistics preparations you accomplished to set up and execute the meeting (scheduling the conference room, printing copies of read-ahead material, stuffing folders for all attendees, making a seating chart, laying out tent cards and folders for all attendees, arranging a teleconference for those unable to attend, making posters and maps, etc.)

5. Date and location of the next meeting

6. Discussion threads (who said what) for each agenda item

7. Concluding recommendations

8. Comments or feedback (hopefully positive) on the meeting's planning and execution

9. Summary of key points made

10. Resulting action items and who is responsible for each

11. Coordinating details of the meeting with participants to include providing read-ahead materials

12. Agenda items

Answer: Items that should make the cut are 3, 7, 9, and 10. Depending on who provided positive feedback, 8 could also be included. Despite the hard work that resulted in a flawless meeting, the boss doesn't need the other details.

Example #9

Before: Team A **met with** Team B **to** discuss the new security training program **that is to be implemented across the corporation** and implementation **plan issues. Good progress was made on the way forward and an** invitation **extended by** Team A to Team B to **accompany their members on visits to** regional offices **pursuant to the corporation's** policy requiring annual security inspections **which was** launched by corporate headquarters two years ago as a means for assessing the **adequacy of** regional offices to comply with corporate regulations **in the Information Security arena. Further** discussions **are in progress** regarding the scope/timing and location of these visits.

After: Team A and Team B discussed the new corporate-wide training program on security and its implementation. The meeting was very productive. Team A invited Team B to participate in annual security inspections of regional offices, as required by corporate policy. Corporate headquarters launched this inspection program two years ago to assess the regional offices' compliance with corporate security regulations. Discussions continue regarding the scope, timing, and location of the site visits.

Analysis: Begin by identifying the core verb: replace *met with . . . to discuss* with *discussed.* Replace *across the corporation* with *corporate-wide.* Avoid using nouns as adjectives: transform *implementation plan issues* to *implementation. Plan issues* is extraneous data. Transform *Good progress was made on the way forward* into more professional terms such as, *The meeting was very productive.* Avoid the passive voice of *an invitation was extended by Team A to Team B* by stating simply *Team A invited Team B.* Shorten *to accompany their members* with *to participate.* Choose a simpler term, replacing *pursuant to* with *required by. Visits to . . . as a means for assessing* equates to *inspections.* Change the *corporation's policy* to *corporate policy.*

Next, avoid the passive voice by revising *was launched by corporate headquarters* to *Corporate headquarters launched. The adequacy of regional offices to comply* equates to *regional offices' compliance. In the Information Security arena* equates to *security regulations.* Also note that *Information Security* was improperly capitalized. *Further discussions are in progress* equates to *discussions continue.* Finally, delete the "/" between *scope/timing* and replace with a comma. By applying *Word Sculpting Tools,* we reduced this paragraph from 104 to 70 words!

Example #10

Before: The **Federal Bureau of Investigation, Drug Enforcement Agency, and Department of Defense** officers briefed our recruits at the quarterly orientation class. Presentations were well received.

After: Officers from the FBI, DEA, and DOD briefed our recruits at the quarterly orientation class. Presentations prompted excellent, substantive questions from the audience.

Analysis: This example chokes the reader by unnecessarily spelling out FBI, DEA, and DOD. It also concludes with a vague summary statement, so we clarified.

CHAPTER 11 EXERCISES—Now You Try!

Exercise #1

Before: Regular staff meetings help to provide shared operational visibility on end-of-the-year financial transactions.

After: _____

Exercise #2

Before: Currently, there is a multiplicity of non-interoperable collaboration IT tools in use across the corporation. This not only limits corporate information sharing potential, but also generates increased costs.

After: _____

Exercise #3

Before: Users should be advised up front what to expect that will be new IT capabilities, what will no longer be available, and the major differences they will see.

After: _____

Exercise #4

Before: She provides office staff thought leadership to projects and process improvement activities.

After: _____

Exercise #5

Before: I gathered information regarding financial management vendors' software and provided a summary of the products.

After: _____

Exercise #6

Before: Conduct technical market analysis, concept idea development, design and functional development of new product ideas to ensure the organizations continued growth, development of white papers from resulting research, software and hardware testing, and maintaining the organization's competitive position in the marketplace.

After: _____

Exercise #7

Before: Demonstrated instructional techniques while conducting quarterly training for directorates in accordance with regulations ABCD-5400.12; EFGH-334.5; XHRZ-4300.2; and Corporate Policy 1002, *Mandatory Annual Training Requirements.*

After: _____

Exercise #8

Before: Ability to synthesize data and prepared, designed, budgetary analysis, manpower data, procurement cost and presented the proposal for a supply depot with cost estimate of 250K to senior level executives.

After: _____

Exercise #9

Before: Successfully automated inventory control through implementation of Inventory Access Control System (IACS), Automated Property Supply (APS), Property Accounting System (PAS), Logistics and Infrastructure System (LIS), and the Inventory and Supply Requirements System (ISRS).

After: _____

Exercise #10

Before: Managed the security program for a CJTF in Operation Enduring Freedom.

After: _____

Now, check your answers in Appendix A.

12. Tethers: In Sentences and Otherwise

To introduce this *Word Sculpting Tool,* envision the following items:

- Child holding the string of a red, helium-filled balloon
- Lady walking her dog on a leash
- Ground station controlling an orbiting satellite
- Commander leading a military unit in combat
- Coach directing a football team on the field

Question: What do they have in common?

Answer: a tether. Whether physical, digital, or conceptual, each item is tethered to a base.

Let's examine this from a literary perspective. A common construct for sentences involves tethering several items to a base concept. The author must ensure each item is properly tethered, making sense when directly associated with its particular base.

The example below demonstrates a functional tether. *Drafted, coordinated, and disseminated* are the items (aka the balloon) and *minutes* is the base (aka the little girl). See how it works.

- *She drafted, coordinated, and disseminated minutes of the meeting.* Validate these tethers by associating each with its base. *Drafted minutes, coordinated minutes,* and *disseminated minutes.* Perfect!

Check these examples following the steps demonstrated above.

- *This software was used to manage production, operating costs, and the delivery schedule.* The tethers are sound: *manage production, manage operating costs,* and *manage delivery schedule.*

- *Developed, coordinated, and monitored processes, procedures, and the tools necessary to allow for identification, development, assignment, implementation, and tracking of fiscal requirements in corporate headquarters and overseas branches.* What a mouthful! But, all tethers in this sentence work. However, this example demonstrates too much of a good thing.

- *The Human Resources Department developed, recruited, and aligned the workforce to achieve corporate goals.* You see the pattern here: *developed the workforce, recruited the workforce,* and *aligned the workforce.*

- *She authored, coordinated, and briefed the report at the quarterly marketing conference.* The tethers work: *authored the report, coordinated the report,* and *briefed the report.*

- *Reviewed and redesigned the company's records management, knowledge management, and content management systems.* This example contains two sets of tethers, and both work.

- *He is responsible for coordinating, developing, editing, and publishing instruction manuals.* The tethers are sound: *coordinating manuals, developing manuals, editing manuals,* and *publishing manuals.* I note one refinement for this last example in the sequence of listed items. The author should place them chronologically: *develop, edit, coordinate,* and *publish.*

The tether also applies to listed items. The base is the word that immediately precedes the colon; the items are the bullets that follow.

This book provides:

- Strategies to write powerfully
- *Word Sculpting Tools* to hone your draft
- 200 exercises to practice teaching points

The tether is also an excellent tool to use at the paragraph level. Examine each sentence (i.e., the item) in context of the topic sentence (i.e., the base). If the tether holds and the sentences correlate, the paragraph is solid. If not, adjust.

Using the examples below, examine the concept more closely. The tethered item (aka, the balloon) is bolded and the base (aka, the child) is underlined.

EXAMPLES

Example #1

Before: She **composed** and **translated** technical information into layman's language.

To verify the soundness of the two tethers, determine if it is possible to *compose information into layman's language.* The answer, "Not so much, because of the word *into*, which implies a change." But it is possible to compose information *in* layman's language. Is it possible to *translate information into layman's language*? Yes. That tether works. Now, we give the child a third balloon, *analyzed*.

She **analyzed**, **composed**, and **translated** technical information into layman's language.

To verify the soundness of the tether, pose the question, "Can someone *analyze information into layman's language*?" The answer, "No." Now, we give the child a final balloon and, you guessed it . . . verify the tether.

She **gathered**, **analyzed**, **composed**, and **translated** technical information into layman's language.

You get the drill now. Can you *gather information into layman's language*? Again, "No." This sentence is completely dysfunctional. To fix it, we tether the balloons, *gathered, analyzed, and composed* to a new base, *technical information*. And, here's the solution.

After: *She gathered, analyzed, and composed technical information and translated it into layman's language.*

Example #2

Before: She develops finance **plans**, transportation **plans** and **assists** in the development of emergency response plans.

After: She develops finance plans and transportation plans and helps develop emergency response plans.

Analysis: At first glance at the *Before* version, the base element *develops* supports three tethers: *develops finance plans, develops transportation plans,* and *develops assists.* You see the third is dysfunctional. We repair this by tethering the first two items to the base *develops: Develops finance plans and transportation plans.* We revise *assists in the development of* to *helps develop,* placing this action in parallel construction with the other base *develops.* Thus, you have *She develops A and B and helps develop C.*

110

Example #3

Before: The supervisor plans the **agenda**, attendee **list**, and the meeting **date**.

After: The supervisor establishes the agenda, attendee list, and the meeting date.

Analysis: The base for the tether is *plan*. Let's validate the tethers. *Plan . . . agenda* works. *Plan . . . list* is a broken tether. *Plan . . . the date* also works. This sentence can be easily fixed by replacing the verb *plans* with *establishes. Establishes the . . . agenda, list, and date.*

Example #4

Before: She **ensured** and **executed** in a professional manner administrative actions in a fast-paced environment.

After: She performed administrative functions professionally in an operationally intense environment.

Analysis: The first tether is dysfunctional. How can someone *ensure administrative actions*? While the second tether, *execute administrative actions,* is valid, the entire sentence is more effectively written as shown above.

Example #5

Before: This office provides financial management **awareness** and **training**.

After: This office provides training on financial management.

Analysis: The first tether is dysfunctional. How can someone *provide awareness*? While the second tether is valid, *provide training,* the entire sentence is more effectively written as shown above. We delete the term *awareness* as redundant; it is encompassed in the term *training.*

Example #6

Before: He conducted **link analysis** and **correlation** of criminal finance activities.

After: He analyzed links and correlated activities associated with criminal finances.

Analysis: In today's bureaucratic-speak, the tether *conducted link analysis* works. The tether *conducted correlation* does not. Recognizing this as an example of a hidden verb, delete *conducted* and focus on the real actions, *analyze* and *correlate.* We also revise this to preclude using nouns as adjectives, preferring *activities associated with criminal finances.*

Example #7

Before: She was tasked to explore **the desire to** and **utility in** forming a committee for the county bazaar.

After: She was tasked to explore the desire to form and the usefulness of a committee for the county bazaar.

Analysis: The base here is *forming.* The problem lies with prepositions attached to each item tethered to the *-ing* verb ending (the gerund form, for you English majors.) Test the first tether: *the desire to form**ing*** does not work. The second tether, *utility in forming* does. So, we revise by shifting the base to *committee,* making *desire to form a committee* and *usefulness of a committee.*

Example #8

Before: This position requires **briefing** senior executives and **draft** accurate detailed production reports.

After: This position requires briefing senior executives and drafting detailed production reports.

Analysis: The base *requires* has two items. The first tether works, *requires briefing*. The second tether is broken, *requires draft*. This is easily remedied by replacing *draft* with the parallel noun *drafting*.

Example #9

Before: Would the company **be able to** or **interested in** expediting the delivery schedule?

After: Would the company be interested in expediting the delivery schedule? Could it do so?

Analysis: The base is *expediting.* Check the tether: *be able to or interested in expediting.* It doesn't work. Writers often break tethers by adding a mismatched preposition preceding the base.

Example #10

Before: **Created** a viable and **implemented** an award program and process for the Project Manager, providing management and oversight support.

After: Created and implemented a viable award program, providing a vehicle for the project manager to oversee the process.

Analysis: This is a bullet based on a resume. Placement of the adjective *viable* interrupts the tether. Move it and the first part of the sentence comes into focus. We rewrote the rest of the sentence to clarify the final thought. Did you notice that *Project Manager* was incorrectly capitalized?

CHAPTER 12 EXERCISES—Now You Try!

Exercise #1

Before: Manages, conducts research, analysis, and provides guidance on responses to public inquiries.

After: _____

Exercise #2

Before: Plans, directs, organizes, and exercises control over all Security Administration processes, procedures and manages staff within the corporate security office.

After: _____

Exercise #3

Before: She reserved the room for, sent invitations, and arranged catering of the annual awards dinner.

After: _____

Exercise #4

Before: The plan focuses on enabling integration of design teams, greater company-wide communication, and on reducing operating costs thru implementation of new software capabilities.

After: _____

Exercise #5

Before: This role caused him to organize, shepherd, and facilitate three Senior Executive "Security Pow Wows" for corporate personnel.

After: _____

Exercise #6

Before: He demonstrated strong writing skills and communications skills with audiences of varying backgrounds and authorities.

After: _____

Exercise #7

Before: He worked to identify program requirements that met tactical, operational, and strategic needs information needs; guided development of roles, missions, and functions; information requirements; products and services; information sources; IT architecture; drafted the Operation's Plan.

After: _____

Exercise #8

Before: Ensured and executed with professionalism numerous administrative actions in a fast paced environment. These actions are medical screening, passports/visas, procurement of mission-related clothing and equipment, and more.

After: _____

Exercise #9

Before: Conducted interviews, employee evaluations, and problem resolution.

After: _____

Exercise #10

Before: Facilitated meetings in the design, development, testing, and training of reporting tools and data base architectures.

After: _____

Now, check your answers in Appendix A.

13. Be Clear:
Who-Does-What-to-Whom?

Snarled writing is difficult to understand, can be tricky to unravel, inflicts needless frustration upon the reader, and undermines your message. Avoid this by clearly stating, "Who (pause) does what (pause) to whom?" Identify the fundamental subject, verb, and object, and then insert amplifying information, as appropriate. This approach transforms *She assisted with document preparation of travel expense reports* to *She helped prepare travel expense reports.*

Here is an example of classic bureaucratic blather: *This team actively participates in corporate initiatives in a manner that fosters collaboration and focuses attention on our common goals and shared commitment to corporate success, regardless of organizational affiliation.* Put that in clear text!

Poor writing techniques we've discussed so far converge to generate this convoluted, unintelligible morass: inappropriate or awkward verbs, the passive voice, misplaced phrases, useless words, redundancy, cart before the horse, and long strings of nouns used as adjectives.

Consider these examples of how *not* to write:

- *This document was originally prepared by the Federal Reserve Board at the request of Congress in this stipulated format.* Imagine reading paragraph upon paragraph written like that! Apply the formula "Who (pause) does what (pause) to whom?" and this results, *The Federal Reserve Board prepared the document in the format that Congress stipulated.*

- *Consider questions a reader might have and ensure every effort is made to compose a report leaving no major questions unanswered in the reader's mind.* Translated we have, *Compose a report that anticipates and answers the reader's questions.*

- *A memo documenting the agreement was made for recordkeeping purposes.* Huh? Here's a much simpler version: *The agreement was documented in a memo* still uses passive voice, so an even better sentence is *They documented the agreement in a memo.*

- *When planned well, end-to-end IT services can drive up to a seventeen-percent reduction in an annual budget.* The revision reads, *Well-planned, comprehensive IT services can reduce an annual budget by up to seventeen percent.*

- *Passengers are requested to report any behavior they have reason to believe may be suspicious to airport authorities.* This can be simplified to, *Report suspicious behavior to airport authorities.*

- *This brochure describes the Computer Security and Risk Management Committee processes.* Try instead, *This brochure describes the processes of the Computer Security and Risk Management Committee.*

EXAMPLES

Example #1

Before: He **researched** and **incorporated best practices** from charters of **other** similar organizations to provide clear roles and responsibilities for each organization in the draft charter.

After: He researched charters of similar organizations, identified best practices, and incorporated these into his own draft charter to delineate organizational roles and responsibilities.

Analysis: The revision more clearly associates each verb with the corresponding object and then orders them sequentially. This answers the questions, "What did he do and why?" "He researched what?" "Identified what?" The word *delineate* replaces the word *provide* because it is sharper and more descriptive of the action taken.

Example #2

Before: A corporate-**level** policy **is** needed on **dealing** with the media.

After: The corporation needs a policy on interfacing with the media.

Analysis: Active voice saves space, is more direct, and is clearer. Replace the word *dealing* with *interfacing*. Why? *Dealing* is too colloquial and is reminiscent of a card game. It also has a negative connotation, as if *dealing with the media* is a bad thing. *Interfacing* is more positive and implies collaboration.

Example #3

Before: **Significant efforts by** the staff **went into** the creati**on of** a new dining facility.

After: The staff worked hard to create a new dining facility.

Analysis: Apply who-did-what-to-whom and the story emerges.

Example #4

Before: Recently, the office manager notified the system administrator that teams overseas reported **that** a size restriction for email attachments was hampering **their** effectiveness. Technicians theorized **that** configuration issues on the distant end were **creating the difficulties. After confirming this**, they communicated the fix to the users.

After: The office manager recently notified the system administrator that a restriction in size for email attachments was hampering the effectiveness of overseas teams. Technicians theorized, then confirmed the cause to be configuration issues on the distant end and communicated the fix to the users.

Analysis: Be kind to the reader and simplify this story line. Begin with the subject, not the adverb *Recently*. Discard *were creating the difficulties,* which is already understood in the thought, *hampering their effectiveness. After confirming this* is reduced to *confirmed.* This revision presumes the central point is the email issue, not the fact that the field units reported it; that data point is not included in the revision.

Example #5

Before: She led the mission **requirements definition, prioritization, and management** process through the **system implementation** lifecycle.

After: She led the process to define, prioritize, and manage the mission's requirements through the lifecycle of the system's implementation.

Analysis: "She led what to do what?" Answer the question and the bureaucratic fog suddenly lifts. This is a classic example of creating confusion and possible misreading by using long strings of nouns as adjectives.

Example #6

Before: **Family, bereavement, and counseling** related to post-traumatic stress **are** covered by the **insurance policy**.

After: The insurance policy covers counseling for families, bereavement, and post-traumatic stress.

or

The insurance policy covers counseling for families and situations involving bereavement and post-traumatic stress.

Analysis: Identify the subject, *policy.* What does it do? It *covers.* What does it cover? Three types of *counseling: family, bereavement, and post-traumatic stress.* The revision states *families,* using the noun instead of using *family* as an adjective to modify *counseling. Counseling* is a central concept and shouldn't be buried in the middle of the sentence. The active voice also helps clarify the thought.

Example #7

Before: Provide inputs for the development of **an information services and data management** policy.

After: Provide input for the development of a policy on information services and data management.

Analysis: The long string *information services and data management* should not be used as adjectives modifying *policy.* Rather, the sentence addresses a policy on these topics. Additionally, this is an example of the cart before the horse because the key thought, *policy*, was placed as the last word in the sentence.

Example #8

Before: [Note to instructor] Explain **the** need to know **who it is that** you are speaking with before providing the data.

After: [Note to instructor] Teaching point: Individuals need to know with whom they are speaking before providing the requested data.

Analysis: To clarify this for the instructor, flag the item as a *teaching point.* This also separates the fact that it IS a teaching point from the information to convey to the students. Using correct grammar, *whom* instead of *who,* also helps.

Example #9

Before: **Ensuring version control of all documentation through multiple layers of review** and revision requiring quick decision-making and sound judgment, flexibility, and creative problem-solving skills.

After: Organized, adjudicated, and incorporated approximately 250 modifications to a key planning document and its three appendices during the course of three major reviews by eight organizations. Meticulously managed the development of the document from initial draft to final signature; regularly updated all contributors on its status. Demonstrated sound judgment, flexibility, and creative problem-solving skills throughout the processes.

Analysis: What is involved in *ensuring version control*? What did the individual do? The *Before* example prompted many questions. For those unfamiliar with developing complex documents, what is *version control*? What is meant by *all documentation*? How many is *multiple layers of review*? The *After* version clarifies the individual's accomplishment.

Example #10

Before: Next week, I **will send** you a **Budget and Analysis Committee Minutes review request**.

After: Next week, I will ask you to review the minutes of the Budget and Analysis Committee.

Analysis: This is another example of a long string of nouns being used as adjectives. One is OK, but many in a row can be confusing, be misread, and frustrate the reader. *Budget and Analysis Committee Minutes review* should not modify (i.e., precede) *request.* To unravel this, first ask, "What will I send?" The answer, a *request.* To do what? *To review the minutes.* Finally, we reduce *send . . . a . . . request* to one word, *ask.*

CHAPTER 13 EXERCISES—Now You Try!

Exercise #1

Before: The inspector noted several annual financial report recordkeeping inconsistencies.

After: _____

Exercise #2

Before: To point out to the employees the many successes of the company this past year, the CEO presented a briefing that addressed the overall goals and objectives at both corporate and regional levels, successful marketing strategies, new product lines developed, customer feedback, and wrapped it up by recognizing those individuals with the highest sales statistics.

After: _____

Exercise #3

Before: Substantial efforts were applied to make certain the corporate leaders were fully informed and engaged.

After: _____

Exercise #4

Before: The purpose of the regulation is to require agencies throughout the corporation to adhere to standardized security standards.

After: _____

Exercise #5

Before: This is no small challenge; it will take the support of all corporate partners to implement this program.

After: _____

Exercise #6

Before: She held her first staff meeting with the decision agreed upon to continue on a monthly basis.

After: _____

Exercise #7

Before: The policy directs that each agency have a successful implementation of procedures to train employees.

After: _____

Exercise #8

Before: He was hired to oversee the Information Security Services capability integration and implementation.

After: _____

Exercise #9

Before: To make an informed decision, comparison of cloud computing implementation plans is essential.

After: _____

Exercise #10

Before: Performed billet management reporting for the Division Chief and provided contact and recall management for division senior leadership.

After: _____

Now, check your answers in Appendix A.

14. Keep the Focus: Shut the Gates

Dear Reader—Poof! You're now a tour guide, leading visitors through an expansive, colorful, and fragrant garden in full bloom. (Stay with me here . . . there's a point!) This garden's main walkway is intersected on both sides by smaller paths offering additional opportunities to further explore nature's beauty. The garden is closing. You must lead your guests directly to the exit; no detours allowed.

This scenario also applies to writing. As the author, you must guide your reader on a journey—convey your message—allowing no distractions. How? Avoid items in your text that lure readers off course, diverting them from your intended message. Here are eight types of gates you should secure.

1. Errors in punctuation, spelling, and capitalization are frustrating to the reader, but also prompt him or her to count the mistakes rather than listen to your message.

- *I worked with the Business Development team (BDT) Operations development staff to organize files. I recomended that a list be created and that all historic proposils have a checklist indicated what is in the file.*

2. Another distraction is inconsistency in presenting terms. To exemplify, I once reviewed a 5-page resume, which mentioned the Department of Transportation fifteen times. The author spelled it out in full the first two times without providing the acronym, DOT. The author spelled it out again the third time, but added *(DOT)*. It was spelled out again the fourth time. The fifth mention was spelled out with *(DOT)*. The next three instances were simply *DOT*. The ninth instance was spelled in full. The next two appearances were *DOT*. The twelfth was spelled again in full. The last three instances were *DOT*. I don't recall anything about the individual's accomplishments but vividly recall the discrepancies!

   I also found these variations in another resume, which question the author's attention to detail.

   - Phase I, Phase One, and Phase 1
   - Fiscal Year 2016, FY2016, FY 2016, and FY16

3. Strange wording, professional jargon inappropriate to the audience, and poorly defined terms or terms that are not defined at all cause the reader to stray, pondering, "Huh? What's that?" such as the following:

   - *Served as "the voice" of this office to counterparts in the organization.*
   - *This team sticks like glue to the customer and has formed a tight bond.*
   - *She is the front door to the office.*

4. Outlandish statements or poor writing might prompt the reader's response, "I can't believe I just read that!"

> *Performed federal financial management and process improvement in support of procedurally solving interest being accrued on federal invoicing.*

5. Stories only partially told force the reader to wonder, "How many? How long? Who signed? What happened as a result?"

6. The narrative inadvertently raises a subject that distracts the reader or tells the wrong story. The item below, based on an individual's input to a performance appraisal, demonstrates a missed opportunity. In this instance, Jane composed and published a brochure. Here's how she characterized her accomplishment:

   > *I created a brochure for people unfamiliar with the organizations on the corporate campus. It describes our organizational structure and identifies leadership down to the branch level. The document also addresses the mission and functions of five other collocated organizations and describes how each functionally relates to the others. The brochure lists points of contact for each organization and contains a map pinpointing key buildings.*

   The story *should* have centered on Jane's operational impact resulting from the brochure. She could have stated:

   - This product was her own initiative
   - Her brochure galvanized leadership into establishing a 1-day orientation class for new employees
   - Her product was regularly distributed at this forum (cite the number of classes and employees who received it)
   - Compliments about the brochure, etc.

7. Improperly presented statistics or failing to put them in context for the reader.

   - 1.5% error free rate

- Increased production by 20%
- Top 5% of my staff

8. Excessive and inappropriate use of metaphors and similes. Of this, I speak from personal—and painful—experience. I once composed a personnel appraisal on a gifted analyst, couching my laudatory comments in terms such as *home run, star batter, pinch hitter,* and *hit it out of the ballpark.* This was a tightly woven metaphor of which I was very proud. In equal measure, I was stunned when my boss rejected it, evidenced by mass quantities of red ink and his stern, written admonition to "abandon these ridiculous metaphoric flights of fancy!"

The lesson . . . metaphors and similes add color and catch the reader's attention. They provide a light touch to a composition, similar to gently tipping a balloon off your fingertips into the air. However, left unchecked, they obfuscate the intended message. Moreover, products in many areas of the corporate and government environments are generally focused, solid, and serious. Are metaphors and similes appropriate there? Not really.

EXAMPLES

Example #1

Before: Jerry directed his first high school play, *The Lion, the Witch and the Wardrobe.* **This was a delightful story, the first in the chronicles of Narnia in which four children discover a magic land through a wardrobe in their uncle's home.** The audience loved the production!

After: Jerry directed his first high school play, *The Lion, the Witch and the Wardrobe*. He managed fifteen complex scene changes, eighteen costume changes, lighting, choreography, and eight rehearsals for the forty cast members. His flawless production of this beloved children's classic was a smash hit and broke all attendance records.

Analysis: The goal, in fact, is to highlight Jerry's successful debut as a drama director. How effective is the *Before* version? Where is the focus? The reader's attention should be directed (pun intended) to Jerry's success as a director, not the story's theme.

Example #2

Before: Intervention by a professional facilitator was exceedingly effective; the **long-standing** dispute was finally resolved.

After: Intervention by a professional facilitator was exceedingly effective; the three-year-long dispute was finally resolved.

Analysis: This example begs the question, "How long did the dispute last?" So, tell the reader!

Example #3

Before: **She accomplished all goals for the client and the customers.**

After: No improved version is possible without interviewing the author.

Analysis: This sentence is based on a resume. Unfortunately, the job applicant doesn't identify the goals or explain the difference between the *client and the customers.* The reader wanders away pondering, "What the heck is the writer trying to convey?"

Example #4

Before: She managed a portfolio of **more than** twelve programs.

After: She managed a portfolio of fourteen programs.

Analysis: This short sentence leaves the reader questioning, "How many, exactly?" The lesson here is to be specific when dealing with such small numbers.

Example #5

Before: She was honored with **multiple awards** for her excellent performance as Team Lead.

After: She was named "Employee of the Quarter," received a Letter of Appreciation from the Deputy Director for Operations, and was presented a financial performance award for her achievements as Team Lead.

Analysis: Do you remember this example from Chapters 4 and 8? The author leaves the garden gate open by failing to elaborate on *multiple awards*. So now we complete the story. If it helps, go back and revisit the example in those contexts.

Example #6

Before: **He drove productivity improvements through highly motivational team supervision; successfully led conversion of goals into a strategic action plan.**

After: A revision is impossible without interviewing the author.

Analysis: This example, based on a resume, is rife with unanswered questions: What improvements did he make? Statistics would help. Exactly how did he motivate his team? How large was his team? What goals did he convert into a strategic action plan? How do you *lead a conversion of goals into a plan*? What does that mean? What did this guy actually do?

Example #7

Before: **The position requires briefing senior executives and draft accurate detailed reports on projected quarterly gains.**

After: Composed detailed reports and briefed senior executives on projected quarterly gains.

Analysis: Yes, we saw a similar item (Example 8) in Chapter 12 on tethers. We previously identified the broken tether. The base is *requires* and the items are *briefing* and *draft,* which we correct to *drafting.* However, this example serves as a foil for other teaching points as well. Recalling that it is based on a resume, it reads as a job description, not an accomplishment. We delete *accurate* as both redundant and leaving the gate open. It is redundant because *accurate* is an understood requirement; it leaves the gate open because the reader thinks, "Who would be tasked to produce an *inaccurate* report?"

We also have the opportunity here to apply lessons from Chapter 10, "Verbs Are Your Friends." Look at the word *draft.* Is the individual responsible only for generating the initial version of these reports? If so, *drafting* is appropriate. If the individual is responsible for generating the initial version, coordinating it, and producing the final product, *drafting* inaccurately conveys the actual effort. *Compose, author,* or *generate* would be more accurate. So, the final version of this job description should read *Individual filling this position is required to compose detailed reports and brief senior executives on projected quarterly gains.*

Example #8

Before: Position required attention to detail, maintaining a team-oriented approach, and the **ability to put aside ego to accomplish some mundane, yet critical tasks** to ensure success of senior tasks and missions.

After: Regularly demonstrated attention to detail, teamwork, and flexibility in working a wide variety of tasks, skills essential to this position.

Analysis: This is based on a resume that again reads like a job requirement as opposed to an accomplishment. It leaves the gate open. *Put aside ego to*—who includes that in a resume? Poorly chosen words such as these could be detrimental in a tight job market, prompting a flurry of questions that divert the reader from the intended message. Is this individual so haughty that *ego* is even mentioned? What does this individual consider *mundane*? What are *senior tasks and missions*? Would the job screener or interviewer want to continue reading this resume? Probably not.

Example #9

Before: **Advanced knowledge** of research programs such as Lexis Nexis and Westlaw, as well as **competence** with Pacer system was required.

After: Demonstrated requisite advanced knowledge of and skills in research programs such as Lexis Nexis, Westlaw, and Pacer.

Analysis: This transposes the cart and horse with *was required* concluding the *Before* version. It is also bewildering and, as such, definitely opens the garden gate. What does *advanced knowledge* mean? Is *advanced* a verb or adjective? Is the author explaining that she enhanced her own knowledge about these three programs? If so, to what degree of proficiency? Or, does the author *advance knowledge* of colleagues by training them on this subject matter? Recall the earlier cautionary note of carefully selecting words to avoid inadvertently sending a mediocre message? Instead of *competence,* the author should state *skill* or *proficiency.* Finally, the author makes a grammatical mistake with the verb. The sentence should read . . . *knowledge and competence . . . were required.* This item again reads as a position description, not a demonstrated skill or accomplishment.

Example #10

Before: **Orchestrated document management tools and processes and conducted office procurement.**

After: Oversaw the process to obtain office supplies.

Analysis: The first part is impossible to revise without understanding the actions that constitute *orchestrated. Conducted office procurement* equates to *Oversaw the process to obtain office supplies.*

CHAPTER 14 EXERCISES—Now You Try!

Exercise #1

Before: Ensured medical records were updated and prepared for surgery and specialist appointments.

After: _____

Exercise #2

Before: Conducted weekly presentations and briefings weekly to corporate seniors as well as outside entities with skill and ease. As well as other warehouse and Central Issue Facilities.

After: _____

Exercise #3

Before: The plan provides programs a specific methodology to document their architectures.

After: _____

Exercise #4

Before: Delivered administrative application training.

After: _____

Exercise #5

Before: She is seasoned with Executive Order 12543.

After: _____

Exercise #6

Before: Mary executes Protocol as well as orchestrates the seating of all Senior Staff Members.

After: _____

Exercise #7

Before: I am the on-site Project Manager for a project at a major corporation. The project helps the finance department by identifies department-wide files that can be destroyed immediately, can be destroyed in the near future, maintained on site or can be sent to offsite storage. Files that are eligible for immediate destruction are listed on an Excel spreadsheet. The spreadsheet is then submitted to departmental management for review. If the files are approved for destruction, they will be placed in bins and sent for shredding. Files marked for offsite storage are placed in boxes and a box content report is prepared electronically. This work is done by a team of eight members which I manage.

After: _____

Exercise #8

Before: Responsible for scheduling staff meetings for Senior Government Staff via Lotus Notes. Responsible for coordinating multiple Senior Government Calendars via Lotus Notes.

After: _____

Exercise #9

Before: Clear and well-defined requirements up front would have minimized the scope creeps, modifications, and project delays.

After: _____

Exercise #10

Before: Participated in Operation NOBLE STEED in charge of briefing more than sixty pilots and Weapon System Operators on air threats in the African Theater.

After: _____

Now, check your answers in Appendix A.

15. Final Steps:
Revise, Edit, and Proofread

So, you think you're done? The text is as smooth as a fine wine, sanded wood, or an aircraft's flawless landing. You've gathered lots of meaningful data. Using *Word Sculpting Tools* presented thus far, you avoided all distracting snags. You are ready to confidently guide the reader on the journey, without a single detour or misstep along the way. Your message is mesmerizing; the reader will be enraptured, nodding in agreement with your every point. Well, almost.

Congratulations—you completed the initial draft! At this point, you've assembled the building blocks of information from which to construct your message. Three critical steps remain: revise, edit, and proofread.

These are neither synonymous nor simultaneous. Each serves a different purpose. Each is essential. Success depends on how effectively you complete them. Failing will compromise your credibility with that audience you've worked so hard to capture and cultivate. Why? If the author is inattentive to the quality of the product, why should the reader invest his or her time reading it?

Step 1 — Revise

You must now painstakingly arrange that content—those building blocks—into the final product. Read your draft slowly and from the audience's perspective. If you *received* this information, how would you respond? Compare the initial draft to your outline. Does it deviate? If so, are the deviations legitimate (meaning, the information supports the thesis) or tangential? Several revisions might be necessary—and that's OK, even advisable. Other points to consider are listed below:

- Know your audience; tailor your product accordingly
- Address the audience's issue(s), question(s), and concerns
- Use form, style, and terminology appropriate to the product and the audience
- Ensure you've defined relevant terms
- State the goal or purpose clearly
- Sequence information logically; rearrange or delete as needed
- Provide supporting evidence for all positions
- Respond to posed questions
- Anticipate and respond to questions **not** posed
- Organize and connect sections
- Identify and respond to counterarguments objectively and factually
- Present balanced, logical arguments
- Eliminate tangential information
- Extend or limit concepts as necessary

- Eliminate bureaucratic blather such as vague, convoluted, or run-on sentences

- Complete the circle: harmonize the opening and conclusion

Step 2 — Edit

Read your revised draft aloud slowly. This adds an important and different dimension to editing. Listen . . . and you will *hear* how words flow . . . or how they don't flow. Verbalization also helps identify thoughts that don't connect and catch words you inadvertently and excessively repeat. In the editing phase, examine your writing sentence by sentence to check for the following:

- Application of all *Word Sculpting Tools* (See Chapters 6–15)

- Clear title, subtitles, headings, and other section dividers (if used)

- Repetitious or misused words

- Sentence structure and syntax

- Rhythm and flow (paragraph to paragraph and sentence to sentence)

- Accuracy of cited references

- Length of document (i.e., conforms to stipulated limits)

Step 3 — Proofread

Ahhh, the final step. The storyline is now tight, arguments well-organized and logically substantiated, and the conclusion is synchronized with the opening. Now, purge the document of mistakes. Carefully check the following:

- Sentence structure, phrases, and clauses

- Grammar (e.g., verb tense, voice, and subject-verb agreement)

- Spelling, punctuation, capitalization, abbreviations, numbering/lettering, and typos

Proofread your work manually; **do not rely exclusively on automated systems like spell checkers**. Why? Automated systems might recognize valid words but will not correct spelling relative to the context. The following sentence is exaggerated for effect but reinforces this point.

*Automated systems will **revue you're hole** product but will **knot** be **two** effective and **they're** observations will often lead **ewe a rye**.*

Here are some suggested approaches:

- **Look for errors—one type at a time.** You risk losing focus when trying to identify all errors simultaneously. Review once for spelling, again for punctuation, etc.

- **Read the paper backwards.** This prevents you from being distracted by the message and losing focus on the task at hand . . . finding errors.

- **Circle and validate every punctuation mark.** As you circle, verify that the punctuation is correct. Be aware, however, this technique is only partially helpful. Why? It doesn't highlight punctuation you accidentally omitted.

See if you can find the errors in these excerpts from actual products, mostly resumes:

- *Demonstrated the ability the ability to balance a customer service facilitator role against stringint security requirements.* (repeated words, *the ability*; corrected misspelling should be *stringent*)

- *Further, coordinated schedules of senior military personnel, across the glove, under wartime stress levels.* (two improper commas; corrected misspelling should be *globe*)

- *Does your agency have a dedicated team to organize the relocation? If, there is no such team, assemble one. Please identify, members assigned to this team.* (two improper commas)

- *Responsible for writing an IMPLEMENTING quality policies.* (corrected misspelling should be *and;* improper use of capitalization)

- *Primary Liason between corporate headquarters and key clients.* (corrected misspelling should be *liaison;* improper capitalization because *liaison* is not a proper noun)

- *creates an environment that encourages collaboration common goals, and shared commitments across the corporation,* (Capitalize *create;* add a comma after *collaboration;* change the comma at the end to a period)

- *Testing continues with no major issues were identified* (delete *were;* add missing period at the end of the sentence)

- *Arraigned travel for conferences and public speaking events.* (corrected misspelling should be *Arranged*)

Take care with email, as well. Consider the following communication with this question in mind, "Would you hire the author as your executive assistant?" Can you identify the errors?

I have been ask to arrange a business lunch for our bosses. This venue could occurr either on the corporate premisis or at a nearby restaurant. We are targeting for about three hours (if tranpsort time is neccessary). Please convey her preferences as soon as conveniently possible.

(The incorrect verb form *ask* should be *asked; venue* (the location of an event) is used incorrectly and should be replaced with *event; targeting for about three hours* should be replaced with *planning on about three hours for this event; convey her* should be replaced with *reply with your supervisor's;* add the word *is* to produce *as soon as is conveniently possible;* and corrected misspellings should be *occur, premises, transport, necessary.*)

The revision below not only corrects the errors, but is also a more professional communication:

I have been asked to arrange a business lunch for our bosses. This event could occur either on the corporate premises or at a nearby restaurant. We are planning on about three hours (should transportation time be necessary). Please reply with your supervisor's preferences as soon as is conveniently possible.

In another example, a large corporation was establishing a governance board; senior executives from all subordinate elements would serve as members. The project office disseminated a draft charter for substantive review.

The document, however, was replete with grammatical errors (missing and inconsistent punctuation, improperly placed commas, and misaligned bullets), poor wording, and content that fit better elsewhere in the document. The office opted to circulate the draft for review without correcting the errors, with predictable results.

Respondents were distracted by and only highlighted the mistakes for correction. Teaching point: The project office opened the garden gate by sending an error-ridden product and did not receive the thorough, expertise-based input it sought.

EXAMPLES

Example #1

Before: **Conducted weekly presentations** weekly **to** corporate leadership.

After: Briefed corporate leadership weekly.

<u>Analysis:</u> Note the duplicate words. Also use a more specific verb, *briefed.*

Example #2

Before: The position required briefing senior executives and **draft detailed accurate** reports on personnel status.

After: The position required briefing senior executives and drafting reports on personnel.

Analysis: This is a simple fix to repair a broken tether. Change *draft* to *drafting* so it parallels *briefing.* We also delete *detailed* as a superfluous word. We delete *accurate* as a redundancy of the "no-duh" type because who would be required to draft an *inaccurate* report?

Example #3

Before: Designed, developed and **teach** a one-day orientation seminar.

After: Designed, developed, and taught a one-day seminar.

Analysis: Use consistent verb tenses. This is a common mistake.

Example #4

Before: Responsible for **all performance quality all contracts.**

After: Responsible for quality control of all contracts.

Analysis: We think the author intends to say, *Responsible for all performance quality* **control on** *all contracts.* However, the writing is poor even with those corrections.

Example #5

Before: Demonstrated excellent **interpersonnal skills and the ability to build and maintain close, positive, and professional relationships.** Served as a liaison for **multiple agencies,** creating synergies across **various organizations** promoting agency policies and interests. Her **interpersonnal skills and ability to build and maintain close, positive, and professional relationships** has led to increased funding.

After: Demonstrated excellent interpersonal skills and the ability to build and maintain close, positive, and professional relationships. Liaised with seven agencies, creating synergy in promoting the agency's policies and interests. Succeeded in increasing funding for her parent organization by $15,000.

Analysis: Delete the duplicated *interpersonal skills and the ability to build and maintain close, positive, and professional relationships.* Use the verb *liaised.* Replace the vague *multiple* with a specific number, adding clarity to the message. *Multiple agencies* and *various organizations* are also redundant. The *Before* version leaves the reader wondering, "Increased funding for whom and by how much?" We add those details to complete the story and close the gate. Did you catch the mistakes? *Interpersonal* is misspelled twice, and *has led* should be *have led.*

Example #6

Before: This company produces **Unmanned Aerial Vehicles** (UAVs); new applications for UAVs include commercial, scientific, and agriculture.

After: This company produces unmanned aerial vehicles (UAVs); new applications for UAVs include commercial, scientific, and agriculture.

Analysis: Capital letters are improper for *unmanned aerial vehicles* because it is not a proper noun.

Example #7

Before: Train and familiarize Congressional **Members** and other **Government Agency Leaders** on procedures supporting **Congressional National Events**.

After: Train and familiarize members of Congress and leaders of other government agencies on procedures relating to congressional national events.

Analysis: First, correct the many mistakes in capitalization: *congressional members, government agency leaders,* and *congressional national events*. Second, trying not to use long strings of nouns as adjectives, we modify to *leaders of other government agencies.* Finally, the garden gate was left open allowing the reader to puzzle, "What are *procedures relating to Congressional National Events*?" The most important of those specific procedures should be added.

Example #8

Before: Develops, **Plans**, **Schedules**, and implements assigned tasks, procedures, and processes.

After: Develops, plans, schedules, and implements assigned tasks, procedures, and processes.

Analysis: Again, capitalize only the first word. Please note, this item doesn't say much substantively.

Example #9

Before: Integrated **Commercial Off-The-Shelf Technology** (COTS) to reduce cost of projects under development.

After: Integrated commercial off-the-shelf technology (COTS) to reduce cost of projects under development.

Analysis: This is another example of the tendency to mistakenly capitalize words because they are used in an acronym. Unless the item is a proper noun, the words should not be capitalized.

Example #10

Before: **Contributor** in creating **Executive Level one page overall** briefing papers.

After: Helped compose text and design graphics for sixteen executive-level briefing papers describing key functions and products of the company. These papers are regularly disseminated in company training venues and at major corporate tradeshows as part of its strategic communications and outreach campaign.

<u>Analysis:</u> Note in the *Before* version the improper capitalization and the missing hyphen in *executive-level* and the missing hyphen in *one-page*. The word *Contributor* opens the garden gate by raising the questions, "How? What did the individual actually do?" The revision specifies the individual's contributions relative to these briefing papers. Sparing the reader unnecessary detail, we do not have to specify the length of the briefing papers. *Overall* is a useless word. We complete the story by stating the number of papers, detailing information they conveyed, and describing their use by the corporation.

CHAPTER 15 EXERCISES—Now You Try!

Exercise #1

Before: Reviewed signature documents of completeness prior to dispatch.

After: _____

Exercise #2

Before: We still need to document all of the steps we completed to in regards to preparing the documents for scanning and shipping.

After: _____

Exercise #3

Before: This memorandum provides guidance for each office that generate, maintains, transmits, stores, or access information on the Information Technology (IT) infrastructure. After confirming that an a breach has occurred, immediately notify the appropriate security officer. To gain better visibility into, and understanding of, how employees currently report possible IT incidents, a study is required.

After: _____

Exercise #4

Before: A joint working group was formed and subsequently conducted a two month study that developed the Funding and Cost Recovery Plan for FY 2013–2016 Staff Paper. The plan includes an anticipated progression in cost recovery from FY2013 through FY 2016 for several mutually-operated systems. Based on input from the working group, a variance of services and best practices were established. Each participating agency identified a budget for their IT resources.

After: _____

Exercise #5

Before: The goal was to move the Hospital Liaison Program, to a point of consistent, operational, sustainability. In that context, a set of monthly milestones were established. One action was to implement a working group, to support the governance framework and, along with the Human Resources department oversees the assignment process (e.g, personnel, shift schedules, duties) as well.

After: _____

Exercise #6

Before: Has excellent reading and comprehensive skills.

After: _____

Exercise #7

Before: Analyzed and effectively summarized information and date in both written and geographic format.

After: _____

Exercise #8

Before: The rescue team complied with all requirements identified in the Community Emergency actions and Response Handbook (CEARH) which services as the go-to standard for rescue teams across the state. This document can be accesed online.

After: _____

Exercise #9

Before: His team has perform some significant results oriented collaborations with other parts of the organization by reaching out to all the teams working with them to give them information on the program, doing boot camps to get them talking on the same page. The team set up a collaboration fourm provide interface. and working to provide mission products like BIMP. Through our new softward, which has allowed the team to really bring mission focus this year through some really great interfaces that the mugs have been very happy to see themselves in the project and help provide a way towards functional integration. It has been a complete Team effort, all helping the others and the groups within the organization and beyond

After: _____

Exercise #10

Before: With more than ten major IT fielding initiatives in a dessert environment, never had a security beach, never impacting a major training operation and never impacted installation operations more than two hours..

After: _____

Now, check your answers in Appendix A.

Part 3

Write to Influence!
Applied Daily

16. The College Application: Essays That Open Doors

This chapter is based on a popular workshop I teach students applying to college. So, I speak directly to them (and their parents, too).

Don't be intimidated by this essay. View it, instead, as an opportunity to shine and reveal something your grades can't—your personality! Embrace the essay and give admission officers what they seek, a sense of who you are.

For many, this essay is the first exposure to "adult writing." By that I mean, communication that will impact your life. This type of writing is constrained by two factors: time and space. The reader's—in this case, the evaluator's—time is measured in seconds; it is fleeting, as are the opportunities you hope to obtain. Physical space refers to the length of the essay, which is also often limited.

Lesson: The individual who best leverages time and space often wins. Therefore, make each word count and every second of the reader's time play to *your* advantage. That is the core premise of *Write to Influence!*

Imagine an inverted triangle—progressing from macro to micro. The macro refers to composing the first draft of the essay; the micro equates to refining it. First, the macro. Select the storyline, develop an outline, gather data, and construct the rough draft. Next, the micro. Refine the draft at the sentence level, applying *Word Sculpting Tools* to hone it into succinct, focused, and gripping text. Provided below are eight steps to compose this all-important essay.

1. Inventory yourself. A showstopper essay begins with quiet introspection. Find a corner and list what makes you *unique*. Reflect on your experiences – fabulous, funny, or frightening. Identify your likes and dislikes; strengths and weaknesses; and goals and dreams. Passions, hobbies, unique family history . . . consider those, too. These questions might stimulate ideas:

- Have you enjoyed a fantastic success? What did you learn and how did you handle it?

- Did you fail at something? What did you learn and how did you respond to *that*?

- What movie, book, or song particularly moved you and why?

- Rub the magic lamp; what might be your three wishes?

This introspection yields valuable insights and vignettes from which to draw when composing the essay. Hint: retain this information; it will pay dividends later as you prepare for job interviews. Questions posed in that context often resemble the essay prompts!

2. Reflect, don't just report. When recalling an occurrence, don't merely relay a factual sequence of events. For example, in describing foreign travel, don't just list the agenda (e.g., on day 1, on day 2) Focus instead on gained insights. How did you return as a different person? Amplify points with detail and examples.

3. Share something personal. The first rule in communication is, "Know your audience." Let's amplify this: "Anticipate and speak to their needs." In this case, the audience is the entrance board. Members want to know, "Who is this applicant, and why should we allow him or her to join our student body?"

Tell them! Draw from that rich treasure trove of information you compiled in step 1. Select a topic that speaks about you and address it from an unusual perspective. Be honest, thoughtful, and inspired.

Remember, these dedicated people invest long hours reviewing stacks upon stacks of applications. Your goal: stand out from the crowd. Hook the fish with a catchy (pun intended!) opening line; reel it in with that captivating story!

4. Don't tackle gigantic problems. Smarter folks than you try to solve world peace and *their* solutions are not space constrained! Avoid grandiose ideas such as:

- "There is so much suffering in the world I feel I have to help people."
- "At the foundation of my character is a deep desire to create peace."
- "I would like to apply my personality traits to make me the most useful I can be as I find my place in the world."

Finally, if your essay opens with, "Throughout history," you're on the wrong track.

5. BOPA! Brainstorm, **O**utline, **P**rioritize, and **A**djust. You now have the essay prompt and a wealth of personal stories from that self-inventory. The next step is to brainstorm. Determine which experiences best fit the prompt.

Now, outline your essay. No fair cutting corners! Reread Chapter 1 and fortify your motivation to complete this step. The outline constitutes your personal roadmap that keeps the storyline on track. Identify three or four key points as the concept evolves. Prioritize and adjust as needed. BOPA is also useful in organizing lengthy compositions or space-constrained writing.

6. Compose your essay like a gourmet meal. Begin with a captivating title and opening sentence (aka, the appetizer) to draw the evaluator into your story. Follow with a well-crafted body of text (aka, the entrée). Take special care with the conclusion (aka, the dessert). Correlate it to your opening statement and ensure it, too, is captivating. Why? This last thought shapes the evaluator's final impression of your essay . . . and you. Don't fade into black like cowboys riding into the distance at a film's conclusion. Instead, end on a dramatic note like Disney's *Lion King*.

7. Word Sculpt the text. Congratulations! You have a draft! You're done now, right? Nope. Many students make this critical error. Like the sculptor contemplating a 6-ft tall block of marble, you must now sculpt your text, discarding words that contribute nothing to and actually detract from your message. Apply the 10 *Word Sculpting Tools* (Part 2 of this book).

8. Take a break, then re-engage. At this point, put the essay down, do something else. Reengage later with a fresh perspective and rejuvenated grey cells. The good news—you're in the home stretch, well on your way to achieving that showstopping essay.

17. Your Resume:
Stand Out from the Crowd

Bang! The race is on. The clock is ticking. You have thirty seconds to snare the potential employer's attention. The resume must sell itself—and you! However, "marketing" themselves is difficult for many people. They don't want to "brag" by accentuating their capabilities and accomplishments. For this reason, composing a resume and submitting input for a periodic performance appraisal are often troublesome and distasteful.

I offer these suggestions. Approach this autobiographical task from a strictly fact-based perspective, applying your newly acquired writing strategies and *Word Sculpting Tools*. First, assemble material from which you will sculpt the product. Ask these questions as the first step, "What did I do?" and "What were my impacts?"

Be specific in identifying this information. Imagine describing the accomplishments of that stellar subordinate whose career you want to advance. Your goal—outshine the competition. Don't kid yourself; the competition is writing with the same objective!

The task is even more challenging because your resume should be two pages in length; some organizations require a single page. How do you cram years of professional experience and education into that limited space?

Individuals well into their careers will likely be experienced in several areas. Develop an in-depth product akin to a functional autobiography; this can be many pages in length. Craft your resume by extracting from that master product sections pertinent to the position for which you are applying.

Play the "Match Game" in tailoring your resume to a specific job. Develop a working aid comprised of three columns. In the first, list required job skills, information about the company, its products, and customers. Identify your skills, education, and experience in the second. In the third, specify your other connections with the position and employer. The goal is to match your skills and experience in terms reflected in the job announcement.

The following thirteen tips will guide you in this endeavor:

1. Don't write a resume that sounds like a job description, enumerating elements of the job or required skills. Instead, convey what you actually did. Many resumes contain bullets that begin with, "Responsible for." This wastes the opportunity to specify real accomplishments. The fact that an individual is responsible for something does not indicate how well he or she fulfilled that responsibility.

Authors often incorporate into their resume lines taken directly from the position announcement to which the resume responds. I found this listed as an accomplishment in a resume, *Experience with and/or demonstrated understanding of agency policies and customer base a highly desired factor.* Do you think the potential employer won't notice?

Ensure the resume answers these questions: What did you do? What were the impacts of your accomplishments? What was your value added . . . in concrete terms?

2. Avoid repetitious opening words. Consider the following, presented exactly as they appeared in the critical, opening half page of a resume. The redundancy and monotony are obvious when read aloud. Rare is the employer who has the time and patience to review such text. Remember, your resume is one of many in the queue!

- Responsible for writing and creating
- Responsible for writing and creating
- Responsible for researching
- Contributor in
- Responsible for all
- Responsible for maintaining
- Contributor of
- Responsible for creating
- Maintain
- Responsible for maintaining
- Responsible for scheduling
- Maintain
- Contributor in

3. Be consistent in the opening words for bullets, whether nouns or verbs. This applies to a series in all product types (resumes, briefings, point papers, reports, etc.). If you open with verbs, maintain a consistent person (e.g., compose vs composes) and tense (e.g., compose vs compos**ed**). The author often shifts not only from line to line, but often within a line.

Examine this list from a single resume that mixes nouns and verbs, verb person and tense. Read aloud and you'll hear the snags in rhythm, distracting from the intended message.

- Provide
- Located
- Extensive knowledge of
- Assist Technical Staff
- Security functions
- Manages
- Provided
- Department Assignments included
- Excellent communication skills
- Extensive event planning and catering
- Coordinates
- Coordinated
- Extensive travel coordination
- Awards Program Administration to include

4. Use descriptive, crisp action verbs to engage the reader. Contrast this "how to" example with the bullets listed above.

- Planned and implemented
- Developed and validated
- Tracked and reviewed
- Drafted
- Formulated and consolidated
- Composed
- Briefed
- Represented

- Served as functional area lead for
- Awarded certificate for
- Named as top performer for
- Led a corporate review of
- Initiated
- Researched and corrected
- Redesigned
- Applied
- Advised decision makers on
- Revitalized
- Organized and directed
- Counseled several senior executives on

5. Follow each verb with hard-hitting facts and "so what" statements that convey impact and value added. Were you specifically chosen for a task? If so, for what and by whom? If you cite an organizational level, expound. For example, *The division chief lauded her report.* That sounds good but elucidate the seniority or scope of responsibility of the division chief. Here are some examples:

- Led four initiatives that increased transparency and integration of the corporation's geographically dispersed R&D laboratories.
- Organized, facilitated, and directed Joint Lab Forums and semi-annual off-sites, resulting in new collaboration across twelve geographically separated S&T laboratories.
- Organized and led five White House briefings for elected officials on a variety of issues, including international exchange rates, foreign trade, and exports/imports.
- Researched issues and wrote testimony for state officials to present to three congressional committees.

- Analyzed cyberattacks, threats, vulnerabilities, and trends; identified 15 mitigations. Wrote a comprehensive report published as a Key Finding and circulated to all corporate leaders.

- Developed and led the public affairs campaign for the U.S. president's economic security, homeland security, and international initiatives, reaching electorates throughout the country.

6. Highlight accolades such as awards, bonuses, and other recognition that differentiate you from peers. Did you receive letters of appreciation or an organizational "coin" for a job well done? If so, for what and from whom? Were you a member of a team recognized for an accomplishment (e.g., member of a four-person team that did such and such)? Were you selected for a competitive position and from how many contenders? Here are some examples from actual resumes:

- Received a commendation and performance award from the executive director.

- One of four officers selected to prepare the nominee for confirmation hearings before Congress.

- Selected through agency-wide competition for coveted award.

- Received the Distinguished Federal Executive Rank Stipend Award upon conclusion of this assignment.

- Named "Salesperson of the Year," selected from 144 peers

- Awards: Team of the Quarter (2019), Manager's Quarterly Award (2019), Pitsenbarger Award from Aerospace Education Foundation (2019), and additional medals and citations.

- Master's degree in Public Administration; Magna Cum Laude. [included because of the stated level of performance]

- Awards:
  - National Aeronautic Corporation President's Special Award for Outstanding Customer Service (2019)

- ABC Agency Meritorious Unit Citation (2019)
- ABC Agency Director Coin and Outstanding Customer Service Award (2019)

7. Quantify your accomplishments. Highlight leadership and supervisory roles. Did you lead a team? If so, how large? Did you operate a facility or equipment? If so, what was the value? Did you manage a program? Scope the value of those assets, as well. Did you give a presentation? To how many people, representing how many organizations? What happened as a result of that presentation? See how details contribute to the bullets below:

- Selected as Airman of the Year from 250 nominees representing an organization of 16,000 members.

- Simultaneously managed 2 divisions and supervised 50+ people; ensured each division met mission requirements without conflict of priorities.

- Taught a refresher class for corporate pay and travel processors; reduced payroll errors by 5 percent; revitalized a customer service program, expediting response time to customer inquiries by 18 percent.

- Developed a training program for 30 junior officers, mentoring them in critical professional skills; coordinated lesson plans across 5 corporate divisions; the Vice President of Operations lauded her initiative in establishing this program.

- Served as senior executive assistant overseeing 5 subordinates; provided daily administrative support to 3 directors and 100 staff members.

- Member of an 8-person team that managed the relocation of 3,500 personnel and telecommunications equipment valued at $75M to a new headquarters building.
  - Developed and maintained a master schedule of 7,090 tasks completed during the 11 months to accomplish the move.

- Received letter of recognition from the Chairman of the Board.

8. Write to stand out from the crowd! The litmus test—If what you wrote applies to most people, you placed yourself in the middle—not in front—of the crowd.

These four observations pertain to the lines below, based on resumes. First, each line applies to a multitude of job applicants. Second, many of the skills highlighted are *expected* by hiring officials and, for that reason, should not be mentioned. Third, you not only lose points mentioning these items, you also forfeit the opportunity, in both the reader's time and space on the resume, to feature your unique capabilities. Finally, if the author touts *writing and communication skills,* the resume had better reflect them!

- Demonstrated and proven leadership ability.

- Consistently demonstrates a tireless devotion to duty.

- Does what is right and takes personal responsibility.

- Treats everyone with kindness and respect.

- Ensures requests are answered and provides additional information as required.

- A model for honest, trustworthy, and ethical behavior.

- Very focused on ensuring that resources are effectively used for intended purposes.

- Has been instrumental in providing results.

- Will provide outstanding support as a valued subject matter expert.

- Self-motivated with military professionalism; distinguished service in the U.S. military.

- Committed to delivering quality customer service.

- Demonstrated ability to work under pressure.

- Demonstrated ability to work with others and secure their cooperation to achieve results.

- Exceptional writing and speaking skills.

9. Write clearly so the reader doesn't wonder, "Huh?" Remember that garden gate in Chapter 14? You must rapidly capture and retain the reader's attention. Don't lose it through ill-defined terms, run-on sentences, unexplained acronyms, or items that make no sense. Vague verbs such as *assist, provide,* and *contribute* prompt the questions, "How? What specifically did you do?" Here are some examples, some replete with errors, to avoid:

- Provided support in the area of security in support of a federal agency.

- Assisted with papers such as white papers, RFPs, proposals, and contracts.

- Provided support to special projects, off-site meetings, retreats, etc.

- Created forms and a product timeline used as a model to set up the automation process being created.

- Worked closely with outside working group and Chief of AKCC in planning, staffing, and coordination. (Unfortunately, AKCC was not spelled out for the reader.)

- Exemplified the strong and effective partnerships that fosters corporate involvement in problem resolution and are role models in the corporation for information sharing. He is consistent in his communications to always focus on the further of the mission. (This is presented exactly as it appeared in the resume and leads beautifully to the next tip, proofread! *Fosters* should be *foster*; resumes should not include personal pronouns such as *he, his, she, her, I,* or *me*; and the *on the further of the mission* should be *on furthering the mission*.)

- Consistently been proactively engaged with the corporation and delivering reusable methodologies, embraced philosophies, and insight into the culture of his project.

- Identified and adopted a standardized organizational model, defined relationships and responsibilities throughout the organization all the way up to the director; introduced effective customer service.

- When classical methods would not have been practical, took a novel approach in building and leveraging relationships with partner organizations to tackle the problem of accounting for progress against goals so that it can be more effectively managed and reported.

- Creates an environment or conducts business in such a way as to encourage collaboration, common goals, and shared communication; actively participates in or leads corporate initiatives; acts selflessly and provides support to or encouragement of others.

- As Security Management Specialist, Mr. Smith is responsible for using various procedures and policies for the production of sufficient records into the security management program. Additionally, as a key security manager he became involved in the development and modification of the systems to ensure the record-keeping requirements are executed properly. With excellent communication experience, Mr. Smith specializes in preparing and delivering presentations to executive staff and offering training and guidance in the matters of Security Management. (Again, this is presented as it appeared in the resume and demonstrates the next tip—Proofread! The applicant's name, *Mr. Smith,* should not appear in the body of the resume; *record-keeping* should be *recordkeeping*; and this bullet entry is too long and should be condensed or broken up into two or three separate bulleted items.)

10. Proofread!! The fastest way to lose the reader—and possibly a new job—is through sloppy proofreading. Note punctuation, capitalization, parallelism, subject-verb agreement, duplication, etc. A mistake-ridden product conveys volumes about your skill, attention to detail, and professionalism. The reader wonders, "If this individual doesn't pay attention to detail on his own resume, will he do any better as an employee?"

Beyond exemplifying poor writing, the items below from resumes contain sixteen errors. Can you find them?

- Create in depth Security Management Trainings to corporate personnel.
- Daily client interaction are regular and sustained, encompassing both formal and informal, routine communication
- provide passengers with pre-security information, location of gates, and airport facilities
- Develop security training for divisions ranging from The Office of the Director, Chief of Staff, Human Resources, Engagements, Facilities. Logistics, Resource Management, And Contracts.
- Create in Depth Training using Sharepoint and other Microsoft tools.
- As a result, the agency will have a state approved security management program

Here are the errors and corrections:

- Create **in depth** Security **M**anagement **T**rainings **to** corporate personnel. (Add a hyphen to *in-depth*; *Security Management Training* should not be capitalized; *Trainings* should be singular; replace *to* with *for* because *Create . . . to corporate personnel* does not make sense. Corrected item: *Create in-depth security management training for corporate personnel.*)

- Daily client interaction **are** regular and sustained, encompassing both formal and informal, routine communication. (Should be the singular verb *is*; delete *regular and sustained* because they are redundant—it already says *daily*; and add a period to the end of listed items—whether they are complete sentences or not—in a resume. Corrected item: *Daily client interaction encompasses both formal and informal, routine communication.*)

- **p**rovide passengers **with** pre-security information, **location of gates, and airport facilities** (Capitalize first word; delete *with*; this also has a broken tether, *Provide information, location, and airport facilities.* The revision—with a period added to the end—reads *Provide passengers information on pre-security, location of gates, and airport facilities.*)

- Develop security training for divisions ranging from **The Office** of the Director, Chief of Staff, Human Resources, Engagements, Facilities**. Logistics, Resource Management, And** Contracts. (Several words were incorrectly capitalized: *The Office* and *And.* The remaining capitalized words are proper names of organizational elements. Corrected version: *Develop security training for divisions ranging from the office of the Director, Chief of Staff, Human Resources, Engagements, Facilities, Logistics, Resource Management, and Contracts.*)

- Create in **D**epth **T**raining using Sharepoint and other Microsoft tools. (Add a hyphen, and correct the capitalization errors in *Depth, Training,* and *Sharepoint.* Corrected version: *Create in-depth training using SharePoint and other Microsoft tools.*)

- As a result, the agency will have a state approved security management program. (Add a hyphen and period. Corrected version: *As a result, the agency will have a state-approved security management program.*)

11. Beware of redundancy. I found instances of individual bullets replicated elsewhere in a resume, sometimes on the same page. I also discovered entire sections duplicated. Perhaps the most egregious example of this last instance was a section of seven bullets— approximately four inches of text—repeated on subsequent pages!

Another resume mentioned the following statement four times in its five pages: *with twenty years military service and twelve years as a support contractor with several federal agencies.* If that weren't enough, the individual added this variation twice: *thirty-two years of experience include* . . . . The reader's response: "OK, already! I get the point!!"

12. Tailor your resume to the job. If it calls for financial expertise, don't inundate prospective employers with your logistics skills. I once screened resumes for an administrative position—someone applied with extensive expertise on another country's military, was fluent in the country's language, and published in his field of expertise. Tremendously talented undoubtedly, but for an administrative position?

13. More is *not* better. Write in bullets not lengthy paragraphs and try to keep the resume to one page, two if you must.

Here are some good "how-to" examples:

- Led diverse 10-person team that oversaw upgrades to both the facility and IT systems needed to support unprecedented growth in mission and manning.
  - Kept the $3.5M project on track while aggressively pursuing a $250K shortfall in program funding.
- Spearheaded administration services for a computer network and completed a 3-year replacement plan of IT hardware, increasing productivity of lab analysis by 140 percent.
- Managed execution of a $7.8M financial plan, achieving the fastest execution rate in the corporation.
- Program manager for a $2.8M deployable platform; delivered capability on time and on budget.

- Handpicked to manage daily operations of a selectively staffed branch of 33 people supporting a special project tasked by the Secretary of Energy.

- Impetus behind a study to procure a $2.8M digital analysis hardware and software capability, resulting in a 700 percent increase in analytical capabilities.

- Led 20 contractors supporting four directorates. Promptly resolved performance issues by coordinating with corporate program managers and the government evaluator.

  - Validated work performed and status of projects. Ensured contractors met required training timelines and were proficient in required skills.

  - All reviews of the Contractor Award Boards resulted in outstanding ratings and performance incentive awards for the company.

- Proficient in drafting talking points, executive summaries, briefings, and supporting documentation for senior executives. Developed four briefings presented to Capitol Hill that successfully gained or maintained support for specific policies and initiatives.

- As team leader for ABC Corporation, expertly supervised nine employees who managed the on-site document control center for the Federal Energy Regulatory Commission.

  - Interfaced daily with government staff, quality controlled data entry, recommended procedures for indexing processes, and maintained records and operational statistics.

18. Grant Submissions: Robust and Compelling

Who doesn't want "free money" to help their cause? People invest incalculable time and effort developing grant submissions. I address this product from the perspective of writing to influence—literally—and present information in three sections: On Your Mark, Get Set, and Go! Each requires diligence, time, commitment, and forethought. While writing a submission is *not* a race, it *is* a competition. Others also want to win! And, while it may seem like free money, receiving a grant is akin to a contract. You agree to perform certain programs and meet specific measurable benchmarks to your investor.

In many ways, writing a grant submission resembles the "Match Game" addressed in Chapter 2, "Know Your Audience – Psychology of the Catch" and again in Chapter 17, "Your Resume: Stand Out from the

Crowd." Leveraging information described below, your objective is to draw as many strong connections as possible between the following:

- **Your organization and the grant.** Don't apply for a grant because it *generally* fits your business. Don't reverse engineer your organization's mission to fit the grant. Apply only for those that seem tailored for you.

- **The grantmaker and your project**. The central questions are twofold: 1) How do the problem and your proposed project align with the grantmaker's mission, values, goals, and objectives? 2) How will your project benefit the grantmaker?

- **Your organization and the grantmaker**. Show how the two organizations align in their stated mission, values, goals, and objectives.

On Your Mark. It's all about preparation. The following sentence states the obvious but for emphasis.
Read . . . the . . . grant . . . application . . . carefully!

1. Highlight critical information. Identify questions you must answer and required materials. Incorporate in your submission key words and phrases to draw subtle but critical parallels between your organization, the proposal, and the grantmaker. Note the color scheme in the grantmaker's logo; consider reflecting them in your graphics.

2. Determine your eligibility. Do you qualify to submit? Some grants require matching funds, submissions from partnering organizations, certifications, or permits. Some have geographic restrictions.

3. Begin early. Check the deadline. Allow time to develop a thorough, well-grounded package. If not, consider submitting in the next round. Don't jeopardize an opportunity with a weak product. "Haste makes waste" is so true!

4. All aboard? In most cases, you can't do this alone. Ensure you have sufficient backing to submit for a grant. Do your organization's leadership and key stakeholders support this project? Have they committed required resources to implement it?

Get Set. Gather the data. This part of the process requires a lot of time, research, and forethought.

5. Know the audience. Research the grantmaker. Review annual reports, websites, other projects it sponsored, terms commonly used in its products, previously accepted proposals, and others' observations about the organization. Your goal is to thoroughly understand its missions, values, goals, and objectives.

6. Establish your credibility. This section demonstrates that you can execute the proposed project. Integrity here is paramount! Be honest. Don't try to "hide" facts that might weaken your proposal. An expert reviewer can detect the dodge and *that* erodes trust.

Describe your organization's missions, values, goals, and objectives. Letters of support and media coverage of your organization's involvement in related areas exemplify documentation that validate your expertise in pertinent areas. Address these items in your submission:

- **Skills:** Explain your organization's skills, knowledge, and ability to complete the project. Include resumes on key staff members and participants in the project.

- **Previous contributions:** Demonstrate contributions your organization made (e.g., financial or volunteer time) to the grantmaker's mission or cause. This evidences your belief in and commitment to the project.

- **The perfect fit:** Describe years of experience in the relevant area or similar projects your organization completed. Show you can deliver the project and demonstrate why your organization is best equipped to do so (without denigrating other agencies).

- **Partnerships:** Identify partnerships with other stakeholders in the area. Include letters of commitment to this project from your partners.

- **Commitment:** Commit your organization to work with the grantmaker even if you don't receive the grant. This affirms you value the grantmaker's mission and better positions you for a future submission.

7. Describe your project. Present the problem and justify why it is sufficiently acute to warrant these resources. Then, provide information about the following: staff members or key personnel on the project; partnering organizations; available resources (including matching funds); amount of funds requested, budget, and a spending plan; methodology for executing the project; benchmarks; timetable; anticipated short-term and long-term results; beneficiaries (immediate, secondary, tertiary, etc.); measures of success and criteria used to make those assessments; and a glance into the future.

Go! Now, put pen to paper. Leverage the strategies and *Word Sculpting Tools* to present a convincing case and clinch the deal. Make each word count and every second of the reader's time play to *your* advantage. The framework described below functions as your roadmap and—at journey's end—your final checklist. It consists of three parts:

- **Cover letter.** Describe how your project will further the grantmaker's mission. Include a summary of your request, the purpose of your project, and the amount of money you seek. Also list the contents of your proposal (i.e., documents included). This single page forms the reviewer's initial impression of you and the project. Your credibility is at stake. Invest as much time and care in this document as the other parts of the grant submission.

- **Executive summary.** Compose this *after* you've completed the form. Some people recommend composing the executive summary first and using it as a roadmap. I disagree. One can't summarize something not yet written. Among other things, answer these questions:

- Who is applying for the grant?

- Where is the soliciting organization based?

- Who is being asked to fund the grant?

- Why is the grant needed?

- On what will the grant money be spent?

- When is the funding needed?

- How much money is requested?

- **Form.** Does the proposal address every item or criterion in the grantmaker's guidelines (even if only to say "Not applicable" or "See item 2.3") in the proper order and under the headings in which they appear in the guidelines? Did you follow every specification? Does the application allow for attachments? Does it require them? Have you verified the package contains all required attachments? Did you clearly label them?

8. Write a summary statement. A one-paragraph description of your request will help shape the project's concept. You might be able to include this summary in the proposal or as the first paragraph of your narrative. It should explain the following: who you are, what your project is, what you plan to do, the amount of requested funds, and how you will spend them.

9. Create an outline. Use the grantmaker's request for proposals (RFP) as the basis for your outline. In that framework, reflect each step of the plan for the project. Expand upon these points as you compose the submission. Ask the grantmaker to review your outline. Not only might you obtain valuable guidance, you will also make a personal contact and perhaps cultivate a relationship.

10. Comply with the application's directions—precisely. Yes, this is a recurring theme for good reason. Failing to follow specifications such as those relating to margins, spacing, type size, word count, or attachments could be considered a technical error and cause for rejection. Note: some organizations now prefer a letter of inquiry prior to receiving the complete submission.

11. Hook the reader. Exude energy and enthusiasm in the title, opening paragraph, and throughout the document. The goal—stand out from the crowd and portray your organization as eagerly leading forward, well-equipped, and committed to resolving the identified problem. Show why your project is unique and innovative, different from and better than other programs or competitors for this grant.

12. Structure your story. Frame your story in three parts. First, introduce the problem and explain why it needs to be resolved. Ideally, you also can provide a short, personalized story or anecdote about a client or incident that helps to build your case for "why." Second, describe your project—the proposed solution—and explain how you can accomplish it. Finally, discuss how your project will resolve the problem in the short and long term, who will benefit, and how the solution can be sustained independent of the grantmaker's financial support.

13. Fill in the detail. Describe the project activities and how you will use the money. A precise explanation increases the likelihood of a positive result. If you have partners, specify their roles and responsibilities in the project.

A common mistake is failing to distinguish between a goal and objective. Goals are broad, overarching, even visionary statements of what you hope to accomplish. According to Beverly Browning in *Grant Writing for Dummies,* objectives should be specific, measurable, attainable, realistic, and time-bound (SMART). Here is an example of a goal and its supporting objective:

> **Goal: Decrease the degree of malnutrition among young children in the southwest region of Baltimore.** (Note the vision of this goal; it's what you hope to accomplish)
>
> **Objective**: By the end of year one, provide 125 mothers in the southwest area of Baltimore a 2-hour training program that will

provide health and nutrition information. (Note how this objective is "SMART").

Source: https://www.thebalancesmb.com/writing-goals-for-grant-proposal-2501951

14. Amplify with a spending plan and budget justification. This will often make or break the proposal. Include a detailed budget and specify how you will spend the funds. Be accurate and detailed in your estimates. For example, identify by category these types of expenses: salaries, purchased services, supplies, rent, communications, travel, equipment, and printing. State the total project cost, amount sought from the grantmaker, and other funding sources, or matching funds you will contribute. The budget justification delineates the calculations supporting the spending plan.

NOTE: Many funders require that you submit both a project budget as well as your organization's current operating budget. If you're requesting "general support," your operations budget is the key submission. However, be sensitive to the funders' process. Plug your data into their form (if they have one) regardless.

15. Look to the future. Show that the project will be self-sufficient after the grantmaker's funding is exhausted. If possible, demonstrate how the project will endure for the long term, either chronologically or by disseminating lessons learned to beneficiaries other than the intended first tier. Like a pebble thrown into a pond, will your project generate lasting and ancillary benefits? How will you fund it in the future?

16. Request a review. Find that valued second set of eyes—an outside party to review your submission—someone who's knowledgeable in the process and understands what a grant reviewer seeks. When reading your proposal, check for the following:

- **Case:** Is the argument for the project clear, concise, and compelling?

- **Objectives:** Are they realistic, achievable, and measurable? This is an area many submitters neglect and, instead, make sweeping statements rather than identify measurable outcomes. These measures will be used to validate the funder's investment when the time for a final report is due.

- **Evidence:** Does the proposal present the problem factually and with supporting data? Does it show why the problem is significant and a high priority? Does it describe previous actions taken by others and why the problem remains?

- **Methods:** Does the submission have a solutions section that clearly states the project's methods? Does it show why these methods were adopted and others were rejected?

- **Schedule:** Does the submission include a realistic project schedule? Is the schedule presented in graphic format?

- **Clarity:** Is your proposal easily understood? Did you avoid gibberish; imbue it with detail to convey depth and impact; purge bureaucratic blather; and close all garden gates?

- **Conclusion:** Did you summarize the problem, your solution, its anticipated impact, cost, your request, and projected benefits? Don't forget: end with a bang!

17. Stay in Touch—Judiciously. Call the grantmaker to ensure the submission arrived and is complete. During the review period, if you achieve a major success in areas of mutual interest . . . tell the grantmaker. In the event of media coverage, provide a copy of the article or the video URL. Good news in related areas always helps!

18. **Prepare for the Final Report.** Timing is critical—meet the deadlines! Failure can seriously erode credibility. Discuss the process for requesting an extension on a deadline. Record data, track expenditures, and gather anecdotes for submission.

19. Email: Polished, Professional, Effective

"Include a section on email!" my friends implored. "My staff can't write. I must proofread all email in draft," was a common complaint. These individuals are not micromanagers. They are professionals and, in many cases, business owners frustrated with the minimal writing skills of their employees. So, to my friends and anyone else who can benefit from tips on composition, addressing, and the general use of email, "This One's for You"!

In email, as with all communication, time and space are critical. The reader's attention is ephemeral and so is your opportunity to convey your message. Here are 18 tips to leverage the reader's time to *your* advantage.

1. Triage, then present the information. This is especially helpful for involved topics and communicating with busy executives. Consider this format or something similar:

- Issue
- Action and due date
- Background

To demonstrate this point, read the email below; raise your hand, figuratively speaking, when you lose interest.

Before: To corporate division chiefs –

SUBJECT: Our New CEO

Russell Brown was recently appointed Chief Executive Officer (CEO) of our corporation. He was previously the CEO of the You're Never Gonna Get Sick (YNGGS) company. During his six-year tenure, he restructured the organization, cut expenses by forty percent, and expanded the clientele by twenty percent. Mr. Brown has extensive background in the field of medical equipment, to include production and distribution, thereof. He is interested in your specific product portfolio, any identified regulatory problems, general and administrative costs, statistics for quarterly production, annual expenses, and gross and net profits. Please prepare a briefing highlighting these areas and please provide it to me by Friday. I will compile them into a book for his review prior to his visit to your sites next week. I'll send the specific date/time to each of you once the schedule is final.

Regards . . . Executive Secretary
[Appropriate signature block]

Applying the suggested format, the revision is far more effective. See the difference?

After: To corporate division chiefs:

SUBJECT: Action—Upcoming Site Visit of the New CEO

Email

Issue: Our new CEO, Russell Brown, will visit your site next week. The specific date and time are to be determined.

Action and due date: Please prepare a briefing for him and forward it to me by Friday. I will compile the briefings into a book for his review prior to the site visits.

The briefing should address:

- Your product portfolio
- Identified regulatory problems
- General and administrative cost
- Statistics for quarterly production
- Annual expenses
- Gross and net profits

Background: Mr. Brown was previously the CEO of You're Never Gonna Get Sick (YNGGS) company. During his six-year tenure, he restructured the organization, cut expenses by forty percent, and expanded the clientele by twenty percent. He also has extensive background in the medical equipment field, including production and distribution.

Regards,

Executive Secretary
[Appropriate signature block]

Analysis: The most critical information was buried at the bottom of the initial email; casual reading could have missed notification of the impending visit and required action. The new boss will visit you and your organization—guess who will be unprepared!

The email needed three structural changes. First, leverage the subject line to highlight required actions. Second, place key facts up front. Third, use the designators *Issue, Action,* and *Background* to prioritize and present the information in more easily read paragraphs, placing some items in a bulleted format.

2. Put the horse before the cart. Open with the critical information—the horse—or the audience might never reach it. When I read aloud the email below to participants in my workshops, they usually raise their hands at the second sentence, indicating loss of interest. Bad news for the writer, who actually needed to relay critical information, highlighted at the email's conclusion. As presented, this communication is completely ineffective; the writer did not achieve the intended objective.

To: Conference Attendees

SUBJECT: *Professional Women in Scientific and Technology Fields Workshop*

All,

*Thank you for taking time out of your busy schedules to attend our workshop, Professional Women in Scientific and Technology Fields. A lot of information was provided and there was some good feedback from the audience. We do not intend for this conference to be a one-way flow of information. We want, and very much need, your ideas and input to continue to facilitate contributions of women in these critical areas. On that note**, there was an important message that I was asked to share and realize that I forgot. If you are aware of an upcoming job vacancy or unique training opportunity, please post that information to our website.***

Jane Smith, Conference Coordinator

One final teaching point . . . I intentionally gave the email above a horrible subject line, reflecting today's proclivity to add noun upon noun upon noun. Isn't it awful?!? Can you compose a better subject line that captures the reader's attention and reflects the writer's intent?

3. Read the entire email. You probably recognize as a professional irritant that individuals whom you email often reply to only one of the two or three points you presented. Of course, the recipient must read the entire item to detect them all. Here is a tip for the sender and recipient:

For the sender: When writing an email, open with an appropriate greeting, then immediately signal the reader the communication contains XX points. For example, *I request your input on three issues*, or *Please note the two questions below*, and then number them.

For the recipient: Read the entire email before responding and address all points. It's amazing how many people don't read and digest the information before replying. If the email poses two questions, respond to both. If you don't, the sender will email you . . . again . . . and you must read *another* email. Avoid this kabuki dance by reading and responding to all points initially conveyed.

4. Ensure the subject line (title) of the email reflects the content. People often hit the reply button—which retains the original email subject line—but then address a completely different topic in the text. This practice complicates subsequent tracking of that material. Precision in titling email is another indicator of polished staff work and effective communication. Take a few moments to retitle the email if the subject shifts.

5. Responding to a question? Referencing an earlier email? Refer to it at the opening of *your* email. This is a professional courtesy to a very busy recipient. Begin your email with, *This responds to your question posed in the email chain below*, and then restate the question. Copy referenced information from the earlier email and place it at the opening of yours. This immediately sets the context, enabling the reader to assimilate your information without dredging through a cumbersome email chain.

6. Sequence attachments to parallel the text in the email. If sending multiple attachments, align them in the order cited in the text. Place those requiring action first, followed by backup material.

7. Edit thyself. Email is a primary means of professional communication. Your transmission reflects not only on your organization, but on you, personally. Therefore, employ all the writing strategies and *Word Sculpting Tools* this book offers to this medium in which brevity is especially cherished. Crisp, concise, and correct writing will also entice the recipient to read your message.

Here are several examples that should have been better proofread. Can you find the mistakes?

- Thank you for all your assistant and I'll send out a meeting update shortly.

- If you are agency is not listed here, your agency does not need to respond.

- This office is dedicated establishing working groups with our members for our members.

- The requirement team need to know if the hard drives are for both network. If so we need a document for each. Also are they just for you're workstations or a colleagues as well.

- I have not been directed to utilizes the new personnel roster.

- If you have any requests. Please tell me.

- I plan to meet with everyone when time permit.

- I put me as the Point of contact person for this issue. Stay tune for more information.

- Thanks for the quick turns around.

- We hope all personnel lists are accurate and current but someone move on yet they still on the list.

- Would you please provide information on charter and process documents for the City Council.

  - to aid me in responding with complete and current information requested from my boss

  - see email chain below for further context

  - my boss is standing a similar body and hopes to leverages your process

- i.e., ensure defined process escalates changes to the appropriate approval authority

Here are the errors and corrections:

- Thank you for **all your assistant and I'll** send **out** a meeting update shortly. (Correction: *Thank you for all of your assistance. I'll send a meeting update shortly.*)

- If **you're** agency is not listed here, your agency does not need to respond. (Correction: *If your agency is not listed here, you do not need to respond.*)

- This office is **dedicated establishing** working groups **with our members for our members.** (Correction: *This office is dedicated to establishing working groups with and for our members.*)

- The requirement team **need** to know if the hard drives are for both **network.** If **so we** need a document for **each. Also are** they just for **you're** workstations or a **colleagues** as well. (Correction: *The requirement team needs to know if the hard drives are for both networks. If so, we need a document for each one. Also, the team needs to know if the hard drives are only for your workstation or for a colleague's workstation as well.*)

- I have not been authorized to **utilizes** the new personnel roster. (Correction: *I have not been authorized to use the new personnel roster.*)

- If you have any **requests. Please** tell **me.** (Corrected: *Please tell me if you have any requests.*)

- I plan to meet with everyone when time **permit.** (Corrected: *I plan to meet with everyone when time permits.*)

- **I put me as** the **Point of contact** person for this issue. Stay **tune** for more information. (Correction: *I am the point-of-contact for this issue, so stay tuned for more information.*)

- Thanks for the quick **turns around**. (Correction: *Thanks for the quick turnaround.*)

- We **hope** all personnel lists **are** accurate **and current but** someone **move on yet they still** on the list. (Correction: *We strive to maintain accurate personnel lists; however, someone departed and the name was not deleted.*)

- Would you please provide information on charter for the city council?

  - **to aid me in responding with complete and current information requested from my boss**

  - **see email chain below for further context**

  - **my boss is standing a similar body and hopes to leverages your experience**

The last item above needed to be rewritten as follows:

Please provide me information on the charter for the city council. My supervisor is establishing a similar body and hopes to leverage your experience. Your assistance will allow me to provide complete and current information, as my supervisor requested. Additional background information is in the email chain below.

8. Be brief in substance. Email is inappropriate for multiple, lengthy paragraphs. Put those in an attachment referenced in the email.

9. Be concise in text. Compose telegraphically as shown below:

- August 10 through August 24 = Aug. 10–24

- 10:30 a.m. through 11:30 a.m. = 10:30–11:30 a.m.

10. Don't include overly personal information. When notifying colleagues that you will be absent from the office and must change the date or time of a meeting, don't include personal information. Colleagues don't need to know about your medical appointment or meeting at your child's school. I was once notified through a group email that an individual was taking emergency leave. Her dear uncle who raised her on his dairy farm recently died . . . and the story continued. Such detail is inappropriate for professional email.

11. Differentiate between the "To" and "CC" address lines. The "To" line equates to action or primary involvement. The "cc" means "carbon copy" and is for information only. Those cc'd aren't expected to respond. Authors often blur this distinction, causing confusion about who is responsible for what. If addressing someone directly, include that individual on the "To," not the "cc" line.

12. Beware of the "Reply All" button! Select this option by exception, not reflex. Does everyone really need to see your response or just the originator of the email to whom you are responding? Empathy has a role here. Do *you* enjoy being on the receiving end of "Reply All"?

13. Watch your language. Because online communication is one dimensional, the reader might not interpret subtleties, such as sarcasm and humor, as the author intended. If the communication is sufficiently informal, emoticons and emoji can help convey the sentiment. However, use them sparingly in professional emails.

14. Don't yell online. Capital letters and bold type equate to shouting and are viewed as rude. Use your writing skills to more professionally convey the message. Also, pause, count slowly to ten, walk away, and consider the repercussions before transmitting.

15. Don't use email to do your dirty work. If you must convey bad news, do so by phone or in person if logistically possible.

16. Send critical email to a back-up addressee. In many cases, email should have more than one addressee. For example, emailing a specific individual in the front office of a senior-level executive is risky. The action stalls if that person is out of the office. If the email conveys critical information and requires an immediate response, address it to several recipients.

17. Don't rely exclusively on email for a short-notice task. If communicating information that requires a quick response, follow up with a phone call. "Well, I sent you an email," is no excuse, nor does it mitigate repercussions.

18. Include your signature block. Conclude with your signature block, comprised of your name, title, telephone number, and email address. Often, companies or agencies also require employees to include a company address, logo, and website. This is the sign of a polished, professional communication and a courtesy to your readers. Provide contact information in case they need it.

20. The Elevator Speech: Essential Tool to Influence

"I only have a few seconds . . . Tell me about your product." Bang! The clock is ticking and you're on!

It's all about marketing. A business needs more than a showstopper product or service. An organization needs more than a worthy cause. An author needs more than a fabulous book. You need more than a stellar resume. Each requires a focused, articulate elevator speech to promote that product, service, cause, book—and yourself—to the audience. And, *that* requires the ability to write to influence!

For my readers unfamiliar with the concept, the term *elevator speech* derives from the time one person might spend with another riding in . . . you guessed it . . . an elevator. The term connotes the briefest amount of time in which to make your pitch—say 60 seconds. Prompts could include:

- For the author—Tell me about your book.
- For the job applicant–Why should I hire *you*?
- For private business—How will your product help *me*?
- For the researcher—Why should I fund *your* project?
- For contractors—What do you offer for this task that others don't?
- For the Department of Defense soliciting funds from Congress—How will this project enhance national security?

Don't have an elevator speech? No problem—let's compose one now. Easy as 1, 2, 3! I'll demonstrate using mine.

1. Strategize your message. My preferred approach is "problem, consequence, and solution." Yours might differ and that's OK. The key is to identify your customers and then explain *why* they need your item or should support your cause. Explain how it will improve *their* lives and how *they* will benefit. Remember . . . focus on the customer, not on your product or cause, and not on yourself.

- **Problem**–Many people are unable to write with precision and focus. This hampers achieving their goals—personal and professional. The problem is rampant, exacerbated by two causes: 1) For years, academic curricula has not sufficiently addressed succinct writing. Consequently, students graduate without these skills. 2) Social media has further blunted the ability to write, formulate, and present cogent, concise viewpoints.
- **Consequence**—This hurts the individual and businesses that seek such skills. Precise communication correlates directly to their *own* marketing success and financial bottom lines.

- **Solution**—*Write to Influence!* My writing strategies and techniques teach people to make each word count and every second of the reader's time play to *their* advantage.

2. Hone your draft. Armed with the story, hone it into an elevator speech using the *Word Sculpting Tools*. With some thought we arrive at a 32-word description and a slightly longer version for other applications.

- **32-Word Description:** Powerful writing changes lives! It is also the lifeblood for successful organizations. *Write to Influence!* teaches people to compose text—clear, concise, and compelling—to beat the competition and achieve their goals.

- **67-Word Description:** Powerful writing changes lives! It is also the lifeblood for successful organizations. *Write to Influence!* teaches people to compose text—clear, concise, and compelling—to beat the competition and achieve their goals. Want to win that academic scholarship, promotion, grant, or business proposal? *Write to Influence!* can tip the balance between success and failure. Tailored for the individual and private business, corporate, academic, government, and non-governmental organizations.

3. Now engage! Like all things, skill and fluency with elevator speeches come with practice. Rehearse until it flows naturally. Then pitch it at every opportunity. This includes talking to strangers in check-out lines at grocery stores, at the post office, on public transportation, even to waiters and cashiers in restaurants! When people inquire, "How are you?" Don't squander that golden opportunity.

This is the cue to deliver your elevator speech. Don't respond flatly with the expected, "Fine" or worse, "It's going." Instead, exude, "Great! My product is selling!" or "Fabulous! I just scored a huge success!" or some other wonderful news related to your situation. This prompts people to inquire further, offering you a platform to elaborate. People instinctively enjoy good news. Don't you? Conclude the encounter by sharing your business card. Never know where *that* might lead!

Are you hesitant to speak to strangers? Get over it. No one knows or believes in your product, service, or issue more than you. *You* are its advocate. *You* must support, defend, and promote it. *You* must trumpet its success. Now, get out there and spread the word . . . with gusto! You'll soon thrill to promote something you *know* will benefit others.

21. Briefings:
Composition and Delivery

Recall the scenarios in Chapter 4, in which you endured a terse interrogation from the judge, your boss, and your father. Now, it's your turn to speak. Addressing an audience places you in that same situation. In preparing your message, you rely on those same strategies in Part One: "Solid Framework," "Know Your Audience," "Set the Hook," "Make the Case," and "Clinch the Deal." You must present material so the audience accepts it as valid and assimilates it for future use (in an information briefing) or accepts your recommendation for an action (in a decision briefing).

A briefing consists of three elements: the message, the slides (text and graphics), and the delivery. Each is critical to the success of the presentation and accomplishment of the task at hand.

1. Develop the message by first answering these questions:

- Who is the audience and to what extent is it familiar with your subject matter?

- What does the audience need to know?

- What is the goal of your briefing? Is it designed to prompt a decision, or is it informational?

- If informational, how might the audience apply it? Have you considered building that bridge into the text, helping the audience make that connection?

- If this task was assigned to you, what does your boss expect you to accomplish?

- How much time is allocated for the presentation?

Decide how to frame your message: macro context to micro detail (like an inverted triangle); the opposite, beginning with detail and building to the larger context; or some other approach. Remember to follow the architectural drawing—your outline—to identify key points that will guide your audience to the desired conclusion.

Next, assemble the construction materials—building blocks of information such as statistics, examples, and other detail that add texture, focus, and validity to your message.

Take care not to lose the audience along the way. I once attended a briefing so poorly presented, it prompted the following four teaching points:

First, an effective presentation requires a trifecta—the message, slides, and delivery must each be spot-on. Failure of one can jeopardize the entire presentation. In this case, the message was badly flawed.

Second, the briefer violated two of my five core writing principles: *tailor the message to the audience's needs* (Principle #2), and *don't burden the audience with unnecessary information* (Principle #4).

Third, the briefing intended to identify a problem, the solution, and the results. However, the presenter opened a large garden gate by *telling the wrong story* (*Word Sculpting Tool*—Chapter 14, "Keep the Focus: Shut the Gates"). She spent 20 of the allocated 45 minutes describing failed attempts to reach the solution and minimal time on the solution itself. She got caught up in her *own* experience and used the podium to tell *her* story, information the audience did not need. Chapter 11, Example #8 speaks to this pitfall.

Fourth, she neglected to apply a central *Write to Influence!* strategy— *triage information to determine what not to share.* All I could think throughout this tedious experience was, "delete . . . delete."

2. Now, let's discuss the slides. As with other products, you must write proportionally both in time (i.e., the amount of time allocated on the agenda) and space (i.e., the slides, themselves). Regarding time, one minute per slide is a good rule of thumb. I always cringe when a briefer appears bearing forty-five slides for a twenty-minute presentation. Don't forget to allow opportunity for discussion or questions and answers in your allocated time.

In writing text, realize that a slide serves two purposes. First, it telegraphs to the audience general points being addressed. Second, it provides the speaker a platform from which to elaborate upon those points; it guides the story. When writing the text, empathize with your audience! Avoid inflicting "death by PowerPoint." Employ the Golden Rule and write a briefing you would like to receive.

Create short, crisp, single-line, telegraphically worded bullets. Data thus presented is refreshing to both the eyes and mind and is far more easily digested. That, by the way, is the intent. Do not reflect every, single detail of substantiating data in your slides. Instead, include this information in the notes page and speak to it.

Now, let's discuss graphics. A picture is worth a thousand words— how true! However, paralleling the advice above, use graphics that are simple and easily understood. Unfortunately, graphics in briefings today present a tsunami of visual effects that are complex, dense, and convoluted. Technology is the enabler. Avoid this temptation.

Do not create a "Turkish carpet" graphic. Turkish carpets are beautiful, especially those made by hand. Many are extraordinary works of art. The intensity of color, depth of detail, complexity of design, and value relate to the number of knots per square inch. Graphics in presentations **are not** Turkish carpets. You receive no points for intensity, density, or complexity. Such graphics detract from, rather than enhance, your message.

Seemingly interminable briefings are often characterized by a double whammy. Slides are packed with paragraphs that suffocate key points in the mire of textual mud, impossible for readers to grasp. This atrocity is often compounded by complex graphics, as mentioned above, making slides overwhelming and horrifying in equal measure. After a bit, audience members, glassy eyed, give up and turn their minds elsewhere.

Finally, close the garden gates. As with other written products, briefings are also susceptible to this malady. Beyond alienating the audience by the interminable briefing described above, inconsistencies in the presentation will also lose the audience. Jumping titles; varying margins; inconsistent spaces between bullets; and errors in spelling, punctuation, and capitalization prompt the ever-fatal question, "How many mistakes can I find on *this* slide?" Follow these tips to close those gates.

- <u>Select</u> a font size to provide sufficient room for text while also accommodating readability. I generally use 28 bold for the title, 24 for the main bullets, 20 for sub-bullets, and 16 for anything below. Note: Consistently apply whatever formula you select to each slide in the presentation. Failing to do so is another common error.

- Strive for brevity. Use bullets, not paragraphs! An audience <u>cannot</u> effectively wade through a paragraph of text on a slide. The brain cannot quickly identify and absorb key points when sandwiched between too much text. Presented with multiple paragraphs, the audience tunes out.

- <u>Compose</u> one-line bullets (i.e., a single thought that doesn't carry over into two lines, as exemplified by this particular sentence). You can sometimes nudge the thought onto one line by slightly adjusting the left and right margins of the text box or by using a shorter word. If the thought is complex and requires several lines, apply *Word Sculpting Tools* and break it into sub-bullets; these are far easier to assimilate.

- <u>Be consistent.</u> Watch for spelling, acronyms, capitalization, punctuation, etc. Are you going to end each bullet with a period? This is optional; but, decide and be consistent.

- <u>Standardize</u> the placement of slide titles and bullets. Be consistent in placement, both horizontally and vertically, on each slide. Inconsistent placement causes the distracting visual effect of these items jumping up and down or right and left as slides progress.

- <u>Don't let visuals step on the text.</u> Watch for graphics or other visuals that overlap text or step on a slide's foundational template.

- <u>Maintain parallelism</u> within a series of bullets or sub-bullets on a particular slide.

    - Start each bullet with either a noun or a verb as seen below but don't mix. This interrupts the rhythm and distracts the audience.

        - *<u>Identifies</u>, prioritizes, and manages incoming requirements*

        - *<u>Provides</u> consistent and timely guidance to all departments*

        - *<u>Allows</u> reallocation of resources to higher priorities*

3. Show time! Now, for the purpose of our discussion, the briefing is written, and you're standing behind the podium . . . "Action!" Briefing is akin to the ancient art of storytelling, partnering with the audience as you tell your tale. Engage the audience and talk *to*—not *at* them. Look around . . . observe, evaluate, and respond to attendees' reactions.

Move around on the stage, if the microphone permits. You're not a statue and you won't be penalized if you step away from the podium.

Apply the fundamental rule in briefing, "Don't read slides to the audience" or use them as a crutch by glancing at them too frequently. Through this practice, the briefer connects with the slides rather than the audience, conveys a sense of insecurity in both presentation skills and knowledge of the material, undermines his or her credibility, insults the audience (they can read, after all), and blows the opportunity to make an effective case.

By all means, use note cards or perhaps even a paper typed in a large font. However, remember eye contact is central to communicating. For that reason, beware of the typed paper, which can also become a crutch. Running a close second to the briefer who reads slides to the audience is the briefer who relies too heavily on notes and achieves eye contact after every third or fourth word. The effect is that of a doll whose head repeatedly bobs up and down as though connected to the shoulders by a spring. This is distracting and gains no credibility with the audience either.

Uncomfortable speaking to an audience? That's normal. As a second lieutenant, I was terrified at the prospect. Several options can help overcome this reticence. Find a conference room and a mentor; practice time and again until you know the material, are comfortable delivering it, and can answer questions. Some people rehearse the entire script. Others learn the material sufficiently to brief from an outline. Others approach a briefing in the role of a storyteller. In doing so, they mentally break the presentation into chapters and either memorize or have the opening sentence on a note card that queues them to the next part of the story.

Whatever your preference, this comfort level doesn't just happen— you must work to achieve it. Ask any actor about rehearsals! Point in fact: you are taking the stage and playing to an audience, so the acting analogy is appropriate. This becomes much easier with practice. I promise!

Part 4

Exercises: Test Your Skills

22. 100 Exercises

Exercise #1

Before: Tom was in charge of the document's coordination effort.

After: _____

Exercise #2

Before: Is this a topic you would like to have addressed in the next meeting of the Parent and Teacher Association?

After _____

Exercise #3

Before: Her involvement entails generating and coordinating the agenda, scheduling the conference room, and developing the seating chart.

After: _____

Exercise #4

Before: The CEO knows that inhibitors to achieve the strategic plan are generally not due to technology rather it is often the policies and practices throughout the corporate structure that have made implementing the plan so challenging.

After: _____

Exercise #5

Before: They discussed the issue for hours before they were able to arrive at an agreement on the solution.

After: _____

Exercise #6

Before: Updates to the Operations Guide must be carefully managed. In order to manage the Operations Guide, the emphasis is on maintaining rigorous change control.

After: _____

Exercise #7

Before: Mr. Jones provides updates to the council on a weekly basis.

After: _____

Exercise #8

Before: Some concern was voiced by several representatives that the festival would cost too much money.

After: _____

Exercise #9

Before: This website provides a list of resources that are available for our use.

After: _____

Exercise #10

Before: After reading the next article, what do you think Congress's role in insuring privacy rights should be?

After: _____

Exercise #11

Before: Word about the fire spread quickly throughout the entire community.

After: _____

Exercise #12

Before: This appears to be a reasonable request. We will put it into action immediately.

After: _____

Exercise #13

Before: The company made progress in the development of plans for the new housing units.

After: _____

Exercise #14

Before: The conference brought together more than 200 attendees.

After: _____

Exercise #15

Before: Due to a flight delay, she had to make adjustments to the itinerary.

After: _____

Exercise #16

Before: Each agency must provide for the protection of its own facility.

After: _____

Exercise #17

Before: Testing resumed on Jan. 17 and was completed on Jan. 21.

After: _____

Exercise #18

Before: Decision-making process that support integrated planning, implementation, and monitoring of the network operations will be established. Innovative acquisition approaches that modernize the network while identifying or eliminating duplication and unwarranted redundancies, will be implemented. Additionally, portfolio management processes that recommend investments based on their potential contributions to achieving mission strategies and priorities will be institutionalized.

After: _____

Exercise #19

Before: Created a file plan to help all personnel effectively maintain records for the appointed Branch/Division level personnel in the Department of Motor Vehicles.

After: _____

Exercise #20

Before: The purpose of this team is to facilitate achievement of corporate strategic goals by utilizing effective communication tactics and methods to inform and persuade key audiences and stakeholders. To that end, the team creates credible, consistent, and transparent communications to advance corporate strategic objectives through effective communications to concerned stakeholders to further corporate priorities to include: business operations, management of human resources, and strategic planning.

After: _____

Exercise #21

Before: To enable expeditious email exchange, various model options are currently being reviewed by the Corporate Communications Working Group (CCWG). A policy will be proposed and coordinated with all partners.

After: _____

Exercise #22

Before: I hold periodic staff meetings.

After: _____

Exercise #23

Before: We know for a fact that this design is similar to one we reviewed last week.

After: _____

Exercise #24

Before: Developed and established a temporary service to supply temporary financial management assistance to established offices and agencies.

After: _____

Exercise #25

Before: It was also my responsibility to answer staff questions related to security management.

After: _____

Exercise #26

Before: The Standard Operating Procedure developed ten years ago remains in use today.

After: _____

Exercise #27

Before: To discourage future attacks, the general prominently displayed a robust, defensive force.

After: _____

Exercise #28

Before: Even after lengthy testimony, many questions remained to be answered.

After: _____

Exercise #29

Before: The Transition Management Plan is a living document that will evolve over time.

After: _____

Exercise #30

Before: Mr. Jones orchestrated three monthly meetings: one meeting each month for technologists; one meeting for the staff; and one meeting for corporate leaders.

After: _____

Exercise #31

Before: In dealing with complex challenges presented by and facing teenagers, parents must have a basic understanding of child psychology.

After: _____

Exercise #32

Before: When sending products out for coordination and comment, include these instructions.

After: _____

Exercise #33

Before: The vice president has approved the attached memorandum, *Financial Impact of Modifications to the Distribution System*, signed by Jane Smith, Director for the Production and Distribution Division, for dissemination.

After: _____

Exercise #34

Before: When registering for the conference, please bring your lunch payment with you.

After: _____

Exercise #35

Before: The Historic Preservation Awareness Tiger Team (HPATT) is coordinating a meeting with several Federal agencies to gather data in support of an ACHP tasker to identify gaps associated with information in the public domain and whether or not the creation and posting on the web of a handbook emphasizing the preservation of America's historic heritage is necessary.

After: _____

Exercise #36

Before: Congress has given the power to the Department of Transportation and the funding to upgrade and repair the nation's highway infrastructure.

After: _____

Exercise #37

Before: With regards to the template standard: Has set the standard within the organization with regards to products being produced to relay the organization's mission message; in doing so, other groups within the organization has adopted the practice and have utilized the template to create their own products.

After: _____

Exercise #38

Before: The report will result in the adoption of best practices across the organization.

After: _____

Exercise #39

Before: Assists organizations in the development of annual budget forecasts.

After: _____

Exercise #40

Before: Responsible for synthesizing large amounts of data to ferret out irrelevant information.

After: _____

Exercise #41

Before: Because the company is understaffed, it does not have a designated representative for each principal customer.

After: _____

Exercise #42

Before: This business reorganization advances the idea that agencies are more effective and efficient collectively than they are individually which will ultimately help to drive down costs while delivering improved mission services.

After: _____

Exercise #43

Before: It would seem individuals strongly believed in their convictions that they choose to overlook data and expert opinion that was counter to their position.

After: _____

Exercise #44

Before: The blame would also lie with John Smith, using the flawed information provided by the finance department, when addressing the Corporate Board when attempting to get support for the new project.

After: _____

Exercise #45

Before: Responsible for the management of senior analysts from federal government offices, as well as academic organizations for fourteen months in Afghanistan in support of multiple clients during Operation Rapid Maneuver.

After: _____

Exercise #46

Before: Demonstrated ability to create and provide direct management of monthly academic development meetings for every financial analyst in the Rutgers Agency to share experience and synchronize client's efforts.

After: _____

Exercise #47

Before:

I advised the office renovation team on the organization and shelving needs for the renovation of the library.

I introduced TFD and NIBED to John Hankins. Hankins was hired as the contractor to organize NIBED IRB financial accounts.

I developed a file system for new shelving in the library. The new shelving is the result of an office renovation.

After: _____

Exercise #48

Before: The strategic plan will be presented for FY17 2nd quarter CEO review.

After: _____

Exercise #49

Before: Ensures all employees have full working knowledge of applicable regulations such as AI15, location and process for storing records by using the standard naming convention and creating PST files.

After: _____

Exercise #50

Before: FOTM Systems, Resource, and Financial Analyses (SRFA)

Led the Analysis, Data, and Standards Team for the Systems, Resource, and Financial Analyses (SRFA) office in the Federal Office of Traffic Management (FOTM) for two years, performing program analysis, financial modeling, and program and budget evaluations.

After: _____

Exercise #51

Before: Temporary position in massive drug litigation required expert depositions, motion preparation, and updating national medical record assembly with medical reports Monday, Wednesday, and Friday, using the Hummingbird and Warbler filing systems.

After: _____

Exercise #52

Before: Professionally delivered presentations and briefings weekly with ease. Promoted integrity of organizational business processes and mission by being customer oriented and proactive manifesting outstanding judgment and experience.

After: _____

Exercise #53

Before: As we did last year, this office will provide you, within two weeks of publication of this data call, with a list of your outstanding actions. You must verify that the information we provide you is correct, correct information you believe is incorrect, and add any items that don't appear on your list. Request you respond on the same day you receive the list from us.

After: _____

Exercise #54

Before: Executed account management process, to include account prioritization development, account resourcing, and account planning with respect to software procurement and maintenance to satisfy business requirements, as the procurement officer by understanding my clients' budgeting and acquisition processes in support of Operation Striking Endeavor.

After: _____

Exercise #55

Before: Her professional history consists of ten years of experience in interagency collaboration, analyzing, producing, and dissemination of information at both the Strategic, Operational, and Tactical levels.

After: _____

Exercise #56

Before: Planned, managed and in many cases configured security implementation on over 5000 computers as well as drafted local policies for the use of 5 security procedures for the corporation.

After: _____

Exercise #57

Before: Effective communication facilitates organizational and behavioral change across the corporation. It results in motivated, engaged personnel who change attitudes and behaviors because they understand it is "the right thing to do" and not in begrudging compliance with a direct activity with respect to the corporate priorities, policies, and strategic plans.

After: _____

Exercise #58

Before: The *Legal Systems in the 20th Century* study was required reading.

After: _____

Exercise #59

Before: The football team scores comparison report effort was a high priority of the university's Athletic Department.

After: _____

Exercise #60

Before: A policy change on sick leave has been approved by the director. Ensure it is read by all of your staff members.

After: _____

Exercise #61

Before: Modifications of business practices continues until a new mode of operation emerges that consistently and effectively makes the most of investments in IT and tangibly maximizes benefits of IT to the mission.

After: _____

Exercise #62

Before: All required emergency medical device (e.g., defibrillators, water rescue equipment, infusion pumps) training listed in the website must be completed by the designated user before equipment will be issued.

After: _____

Exercise #63

Before: The goal is producing an estimated annual paperwork burden reduction of millions of hours.

After: _____

Exercise #64

Before: Ability to work in a matrix team environment and exercised strong technical proficiencies while generating charts and graphs from raw data; prepared presentations, proposals, and reports.

After: _____

Exercise #65

Before: In an automatic dial telephone that is useable in a motor vehicle, when a voice input is provided during a period in which input of the names of called parties is awaited, a voice pattern of the name of the called party is compared with reference patterns of called parties stored in reference pattern storing device, to determine the degree of the similarity therebetween. The names of the called parties are output to a user in the order of decreasing degree of similarity. Each time the name of a called party is output, a command word for confirmation is waited from a user for a predetermined time period. When a voice confirmation command is input and is recognized during this waiting period, a telephone number corresponding to the name of the called party is supplied to a channel. Consequently, the command word for confirmation may be input only if the name of the called party outputted is one desired by the user.

After: _____

Exercise #66

Before: The Chief of Security was quite busy dealing with the data breach follow-on issues.

After: _____

Exercise #67

Before: A goal is to provide updated procedures and guidance to subordinate units for data spillages.

After: _____

Exercise #68

Before: Researched, analyzed, and presented financial data in the form of a daily FINALSUM.

After: _____

Exercise #69

Before: Produced and disseminated the company's first brochure marketing its latest product line. The brochure identifies each item, its price to the consumer, and benefits to all who use these products. It identifies where the product is made, where it might be purchased both physically and online.

After: _____

Exercise #70

Before: The role of the Congress in overseeing the Department of Transportation is to provide the purse for the department to conduct their mission.

After: _____

Exercise #71

Before: Led a team responsible for the successful adaptation, design, and deployment of a web-based application serving many users at several locations.

After: _____

Exercise #72

Before: Lead, Facilitate, and Participate in a group responsible for the future development, maintenance, and deployment of multiply communication networks that will integrate current and future capabilities to supports all communication requirements for several Corporate Agencies. Integrating Commercial Off-The-Shelf (COTS) products to insure interoperability with other Agencies. Trained senior level Agency Leaders on these systems.

After: _____

Exercise #73

Before: She serves as the organizations communication representatives ; provides feedback to customers around the agency headquarters along with units located around the world; provide customers with information on the security process, and role of the security officer; manage two different SharePoint sites.

After: _____

Exercise #74

Before: Held division chiefs accountable for budget and suspense's, and ensured the daily interactions of divisions with-in the office were effective in their execution of the daily mission. Provides daily status update to the director which in-turn ensured the director maintained daily situational awareness. Highly organized and acurate communicator.

After: _____

Exercise #75: Make the Case. Use six lInes to incrementally add detail to tell a more impressive story about the salesman of the month.

- Named salesman of the month

Exercise #76: Does the sentence below set the context for the reader? If so, how?

Selected from five candidates to serve as the aide to the Vice President of the United States.

Exercise #77: Identify the series—A, B, or C—that does not flow smoothly. Explain why.

A. • Manages a team . . .

   • Conducts comprehensive quality assurance to ensure . . .

   • Serves as principal organizational representative . . .

   • Serves as training lead . . .

- Oversees implementation and use of . . .

- Independently completes translations and summaries of . . .

- Applies analytical tradecraft in researching . . .

B. • Manages a . . .

- Responsible for scheduling . . .

- Project manage trainer development and performance to ensure client satisfaction.

- Monitored and reported on . . .

- Supports business growth . . .

- Responsible for . . .

- Create and deliver . . .

- Produce, write, and analyze . . .

C. • Co-edited major reference guide . . .

- Helped develop marketing strategies and promotional products . . .

- Translated and copyedited . . .

- Assisted in the organization and administration of scholarly conferences and lectures.

- Developed and maintained contact with leading scholars . . .

- Handled public inquiries through email and in person on . . .

Exercise #78: Add detail to further explain the significance of this accomplishment.

Before: She tech edited a document.

After: _____

Exercise #79: Add detail to further explain the significance of this accomplishment.

Before: She adjudicated and incorporated comments into the draft document.

After: _____

Exercise #80: Add detail to further explain the significance of this accomplishment.

Before: Project officer for the company's participation in the annual National Computer Security Convention. Coordinated with elements throughout the agency participating in the event. Composed detailed memos and coordinated scheduling details with several executive assistants. Senior VP for Production emailed, "Our corporate representation throughout the event was flawless due to your outstanding prep work—very much appreciated!"

After: _____

Exercise #81: Add statistics to more fully scope the significance of this accomplishment.

Before: Largely responsible for the complete restructure and redesign of the corporate homepage. Took the initiative to regularly populate it with information perfectly suited for customers' needs. Her boss stated, "I'm sure glad you updated this page because I certainly have not had time to do so!" Redesign of this page was a high priority of the Division Chief.

After: _____

Exercise #82: Find the most important sentence and rewrite the paragraph beginning with that fact.

Before: Each year, corporate headquarters requires subordinate divisions to conduct and submit annual security self-assessments. The goal of the self-assessment is to determine whether divisions are compliant with statutory and regulatory security management requirements. Our response to the survey follows the pattern of improving the score in each of the 3 years that we have been tasked to complete the self-assessment. Although corporate-wide results are yet to be released, this year our division received 90 out of 100 points, which, by past results, places our division higher than many longer-established organizational elements.

After: _____

Exercise #83

Before: After reading the article, post your thoughts on who you think is to blame for the debacle.

After: _____

Exercise #84

Before: Mr. Smith demonstrated superior leadership and interpersonal skills in stabilizing his branch when it experienced a 70% turnover of personnel within a single year, resulting in significant loss in operational continuity. A mentor extraordinaire, he implemented an internal training program, developed new working aids, and established continuity books. This noticeably increased the morale and confidence in his leadership.

After: _____

Exercise #85

Before: Largely responsible for establishing the working group that the CEO charged with identifying solutions to distribution challenges affecting all thirty-two stores in the chain coast-to-coast.

After: _____

Exercise #86

Before: Participated in and provided input to senior-most corporate leadership regarding Human Resource policy issues on hiring, maternity leave, and privacy rights.

After: _____

Exercise #87

Before: This office will advise and assist all corporate components on the agenda, logistics, and arrange the details for official travel to the conference.

After: _____

Exercise #88: Explain the difference in meaning of the two sentences below, based on the placement of the comma.

She is skilled in organizing large community events.

She is skilled in organizing large, community events.

After: _____

Exercise #89: Add details to create a more riveting sentence.

Before: Mr. Smith's many accomplishments were lauded to corporate leadership.

After: _____

Exercise #90

Before: In the past week or so, we've met direct with the CEO on five separate occasions, represented the CEO in a DC and multiple corporat-equivalent events. Our officers routinely brief major toy manufacturers, national-level toy conventions and with senior vice presidents throughout our company.

After: _____

Exercise #91

Before: We manage some of the most high profile advertising accounts in the company including Hotintot cereal, Wanna-Go-Faster toy cars, and the Blocks-a-Plenty construction set. We also manage the game, *Take the Stand*, where individual players pitch their case-and convince opposing players of the plausibility of their alibi. We also manage lesser known accounts as well.

After: _____

Exercise #92

Before: Responsible for best practice identification, designing patterns for infrastructure & cloud solutions, and creating global strategies to evolve the infrastructure from its current orientation to a global multi-national and Federally acceptable architecture and design that insures alignment and usage of Technology to achieve business strategies and by improving the overall value chain of the organization.

After: _____

Exercise #93

Before: Conducted meetings/presentations/seminars to the county's first responders on how other units were succeeding throughout the state providing issue papers, guided technical discussions, leading to a decrease in response times and increase in the number of calls answered..

After: _____

Exercise #94

Before: Successfully collaborating with other technology leaders, including globally dispersed leaders, on multiple enterprise-wide initiatives simultaneously, in a highly matrixed environment.

After: _____

Exercise #95

Before: Assist the Office of Computer Defense with technical and programmatic support of the portfolio with over $400 Million in annual budget. Develop numerous highly technical proposals and presentations through substantial research and analysis of data from multiple sources to inform Senior Computer Officials and gain further support in delivering improvements to existing technology and the development of new technology aimed at keeping corporate computer networks ahead of the adversary.

After: _____

Exercise #96

Before: I think that because I come from a charitable organization background I tend to look at all sides of a situation and do not feel that I am in a position to make judgments on anyone, but logical thinking, instead of emotional response are the only way we are going to get the most effective results.

After: _____

Exercise #97

Before: First off, thanks for the article suggestion. Second, for many of us who have not experienced or are unfamiliar with ghetto crime I would definitely try to state the facts first. Known facts, not conjecture or speculation into what could be or could have been the motivation if this is unknown or unclear. Secondly, I was watching a CNN report that went into neighborhoods and interviewed people who had been victimized, those who had been stopped by the police as possible suspects, based on their appearance and those who knew people who were gang members.

After: _____

Exercise #98

Before: The program that I was watched was with Anderson Cooper

After: _____

Exercise #99

Before: I will say that the most reliable books are the ones that features reputable experts in the field of financial management, The one expert that I think is phenomenal at keeping drama at bay in general is John Smith.

After: _____

Exercise #100

Before: The guest included John Smith, financial analyst, Mary Jones, financial reporter and Harry Peters, Securities Broker. They conversation was on the speculation about the impact that the housing market was going to have on the stock market, which was suggested by the Chairman of the Federal Reserve.

After: _____

23. Answers to 100 Exercises

Exercise #1

Before: Tom **was in charge of** the document's coordination **effort**.

After: Tom was responsible for coordinating the document.

or

Tom coordinated the document.

Analysis: *In charge of* can be discarded, unless you want to identify Tom's role in the process. In that case, replace *in charge of* with *responsible for* because it is more professional. The word *effort* is useless.

Exercise #2

Before: **Is this a** topic **you would like to have** addressed in the next meeting **of the** Parent and Teacher Association?

After: Should the Parent Teacher Association address this topic at its next meeting?

Analysis: Beginning with *Should* allows you to discard the useless words, *Is this* and *you would like to have.* Use a more solid subject, the *Parent Teacher Association* (and delete the word *and* in the official title) to provide a cleaner construction of verb, subject, direct object.

Exercise #3

Before: **Her involvement entails** generating and coordinating the agenda, scheduling the conference room, and developing the seating chart.

After: She generates and coordinates the agenda, schedules the conference room, and develops the seating chart.

Analysis: This is an example of hidden verbs and useless words. By deleting *Her involvement entails,* the author gets right to the action, *generates, coordinates, schedules,* and *develops.*

Exercise #4

Before: The CEO **knows that inhibitors to achieve** the strategic plan **are generally not due to** technology **rather it is often** the policies and practices **throughout the** corporate **structure** that **have made implementing the plan so challenging.**

After: The CEO realizes that technology is not the primary impediment to the strategic plan. Corporate policies and practices have also hindered its implementation.

Analysis: *Inhibitors to achieve . . . are generally not due to . . . rather it is often* are useless words. Reading again, we learn that technology is not the only bad guy. What else causes problems? Divide this into two manageable sentences and begin the second with the other culprits, *policies and practices.* We reduce *throughout the corporate structure* to *corporate* and replace *have made implementing the plan so challenging* with *hindered.* Also, notice the run-on sentence: *. . . due to technology rather it is often. . . .* This can be corrected by forming two sentences with a period and uppercase *Rather,* as in *. . . technology. Rather . . .* or by adding a semicolon as in *. . . technology; rather. . . .*

Exercise #5

Before: They discussed the issue for hours before **they were able to arrive at an agreement on the** solution.

After: They discussed the issue for hours before agreeing on a solution.

or, even better

They discussed the issue for hours before reaching a solution.

Analysis: Discard the useless words *they were able to.* Replace *arrive at an agreement* with the verb *agreeing.* Delete the second use of *they* as it is redundant. When possible, replace two words with one, i.e., *agreeing on a solution* equates to *reaching a solution.*

Exercise #6

Before: Updates to the Operations Guide must be carefully managed. **In order to manage the Operations Guide, the emphasis is on maintaining** rigorous change control.

After: Updates to the Operations Guide must be carefully managed by rigorous change control.

or, even better

Changes to the Operations Guide must be rigorously managed.

Analysis: As originally written, this sentence almost repeats itself. We reduce the length by half!

Exercise #7

Before: Mr. Jones **provides updates** to the council **on a weekly basis**.

After: Mr. Jones updates the council weekly.

Analysis: *Provides updates* equates to *updates,* and *weekly basis* is simplified to *weekly.*

Exercise #8

Before: **Some concern was voiced by** several representatives that the festival would **cost too much money**.

After: Several representatives expressed concern that the festival would be too expensive.

Analysis: Substitute the passive *some concern was voiced by* with the active voice *expressed concern*. Also substitute *cost too much money* with *be too expensive.*

Exercise #9

Before: This website **provides a list of** resources **that are** available **for our use**.

After: This website lists available resources.

Analysis: The hidden verb is *lists.* Discard the useless words *provides* and *that are.* The concept *for our use* is redundant, otherwise the information would not have been posted on the website.

Exercise #10

Before: **After** reading the next article, what **do you think** Congress's role in **insuring** privacy rights **should be**?

After: Read the next article. What role should Congress play in ensuring citizens' privacy rights?

Analysis: Delete the *after* construction and begin with the imperative *Read.* Delete as redundant, *do you think.* By posing the question, the author inherently requests the reader's thoughts. Replace *should be* with one word, *play.* Correct *insuring* to *ensuring.*

Example #11

Before: Word about the fire spread quickly **throughout the entire** community.

After: Word about the fire spread quickly across the community.

Analysis: The redundancy lies with *throughout* and *entire*, so we delete *entire.* Then, replace *throughout* with *across* to save space.

Exercise #12

Before: This **appears to be a** reasonable request. We will **put it into action** immediately.

After: This request seems reasonable. We will implement it immediately.

Analysis: The verb *seems* replaces *appears to be. Implement* replaces *put into action.*

Exercise #13

Before: The company **made progress in the development of** plans for the new housing units.

After: The company progressed in developing plans for the new housing units.

Analysis: The verb is changed to *progressed,* and *the development of* is replaced with *developing* to save space.

Exercise #14

Before: The conference **brought together** more than 200 **attendees**.

After: More than 200 people attended the conference.

Analysis: The modified version is crisper and shorter.

Exercise #15

Before: Due to a flight delay, she **had to make adjustments** to the itinerary.

After: Due to a flight delay, she had to adjust the itinerary.

or

She adjusted her itinerary due to a flight delay.

Analysis: The hidden verb is *adjust.* The second *After* example reads more smoothly and is preferred, unless it is important to stress *due to a flight delay*. In that case, use the first solution. We also delete *had to* in the final version.

Exercise #16

Before: Each agency must **provide for the protection of** its own facility.

After: Each agency must protect its own facility.

Analysis: The hidden verb is *protect.*

Exercise #17

Before: Testing resumed on **Jan. 17 and was completed on Jan**. 21.

After: Testing resumed on Jan. 17 and continued four more days.

Analysis: Calculate the length of time for the reader.

Exercise #18

Before: **Decision-making process that support integrated planning, implementation, and monitoring of the network operations will be established. Innovative approaches that modernize the network while identifying or eliminating duplication and unwarranted redundancies, will be implemented. Additionally, portfolio management processes that recommend investments based on their potential contributions to achieving mission strategies and priorities will be institutionalized**.

After: The corporate board will establish a decision-making process that enhances integrated planning, monitoring, and evaluating network operations. The board will employ innovative approaches to modernizing and streamlining the network. Additionally, the board will require Portfolio Managers to specify how recommended expenditures will improve operations and enhance corporate profit margins.

Analysis: The *Before* example is characterized by bureaucratic writing, passive voice, nouns used as adjectives, and cart before the horse. To remedy, identify the subject and verb. We had to specify the subject, *corporate board.* Use active instead of passive voice. Eliminate useless words. For example, we replace *identifying or eliminating duplication and unwarranted redundancies* with one word, *streamlining.* Did you find and correct the grammatical mistake in subject-verb agreement? The beginning phrase in the *Before* version should say *Decision-making process that supports. . . .*

Exercise #19

Before: Created a file plan **to help all personnel** effectively maintain records **for the appointed Branch/Division level** personnel in the Department of Motor Vehicles.

After: Created a file plan enabling the Vehicle Transfer Division of the DMV to effectively maintain its records.

Analysis: First, eliminate as useless words *to help all personnel* and replace with *enabling*. Clarify *for the appointed Branch/Division level* by specifying which organization, such as *the Vehicle Transfer Division.* Most readers will recognize the acronym *DMV,* thus obviating the need to use the full name. Finally, *personnel* is understood, so we do not need to use that word. Please note two mistakes in the *Before* version: *Branch/Division* should not be capitalized and a hyphen is required between *division* and *level.*

Exercise #20

Before: **The purpose of this** team is to facilitate achievement of corporate strategic **goals by utilizing effective communication tactics and methods to inform and persuade key audiences and stakeholders. To that end,** the team **creates credible, consistent, and transparent communications to** advance corporate strategic objectives **through effective communications to concerned stakeholders to further corporate priorities** to include: business operations, management of human resources, and strategic planning.

After: This team advances the corporation's strategic goals. It conveys skillfully crafted information through various media (e.g., brochures, videos, and newsletters) to key audiences. Principal topics include: business operations, management of human resources, and strategic planning.

Analysis: This has multiple problems: No solid opening hook, bureaucratic lingo, useless words, and redundant terms. *The purpose of* are useless words. *Facilitate achievement of* equates to *advances.* *Effective* is unnecessary because if *communications* weren't *effective,* they wouldn't achieve strategic goals. *Utilizing effective communications tactics and methods* equates to *conveys skillfully crafted information through various media.* Discard *stakeholders,* allowing the word *audiences* to carry the thought. *Credible, consistent, and transparent communications* equates to *skillfully crafted. To that end* is a useless phrase. The revision adds detail describing the types of media, enhancing the fidelity of this piece. Not only is the revision more potent, it is shorter by half!

Exercise #21

Before: **To enable expeditious email exchange, various model** options are currently **being** reviewed by the Corporate Communications Working Group (CCWG). A policy will **be** proposed and coordinated with all partners.

After: The corporate Communications Working Group is reviewing options to expedite email. It will propose and coordinate a policy with all partners.

Analysis: Who-does-what-to-whom? *Enable expeditious email exchange* equates to *expedite email. Currently* is redundant because *is reviewing* is already in the present tense. Use the active voice throughout.

Exercise #22

Before: I hold **periodic** staff meetings.

After: Hold staff meetings.

Analysis: This is based on a bullet in a resume. Resumes should not contain personal pronouns, such as *I.* Also, if this resume is for a management position, it could be deleted completely because it wastes space; this action is expected of any manager.

Exercise #23

Before: **We know for a fact that** this design **is similar to** one we reviewed last week.

After: This design definitely resembles one we reviewed last week.

Analysis: The redundancy lies with the words *We know for a fact.*
That the author makes this statement is, in itself, a fact. The simple
and direct verb *resembles* replaces *is similar to.* The author can add
emphasis, if necessary, with the word *definitely.*

Exercise #24

Before: **Developed and established** a **temporary** service to supply
temporary financial management assistance to established offices and
agencies.

After: Established a temporary service to assist customers with financial
management.

Analysis: Another example based on a resume, this contains two
redundancies. First, *developed* and *established* are synonymous in
this context, so we select one. Second, we discard one instance of
temporary. We sculpt *established offices and agencies* into a single
word, *customers.* Another option would be *business clients.* Can one
supply . . . assistance? We select *assist* instead.

Exercise #25

Before: **It was also my responsibility to answer staff questions related
to security management.**

After: None possible without interviewing the author for additional
detail.

Analysis: This is redundant for two reasons. First, *"It was also my
responsibility"* is understood because this is a bullet based on a resume.
Second, a professional is expected *to answer staff questions,* so this
should not be included at all.

Exercise #26

Before: The Standard Operating Procedure developed ten years ago
remains in use **today.**

After: The Standard Operating Procedure developed ten years ago remains in use.

Analysis: The redundancy is simple. The present tense of *remains* negates the need for *today.*

Exercise #27

Before: To discourage **future** attacks, the general prominently displayed a robust, defensive force.

After: To discourage attacks, the general prominently displayed a robust, defensive force.

Analysis: *To discourage* implies *future,* so we can delete this word.

Exercise #28

Before: Even after lengthy testimony, many questions remained **to be answered**.

After: Even after lengthy testimony, many questions remained.

Analysis: Delete *to be answered* because that is inherent in the term *remained.*

Exercise #29

Before: The Transition Management Plan **is a living document** that will evolve over time.

After: The Transition Management Plan will evolve over time.

Analysis: By definition, a *living document* evolves over time. No need to state it twice.

Exercise #30

Before: Mr. Jones orchestrated three monthly meetings: **one meeting each month for** technologists; **one meeting for** the staff; and **one meeting for** corporate leaders.

After: Mr. Jones organized three monthly meetings, one each for technologists, the staff, and corporate leaders.

Analysis: In the beginning, the author states *three monthly meetings.* Therefore, repeating *month, meeting,* and *for* is unnecessary. Also, note the punctuation. A comma should separate the items because, in this case, use of the semicolon is incorrect.

Exercise #31

Before: In dealing with complex challenges presented by and facing teenagers, **parents must have a basic understanding of child psychology.**

After: Parents must understand the basics of child psychology in dealing with complex challenges presented by and facing teenagers.

Analysis: Place the horse before the cart, beginning with the subject, *parents.* Next, find the hidden verb *understand,* and the rest falls into place.

Exercise #32

Before: When sending products out for coordination and comment, **include these instructions**.

After: Include these instructions when sending products for coordination and comment.

Analysis: Two points here. First, don't keep the reader in suspense with a long lead-in. Cut to the chase and begin with the imperative telling the reader what to do. Second, reduce the verb from two words to one by changing *sending out* to *sending.*

Exercise #33

Before: The vice president has approved the attached memorandum, *Financial Impact of Modifications to the Distribution System*, signed by Jane Smith, Director for the Production and Distribution Division, **for dissemination.**

After: The vice president approved the dissemination of the attached memorandum, *Financial Impact of Modifications to the Distribution System*, signed by Jane Smith, Director for the Production and Distribution Division.

Analysis: Another example of cart before the horse. Move the key word *dissemination* to the front of the sentence. That is, after all, the heart of this communication.

Example #34

Before: When registering for the conference, please bring your lunch payment **with you**.

After: When registering for the conference, please bring your lunch payment.

Analysis: Again, the redundancy is simple. The instruction is directed at the reader. So, we can delete *with you.*

Exercise #35

Before: **The Historic Preservation Awareness Tiger Team (HPATT) is coordinating a meeting with several Federal agencies to gather data in support of an ACHP tasker to identify gaps associated with information in the public domain and whether or not the creation and posting on the web of a handbook emphasizing the preservation of America's historic heritage is necessary**.

After: The Historic Preservation Awareness Tiger Team (HPATT), in coordination with several federal agencies, is determining whether the public has access to sufficient information about its roles and responsibilities. It is also determining the need to create and post on the Internet a handbook, *Preservation of America's Historic Heritage*. HPATT is responding to a task levied by the Advisory Council on Historic Preservation.

Analysis: The opening *coordinating a meeting . . . to gather data in support of* is weak and does not entice the reader to continue. We skip these interim steps and open with the main point, *determining whether the public has access*. The author does not specify what gaps *associated with information*, so we add *about its roles and responsibilities*. We follow with the next key point, *determining the need to create and post*. To avoid hogging space, we shorten *necessary* to *need*. In summary, these are the key transitions:

1. Remember the "Who (pause) does what (pause) to whom" formula. The HPATT has two tasks, now clearly stated.

2. The *Before* version consists of one exceedingly long sentence, made all the worse with a key verb comprising the last two words, *is necessary*—the classic cart before the horse.

3. The *Before* version misuses acronyms. It states *(HPATT)* even though the name of the organization is not referenced a second time, making the acronym unnecessary. On the other hand, the author includes *ACHP* without ever spelling out that acronym.

4. Finally, we relegate to the end of the paragraph as background information the fact that the ACHP tasked this action.

Exercise #36

Before: Congress **has given the power** to the Department of Transportation and the funding to **upgrade and repair** the nation's highway infrastructure.

After: Congress granted authority and appropriated funds to the Department of Transportation to overhaul the nation's highway infrastructure.

Analysis: To begin, Congress doesn't *give power;* it *grants authority.* Nor, does it, *give . . . funding;* rather, it *appropriates funds.* The author splits the actions Congress took, so we modify that, as well. Finally, we revise *upgrade and repair* to a single verb, *overhaul.*

Exercise #37

Before: **With regards to the template standard: Has set the standard within the organization with regards to products being produced to relay the organization's mission message; in doing so, other groups within the organization has adopted the practice and have utilized the template to create their own products.**

After: His many products not only set the bar, they raised it. Other elements in the organization are following suit, using his templates as examples to reach their own customers.

Analysis: This is based on a personnel appraisal, so it's appropriate to use personal pronouns. Sequentially, we notice the cart preceding the horse with the lengthy and squishy introduction, *With regards to the template standard: Has set the.* Redundancy is an issue with *products being produced.* The example contains a grammatical error and inconsistency of *groups . . . has adopted . . . and have utilized.* Finally, the paragraph in its entirety benefits from using our who-does-what-to-whom formula.

Exercise #38

Before: The report will **result in the adoption of** best practices across the organization.

After: The report will promulgate best practices across the organization.

Analysis: One strong verb, *promulgate,* replaces many weaker words.

Exercise #39

Before: **Assists** organizations **in the development of annual budget forecasts.**

After: Helps organizations develop annual budget forecasts.

or

Helps organizations forecast annual budgets.

Analysis: *"Helps . . . develop"* replaces *"assists . . . in the development of.* If the *development* step is not central to the message, skip it and cut directly to the key action *forecast.*

Exercise #40

Before: Responsible for synthesizing large amounts of data to **ferret out** irrelevant information.

After: Responsible for synthesizing large amounts of data to identify irrelevant information.

Analysis: *To ferret out* has no place in a professional document. Use a verb such as *identify* or *eliminate* based on the intent of the message.

Exercise #41

Before: Because the company is understaffed, it does not **have a designated** representative for each principal customer.

After: Because the company is understaffed, it does not designate a representative for each principal customer.

Analysis: Find the hidden verb. *Does not have a designated* is replaced with *does not designate.*

Exercise #42

Before: This **business** reorganization advances the idea that agencies are more effective and efficient collectively than **they are** individually which will ultimately **help to drive down** costs while **delivering** improved **mission** services.

After: This reorganization advances the idea that businesses are more effective and efficient collectively than individually, which will ultimately reduce costs while improving services.

Analysis: We eliminate a minor redundancy with *business* and *agency.* Eliminate *they are* as useless words. Add a comma following *individually.* Replace *help to drive down* with *reduce* and delete *delivering* by using *improving.* We also eliminate *mission* as redundant because what other services would *businesses* offer?

Exercise #43

Before: **It would seem** individuals strong**ly believed in their** convictions **that they choose to overlook** data and **expert** opinion **that was counter to their position**.

After: Individuals with strong convictions purposefully disregarded contradictory data and opinions of experts.

Analysis: Delete the useless words *It would seem.* Delete *believed in their* as redundant to *convictions. That they chose to overlook* is replaced by *purposefully disregarded.* Please note, the key action is not that they *chose* but that they *overlooked.* The interim step, *choosing,* is superfluous. Finally, we replace *that was counter to their position* with *contradictory to their own.* Within this last modification, *that was* is actually incorrect and should be *that were* because it refers to *data and opinions.* However, we delete those words as useless. *To their position* is redundant with *convictions.*

Exercise #44

Before: **The blame would also lie with** John Smith, using the flawed information **provided by** the finance department, **when addressing** the Corporate Board **when attempting to get support** for the new project.

After: John Smith was also at fault, asking the Corporate Board to endorse the new project, but basing his presentation on flawed information from the finance department.

Analysis: Too many words! *The blame would also lie with* is replaced with *was also at fault.* Replace *provided by* with *from.* Dual use of *when* is very cumbersome. *Attempting to get support* is replaced with a more polished, *asking the Corporate Board to endorse.*

Exercise #45

Before: **Responsible for the management of** senior analysts from federal **government offices, as well as** academic organizations for fourteen months in Afghanistan **in** support **of multiple** clients **during Operation Rapid Maneuver.**

After: Managed fifteen senior analysts from federal and academic organizations supporting eight clients for fourteen months in Afghanistan.

Analysis: Find the real verb and discard excess words, *responsible for the management of.* More useless words: *government offices, as well as.* Don't say *multiple* as this contributes nothing to the sentence. *Operation Rapid Maneuver* is a fine example of gibberish; don't use titles that signify nothing to the readers. The key fact is *in Afghanistan,* making the title superfluous. The author should state how many analysts he managed.

Exercise #46

Before: **Demonstrated ability to** create and **provide direct management of** monthly **academic development meetings** for **every** financial analyst **in the Rutgers Agency to share experience and synchronize client's efforts.**

After: Created and managed a monthly forum for the 30 financial analysts in the 2,000-person agency. Provided a unique opportunity for employees to network, leverage advances in software, and benchmark business processes.

Analysis: What does the individual do? Skip the step of *demonstrated* and begin with *created. Provide direct management* masks the real verb, *managed.* Delete *academic development* as unnecessary. What is the Rutgers Agency? We identify it by describing the scope and also by specifying the number of financial analysts it employs. *Experience* should be plural, but we don't need it in the improved version. Finally, we eliminate the last few words and better explain the benefit of this forum (better word than *meetings*) that the individual initiated.

Exercise #47

Before:

- **I** advised the office renovation team on the organization and **shelving** needs for the renovation of the **library**.

- **I** introduced **TFD and NIBED to John Hankins**. Hankins was hired as the contractor to organize NIBED IRB financial accounts.

- **I** developed a file system for **new shelving in the library. The new shelving** is the result of an office renovation.

After: Advised the renovation team on shelving requirements for the library; developed and implemented a new filing system when renovations were completed.

Analysis: This is based on three consecutive bullets from a resume. Collectively, they demonstrate two instances of redundancy. First is dual use of *renovation* in the first bullet. Second is triple mention of *shelving*. We discard the second bullet as it is unintelligible and leaves open several garden gates. Acronyms are not spelled out, leaving the reader clueless. Presentation of this bullet is so odd, it seems the author functions as a matchmaker, introducing A and B to *John Hankins*. Who is John Hankins, anyway? Only on the next page of the resume, does the reader learn that *John* is not who, but what. *John Hankins* is a contracting firm. Therefore, to clarify, the second bullet should at least state, *John Hankins was hired as the contracting firm.*

Exercise #48

Before: The strategic plan will be presented for **FY17 2nd quarter** CEO review.

After: The strategic plan will be presented to the CEO for review between Jan.–Mar. 2018.

Analysis: In this case, we choose not to use nouns as adjectives, as in *CEO review.* Instead, state *to the CEO for review.* Now for the gibberish: to help the reader, translate *FY17 2nd quarter* into Jan.–Mar. 2018.

Exercise #49

Before: Ensures all employees **have full working knowledge** of applicable regulations such as **AI15,** location and process for storing records by using the standard naming convention and creating **PST** files.

After: Ensures all employees are fully versed in applicable regulations, the location of and process for storing records by using the standard naming convention, and creating Personal Storage Table (PST) files.

Analysis: This is based on a line from a resume. We replace *have full working knowledge* with *are fully versed.* Delete *AI15* as both gibberish and unnecessary. It also requires too much space to define. Referring to *regulations* will suffice. Finally, we spell out the acronym.

Exercise #50

Before: **FOTM Systems, Resource, and Financial Analyses (SRFA)**

Led the Analysis, Data, and Standards Team for the Systems, Resource, and Financial Analyses (SRFA) office in the Federal Office of Traffic Management (FOTM) for two years, performing program analysis, financial modeling, and program and budget evaluations.

After: Federal Office of Traffic Management (FOTM)—Systems, Resource, and Financial Analyses (SRFA).

Led a team for two years, performing program analysis, financial modeling, and program and budget evaluations.

Analysis: Because the organization is identified in the header, repeating the lengthy and cumbersome titles in the body of the text is unnecessary and counterproductive. It forces the reader to wade through a lot of mud before reaching terra firma! By the way, how big was the team? The author misses the opportunity to include that data point.

Exercise #51

Before: Temporary position in a **massive** drug litigation required expert depositions, motion preparation, and updating the national medical record assembly with medical reports **Monday, Wednesday, and Friday, using the Hummingbird and Warbler** filing systems.

After: Temporary position in a drug litigation required expert depositions, motion preparation, and updating the national medical record assembly several times weekly using automated filing systems.

Analysis: This is a fine example of gibberish. The reader probably doesn't need to know the specific days on which the assembly is updated or the names of the two systems used to do so. Purge such data.

Exercise #52

Before: **Professionally delivered presentations and briefings weekly with ease. Promoted integrity of organizational business processes and mission by being customer oriented and proactive manifesting outstanding judgment and experience.**

After: Proficient at briefing clients weekly. The rest is unintelligible.

Analysis: This is based on another bullet from a resume and leaves the reader asking, "What??" The first word, *Professionally,* is "no-duh" and should be deleted. Actually, the entire bullet should be deleted because it wastes the reader's time. The fact that one performs *professionally* is assumed, as is *being customer oriented* and so forth. How does one *promote integrity of processes*? *Proactive manifesting outstanding judgment and experience*—Honestly! What does that mean?

Exercise #53

Before: **As we did last year,** this office will provide **you, within** two weeks **of publication of this** data call, **with** a list of your outstanding actions. **You must** verify **that the information we provide you is correct, correct information you believe is incorrect, and add any items that**

don't appear on your list. Request **you** respond on the same day **you receive the list from us.**

After: This office will provide a list of your outstanding actions two weeks prior to issuing the formal data call. Please validate and update the information. Request same day response.

Analysis: First, delete the opening words *As we did last year* as unnecessary. Next, determine that the *Before* version is a perfect example of gibberish because it essentially tells the reader how to breathe. It is completely unnecessary to detail each step in the review process. Finally, the *Before* version mentions *you* or *your* eight times!

Exercise #54

Before: **Executed account management process, to include account** prioritization development, **account** resourcing, and **account** planning **with respect to** software procurement and maintenance **to satisfy business requirements**, as the procurement officer by understanding my clients' budgeting and acquisition processes in support of **Operation Striking Endeavor.**

After: As procurement officer in Afghanistan, effectively managed the account process (prioritizing, resourcing, and planning) to procure and maintain software for clients.

Analysis: This demonstrates the open garden gate, redundancy, gibberish, wasted words, and cart before the horse. *Executed account management process* sounds like this poor creature was blindfolded and shot! No need to state *account* three times. *With respect to* are useless words as are *to satisfy business requirements*. The piece that sets the context is buried in the original text; so, we begin the revision with *As procurement officer* and add *in Afghanistan* instead of using the title of the operation, which likely means nothing to the reader. The rest of the sentence is useless and, in fact, is expected as part of the job; we replace it with one word, *effectively.* The author should also have scoped the level of effort by stating the number of clients.

Exercise #55

Before: **Her professional history consists of** ten years of experience in interagency **collaboration, analyzing, producing, and dissemination of information at both the Strategic, Operational, and Tactical levels.**

After: She has ten years' experience with interagency collaboration and with analyzing, producing, and disseminating information at the strategic, operational, and tactical levels.

Analysis: This is based on a line from a professional letter of recommendation. In that context, delete as redundant *Her professional history consists of.* We change *dissemination* to *disseminating* to achieve a parallel construction of *analyzing, producing, and disseminating.* Next, validate the tethers against the base, *information. Analyzing, producing, and disseminating information* works well. However, *interagency collaboration . . . of information* doesn't. Separate this data point from the tether by adding *and with.* We now have *She has experience with collaboration and with analyzing . . . .* The *Before* example contains blatant mistakes in capitalization. Finally, and leaving a bad professional impression, the author states *at both,* implying a sequence of two items . . . except there are three! Not a good letter of recommendation, which could hurt the applicant's chances for promotion or a new job.

Exercise #56

Before: **Planned, managed** and in many cases **configured** security **implementation** on over **5000** computers **as well as** drafted **local** policies for the use of 5 security procedures for the corporation.

After: Planned, managed, and, in many cases, configured security software on more than 5,000 computers; drafted corporate policies to implement 5 local security procedures.

Analysis: We begin by correcting commas. Place a serial comma after *managed.* The words *in many cases* should be bracketed in commas. Next, we ponder, "Can someone configure implementation?" Thinking that unlikely, we revise the sentence to read, *configured security software.* The number *5000* should read *5,000.* Also, when using a specific numeral, use *more than* instead of *over*. As written in the *Before* version, a comma should be placed between *computers* and *as well as*. However, that wording is awkward and unnecessary, so we eliminate *as well as* and join the thoughts with a semicolon.

Exercise #57

Before: **Effective communication facilitates organizational and** behavioral change across the corporation. **It results in motivated, engaged personnel who** change **attitudes and** behaviors **because they understand it is "the right thing to do" and not in begrudging compliance with a direct activity with respect to the** corporate priorities, policies, and strategic plans.

After: Communication works wonders! Effectively presented, it can boost morale, stimulate productivity, and foster other behavioral changes throughout a corporation. People react positively on their own volition, not because modified behaviors are mandated by corporate priorities, policies, and strategic plans.

Analysis: The *Before* version is bureaucratic mush. It has no opening hook and is replete with boring text, useless words, and convoluted construction. "*Personnel*" is bland, so call them what they are . . . *people.* The *After* version has a much more positive slant. Although it's only nine words shorter than the original, what a difference!

Exercise #58

Before: The *Legal Systems in the 20th Century* **study** was required reading.

After: The study, *Legal Systems in the 20th Century*, was required reading.

Analysis: This is another example of a long string of nouns used as adjectives, which leads to misreading. So, the *After* version is much clearer and direct.

243

Exercise #59

Before: **The football team scores comparison report effort** was a high priority of the university's Athletic Department.

After: The report comparing scores of football teams was a high priority of the university's Athletic Department.

Analysis: This is another example of a long string of nouns used as adjectives that can sometimes create confusion and misreading. Begin with *report* as the subject. Discard *effort* as a useless word. *Comparing* describes what the report does and should follow next in the story line. Comparing what? *Scores.* Thus, the sentence is unraveled.

Exercise #60

Before: A policy change on sick leave **has been approved by** the director. Ensure **it is read by** all of your staff **members**.

After: The director issued a change to the policy on sick leave. Ensure your staff reads it.

Analysis: Write in the active voice and ask, "Who did what?" Delete redundant words, *all of . . . members.*

Exercise #61

Before: **Modifications of** business practices continues **until a new mode of operation emerges that consistently and effectively makes the most of** investments in IT and **tangibly** maximizes **benefits of IT to the mission**.

After: The company continues to refine its business practices by seeking new ways to leverage IT investments and maximize profit margins.

Analysis: Present a clear subject and verb. In this case, we must provide them, *The company continues*. Replace *until a new mode of operation emerges* with *by seeking new ways* as a shorter alternative. *Make the most of* is colloquial language slipping into a professional product; *leverage* is much more appropriate. Delete *tangibly,* which refers to the

244

tactile sense. How does that apply here? Be more specific in referring to *benefits of IT to the mission* by stating *maximizes profit margins.* Discard *consistently* and *effectively* and use *maximizes* instead. Did you notice the mistake in the subject and verb agreement in the *Before* version, *Modifications . . . continues?*

Exercise #62

Before: All required emergency medical **device** (e.g., defibrillators, water rescue equipment, and infusion pumps) **training** listed in the website **must be completed by** the designated user before equipment will be issued.

After: Designated users must complete requisite training on emergency medical devices (e.g., defibrillators, water rescue equipment, and infusion pumps) listed on the website before equipment will be issued.

Analysis: Who-does-what-to-whom? Avoiding passive in favor of active voice, we find *designated users must complete training*, and the rest of the sentence falls into place. We shorten *all required* to *requisite.* We also correct the mistake, *all . . . device* by using just *devices.*

Exercise #63

Before: The goal is **producing an estimated** annual paperwork burden reduction of millions of hours.

After: The goal is to reduce the annual burden of paperwork by millions of hours.

Analysis: Find the actual verb. Is it *produce* or simply, *reduce?* In this case, don't use nouns as adjectives because *paperwork burden reduction* is pure bureaucratic writing. We find the solution by applying the formula, who-does-what-to-whom.

Exercise #64

Before: **Ability to** work in a matrix team environment and **exercised** strong technical **proficiencies while generating charts and graphs from raw data;** prepared presentations, proposals, and reports.

After: Skilled in working in a matrix team environment; regularly demonstrated strong technical proficiencies; skilled in preparing presentations, proposals, and reports relied upon by corporate leadership and other business partners.

Analysis: This is based on a bullet from a resume. *Ability to work* is a boring and mediocre opening. Therefore, the revision opens with *Skilled in working,* relying on the understood subject and helping verb, *she is.* How does one *exercise proficiency*? Replace with, *regularly demonstrated strong technical proficiencies.* We correct mistakes in punctuation. The reader does not need the excessive detail, *while generating charts and graphs from raw data.* Finally, the *After* version provides the critical "so what" missing in the original.

Exercise #65

Before: **In an automatic dial telephone that is useable in a motor vehicle, when a voice input is provided during a period in which input of the names of called parties is awaited, a voice pattern of the name of the called party is compared with reference patterns of called parties stored in reference pattern storing device, to determine the degree of the similarity therebetween. The names of the called parties are output to a user in the order of decreasing degree of similarity. Each time the name of a called party is output, a command word for confirmation is waited from a user for a predetermined time period. When a voice confirmation command is input and is recognized during this waiting period, a telephone number corresponding to the name of the called party is supplied to a channel. Consequently, the command word for confirmation may be input only if the name of the called party outputted is one desired by the user.**

After: This describes the operation of an automated telephone system used in motor vehicles. The user states the name he/she intends to call. The automated system then seeks a match of that voice pattern with stored voice patterns. It provides a list of names in order of decreasing similarity that correlate to the requested name. The system will wait for a specified time for the user to confirm the name. It will then dial the number.

Analysis: This almost requires *Word Sculpting Tools* on steroids! Using the who-does-what-to-whom motif and taking the original paragraph in sound bites, this can be translated into understandable English. By the way, *therebetween* is not a typo; it was written as such in the original text.

Exercise #66

Before: The Chief of Security was **quite** busy **dealing** with the data breach **follow-on issues.**

After: The Chief of Security was busy with issues resulting from the data breach.

Analysis: Delete the word *quite* as an unnecessary, judgmental assessment. State the fact, *The Chief of Security was busy* without the editorial comment. Next, delete *dealing with* as redundant and subsumed in the essence of *busy.* Now ask, "Busy with what?" Response, "Busy with issues." *Follow-on* equates to *resulting from.*

Exercise #67

Before: A goal is to provide updated procedures and guidance **to** subordinate units **for data spillages.**

After: A goal is to provide updated procedures and guidance, enabling subordinate units to better respond to data spillages.

Analysis: Beware of unintended messages. The *Before* example almost suggests that the procedures and guidance were to help units spill data.

By adding a few words, *enabling subordinate units to better respond to* the proper message is delivered.

Exercise #68

Before: Researched, analyzed, and presented financial data in **the form of** a daily **FINALSUM**.

After: Researched, analyzed, and presented data in a daily financial summary.

Analysis: This is also based on a resume bullet. First, delete *in the form of.* Next, instead of using the cumbersome term, *FINALSUM,* explain that the product is *a daily financial summary.* This sentence also begs questions, distracting the reader who wonders, "To whom did the individual present the financial summary—a branch chief or president of the company?" This could be a significant gold nugget! Consider this alternative: *He researches and analyzes raw data, then generates a daily financial summary read by senior executives throughout the corporate headquarters.*

Exercise #69

Before: Produced and disseminated the company's first brochure marketing its latest product line. **The brochure identifies each item, its price to the consumer, and benefits to all who use these products. It identifies where the product is made, where it might be purchased both physically and online.**

After: Produced and disseminated the company's first brochure marketing the latest product line. Conducted extensive research on each product described therein, composed the text, originated the graphics, and designed the layout for the brochure. Disseminated 50,000 copies as part of a strategic marketing campaign. Initial sales exceeded expectations by 45%.

Analysis: The author leaves the gate open by telling the wrong story. The point is not the brochure's content, but what that individual did to generate it and the results.

Exercise #70

Before: **The role of** the Congress **in overseeing** the Department of Transportation **is to provide the purse for the department to conduct their mission.**

After: Congress approves funding for the Department of Transportation.

Analysis: Reduced to eight words from twenty-three! We replace, *is to provide the purse for* with a single phrase, *approves funding.* After all, *provide the purse* sounds like financing a horse race! *To conduct their mission* is grammatically incorrect, as it should be *its mission.* Moreover, these words are gratuitous. What else would the department do with the money besides *conduct its mission?*

Exercise #71

Before: Led **a team** responsible for the successful adaptation, design, and deployment of a web-based application serving **many** users at **several** locations.

After: Led a 5-person team responsible for the successful adaptation, design, and deployment of a web-based application serving 200 users at the Department of Homeland Security at 16 locations.

Analysis: The author leaves the gate open and the reader to wonder, "How large a team, how many users, at how many locations?"

Exercise #72

Before: **Lead, Facilitate, and Participate** in a group responsible for the future development, maintenance, and deployment of **multiply** communication networks that will integrate current and future capabilities to **supports** all communication requirements for several **Corporate Agencies. Integrating Commercial Off-The-Shelf (COTS)** products to **insure** interoperability with other **Agencies.** Trained **senior level Agency Leaders** on these systems.

After: Led, facilitated, and participated in a group responsible for the development, maintenance, and deployment of multiple communication networks. These networks will integrate current and future capabilities to support all communication requirements for several corporate agencies. Integrated commercial off-the-shelf (COTS) products to ensure interoperability with other agencies. Trained senior-level agency leaders on these systems.

Analysis: First, select the preferred verb tense, present or past, and standardize. Remove capitalization from *Facilitate, and Participate, Corporate Agencies, Commercial Off-The-Shelf, Agencies, Agency Leaders.* Replace *multiply* with *multiple.* Break the first sentence into two because of the length. Revise *supports* to the infinitive, *to support.* Replace *integrating* with *integrated.* Replace *"insure"* with *"ensure."* Hyphenate *senior level.*

Exercise #73

Before: She serves as the organizations communication representatives ; provides feedback to customers **around the** agency headquarters **along with** units located **around the world**; provide customers **with** *information* on the security process, and role of the security officer; manage two **different** SharePoint sites.

After: Represents the organization on communications issues, provides feedback to customers at agency headquarters and units worldwide, educates customers on the security process and role of the security officer, and manages two SharePoint sites.

Analysis: This example is also based on a resume, so we delete the personal pronoun *she.* It contains multiple errors and instances of imprecise writing. Note that verbs switch voice endings: *serves* to *provides* to *provide.* This occurred throughout the document, resulting in a cumulative and distracting rhythm. The author should use one voice form. It lacks the possessive apostrophe in *organizations,* another error repeated throughout the document. *Representatives* should be singular; note the extra space between *representatives* and the semicolon. To save space, *"Around the"* is replaced by *"at."* Use *along with* instead of *and.* Use *worldwide* instead of *around the world.* Delete the word *with* that accompanies *provides,* as it is unnecessary. Replace *provide* *with inform*ation with the singular verb *educate.* A comma should not follow *security process.* The word *different* is extraneous. Finally, compounding the poor impression made on the potential employer, the author repeats this bullet in its entirety on the same page, both entries separated by only two inches.

Exercise #74

Before: Held division chiefs accountable for budget and **suspense's**, and ensured the daily interactions of divisions **with-in** the office were effective in their execution of the daily mission. **Provides** daily status update to the **director which in-turn** ensured the director maintained daily situational awareness. Highly organized and **acurate** communicator.

After: Ensured division chiefs accomplished the mission. Updated the director daily to ensure his situational awareness. Highly organized and accurate communicator.

Analysis: While the opening words were not incorrect (yes, I realize this is a double negative), they can be improved. *"Suspense's"* should not be possessive. We revise it to more effectively replace *budget and suspense's* with the more encompassing *accomplished the mission.* Eliminate the rest of the first sentence as redundant to the revision. *Provides* changes verbal tenses, switching from the past tense used in the first sentence. We replace it with the more precise verb, *Updated.* Hyphens are incorrect in both *with-in* and *in-turn.* Finally, we correctly spell *accurate.*

Exercise #75: Make the Case. Use six lines to incrementally add detail to tell a more impressive story about the salesman of the month. Additional specifics were added to each line as shown here in bold:

- Named salesman of the month.
- Named salesman of the month **from among twenty-five peers.**

- Named salesman of the month from among twenty-five peers **for the third consecutive month.**

- Named salesman of the month from among twenty-five peers for the third consecutive month; **doubled the output of nearest competitor.**

- Named salesman of the month for the third consecutive month from among twenty-five peers; doubled output of nearest competitor, **bringing in $35K in revenue.**

- Named salesman of the month for the third consecutive month from among twenty-five peers; doubled output of nearest competitor, bringing in $35K in revenue, **and set the annual record for the store**.

- Named salesman of the month for the third consecutive month from among twenty-five peers; doubled output of nearest competitor, bringing in $35K in revenue, set the annual record for the store, **and tied the statewide record for the chain.**

Exercise #76: Does the sentence below set the context for the reader? If so, how?

Selected from five candidates to serve as the aide to the Vice President of the United States.

<u>Analysis:</u> One out of five, at face value doesn't sound so impressive. However, the context and "wow factor" is *to serve as the aide to the Vice President*. That fact and reaching that level of competition set the context for the accolade. It also, by definition, conveys the large pool from which those five candidates were identified.

Exercise #77: Identify the series—A, B, or C—that does not flow smoothly. Explain why.

- A. • Manages a team . . .
  - Conducts comprehensive quality assurance to ensure . . .
  - Serves as principal organizational representative . . .

- Serves as training lead . . .

- Oversees implementation and use of . . .

- Independently completes translations and summaries of . . .

- Applies analytical tradecraft in researching . . .

B. • **Manages a** . . .

- **Responsible for scheduling** . . .

- **Project manage trainer development and performance to ensure client satisfaction.**

- **Monitored and reported on** . . .

- **Supports business growth** . . .

- **Responsible for** . . .

- **Create and deliver** . . .

- **Produce, write and analyze** . . .

C. • Co-edited major reference guide . . .

- Helped develop marketing strategies and promotional products . . .

- Translated and copyedited . . .

- Assisted in the organization and administration of scholarly conferences and lectures.

- Developed and maintained contact with leading scholars . . .

- Handled public inquiries through email and in person on . . .

Analysis: Item B should be rewritten so each item opens consistently with a verb and in the same tense, as seen in the other two items in this exercise. Item B not only uses verbs of differing tenses (present and past), one line opens with a noun, and incorrectly at that. Reading aloud, do you hear how the rhythm snags and distracts the reader?

Note: Lines can also begin with nouns, as long as they open that way consistently.

Exercise #78: Add detail to further explain the significance of this accomplishment.

Before: She tech edited a document.

After: She tech edited a 33-page document, making 392 grammatical corrections and other literary modifications, working four intense hours to make the deadline. Leadership accepted 95% of her recommended changes.

Analysis: Again, what a difference the details make!

Exercise #79: Add detail to further explain the significance of this accomplishment.

Before: She adjudicated and incorporated comments into the draft document.

After: She adjudicated and incorporated into the draft document ninety comments from six organizations.

Analysis: The statistics add depth to this individual's accomplishment.

Exercise #80: Add detail to further explain the significance of this accomplishment.

Before: Project officer for the company's participation in the annual National Computer Security Convention. Coordinated with elements throughout the agency participating in the event. Composed detailed memos and coordinated scheduling details with several executive assistants. Senior VP for Production emailed, "Our corporate representation throughout the event was flawless due to your outstanding prep work—very much appreciated!"

After: Project officer for the company's participation in the annual National Computer Security Convention, attended by 20,000 people. During the 5 months preceding the event, coordinated participation by

26 senior and mid-level executives in all facets of the event. Coordinated scheduling details with executive assistants in 7 divisions to include identifying who would brief during the schedule of events. Forwarded the presentations to and confirmed receipt by the staff organizing the convention. Composed 6 memos providing extensive updates on registration, hotel and transportation accommodations, conference schedule, development and presentation of briefings, IT logistics, and participation in panel discussions. The Senior VP for Production emailed, "Our corporate representation throughout the event was flawless due to your outstanding prep work—very much appreciated!"

Analysis: What a different tale we have! Like adding spices to a recipe, details give a completely different dimension to an otherwise bland paragraph. The degree of accomplishment is heightened by the fact that the individual worked on the project for five months.

Exercise #81: Add statistics to more fully scope the significance of this accomplishment.

Before: Largely responsible for the complete restructure and redesign of the corporate homepage. Took the initiative to regularly populate it with information perfectly suited for customers' needs. Her boss stated, "I'm sure glad you updated this page because I certainly have not had time to do so!" Redesign of this page was a high priority of the Division Chief.

After: Largely responsible for the complete restructure and redesign of the corporate homepage, serving 18 subordinate organizations and with a daily average of 7,500 hits. Took the initiative to regularly populate it with information suited for customers' needs. Her boss stated, "I'm sure glad you updated this page because I certainly have not had time to do so!" Redesign of this page was a personal priority of the corporate CEO.

Analysis: This is also a solid bullet based on a professional letter of recommendation, but how much more momentous if you add the fact that this homepage supports 18 organizations subordinate to the corporate headquarters and is visited daily by 7,500 people! In actuality, this project was a priority of the division chief because it was, in fact, the priority of the company's CEO. What a difference!

Exercise #82: Find the most important sentence and rewrite the paragraph beginning with that fact.

Before: Each year, corporate headquarters requires subordinate divisions to conduct and submit annual security self-assessments. The goal of the self-assessment is to determine whether divisions are compliant with statutory and regulatory security management requirements. Our response to the survey follows the pattern of improving the score in each of the 3 years that we have been tasked to complete the self-assessment. Although corporate-wide results are yet to be released, this year our division received 90 out of 100 points, which, by past results, places our division higher than many longer-established organizational elements.

After: Corporate headquarters rated our office with 90 out of 100 points on our annual security self-assessment. If past statistics hold constant, we scored higher than most of our 30 organizational counterparts. This marks the third consecutive year that we have improved our score. As background, each division is required to conduct and submit an annual self-assessment, the goal of which is to determine its degree of compliance with statutory and regulatory requirements for security management.

Analysis: The lead line was buried, so we raise it to the fore and add statistics to scope the magnitude of this accomplishment. *Each year* is redundant to *annual*. Repeating *self-assessment* in each of the opening sentences is also redundant. Striving for precise expression, the goal of the inspection is not to determine *whether* an organization complies with regulatory requirements, but the degree to which it does so. We delete as extraneous the fact that the 30 counterparts are older than the subject organization.

Exercise #83

Before: **After** read**ing** the article, post **your thoughts on** who **you think** is to blame for the debacle.

After: Read the article and post your response to, "Who is to blame for the debacle?"

or, if *posting* is unessential to the thought, simply state:

Read the article and answer, "Who is to blame for the debacle?"

<u>Analysis:</u> This contains many useless words and one redundancy. Simplify by stating the task in sequence, *Read . . . then post.* The redundancy is *your thoughts on* and *you think.*

Exercise #84

Before: Mr. Smith **demonstrated superior leadership and interpersonal skills** in stabilizing his branch **when it experienced** a seventy percent turnover of personnel **within a single year, resulting in significant loss in operational continuity. A mentor extraordinaire**, he implemented an internal training program, developed new working aids, and established continuity books. **This noticeably increased** the morale and confidence in his leadership.

After: Mr. Smith masterfully stabilized branch operations when beset with a seventy percent turnover in personnel. He implemented an internal training program, developed new working aids, and established continuity books. The staff's morale and confidence in his leadership skyrocketed!

<u>Analysis:</u> The fact that Mr. Smith *demonstrated superior leadership* is not the bell ringer here. What did he do that was so noteworthy? *He stabilized branch operations.* Now, explain under what circumstances and how he accomplished this feat. One can argue that *superior leadership* entails *interpersonal skills,* making those words redundant. We replace the almost invisible words, *when it experienced* with a more dramatic and descriptive verb *beset. Within a single year* might scope

the challenge, but is not significant to the story; we delete that detail. To explain some changes, a *seventy percent turnover of staff* inherently implies a *significant loss in operational continuity,* making those words redundant. Acknowledgment of his leadership is a fitting and solid conclusion to this item. We replace the bland *noticeably increased* with *skyrocketed*, a much more descriptive verb. As a result of that concluding line, the words *a mentor extraordinaire* are also redundant. As a final assessment, the *Before* version has 426 characters, while *After* has only 270 yet is much more to the point and potent!

Exercise #85: Add detail to further explain the significance of this accomplishment.

Before: Largely responsible for establishing a working group that the CEO charged with identifying solutions to distribution challenges affecting all thirty-two stores in the chain coast-to-coast.

After: One of three people the CEO charged to establish a corporate-wide working group. The mission was to develop and implement a plan that identifies and resolves distribution problems afflicting thirty-two stores coast-to-coast.

- Tasked each store to identify a project officer, and then arranged the logistics and agenda for the inaugural meeting, which all attended.

- Volunteered to lead the functional team examining training; the team has already identified eight major issues.

Analysis: The first few words open the garden gate by prompting the reader to wonder, "How was she largely responsible? What did she do?" We scope the situation, stating she was *one of three people*. We clarify the task given to them by using *develop and implement a plan.*

Exercise #86

Before: **Participated in and provided input to** senior-**most** corporate leadership **regarding Human Resource policy issues** on hiring, maternity leave, and privacy rights.

After: Helped generate and provided input to senior corporate leadership on the policies for hiring, maternity leave, and privacy rights.

Analysis: This is a fine example of broken tethers, specifically *participated in and provided input to.* The base as originally written is *senior-most corporate leadership.* To test the viability of the tether, ask if one can *participate in . . . senior-most corporate leadership.* This tether is broken. The second tether works because one can certainly *provide input to senor-most corporate leadership.* We repair the broken tether by making *input* the base. Thus, you have functional tethers, *helped generate input* and *provided input.* Regarding the rest of the sentence, we simplify *senior-most* to *senior.* We reduce *regarding* to *on* to save space. That these are *Human Resources policies* is gratuitous information, so we delete that fact and also delete *issues,* preferring the most accurate term, *policies.*

Exercise #87

Before: This office will **advise and assist** all corporate components on the **agenda, logistics, and arrange** the details for official travel to the conference.

After: This office will advise and assist all corporate components on the agenda and logistics for the conference and arrange details for official travel.

Analysis: This contains a broken tether. Its base is *advise and assist* and the tethers are *on the agenda, logistics, and arrange.* One can *advise and assist* on the *agenda* and *logistics*, but cannot *advise and assist* on *arrange.* The remedy is simple; add the word *and* along with a separating comma, as shown above.

Exercise #88: Explain the difference in meaning of the two sentences below, based on the placement of the comma.

She is skilled in organizing large community events.

She is skilled in organizing large, community events.

Analysis: In the first sentence, *large* describes *community*. Thus, there is an *event* associated with a *large community*. In the second, the event is *large* and it is associated with the *community*.

Exercise #89: Add details to create a more riveting sentence.

Before: Mr. Smith's many accomplishments were lauded to corporate leadership.

After: On twenty-nine occasions, the division chief lauded Mr. Smith's accomplishments to the CEO in detailed submissions to his Weekly Activity Reports.

Analysis: The author opens the garden gate by leaving the reader to wonder how many *accomplishments* and to whom in *corporate leadership* were they mentioned.

Exercise #90

Before: **In the past week or so,** we've met **direct** with the CEO **on five separate occasions, represented the CEO in a DC and multiple corporat-equivalent events.** Our officers routinely brief major toy manufacturers, national-level toy conventions and with senior vice presidents throughout our company.

After: We met with the CEO five times this past week. We represented the CEO [unintelligible]. Our officers routinely brief major toy manufacturers at national-level toy conventions and communicate with senior vice presidents throughout our company.

Analysis: Sloppy wording: *In the past week or so* is a weak and unspecific beginning. Begin with the central point, *We met.*

Mistake: *Direct* should be *directly,* but we delete it as unnecessary.

Sloppy wording : Reduce *on five separate occasions* to *five times.*

Unintelligible: We can't make sense of *represented the CEO in a DC and multiple corporat-equivalent events.*

Mistake: The word *corporat* is misspelled.

Broken tether: *Our officers routinely* **brief** *major toy manufacturers, national-level toy conventions and with senior vice presidents throughout our company.*

- *Brief . . . toy manufacturers* works.
- *Brief . . . national-level toy conventions* doesn't really work, but *brief . . . at . . . toy conventions* does.
- *Brief . . . with senior vice presidents* does not work.

Exercise #91

Before: We manage some of the **most high** profile advertising accounts in the **company including** Hotintot cereal, Wanna-Go-Faster toy cars, and the Blocks-a-Plenty construction set. We also manage the game, *Take the Stand*, **where** individual players pitch their **case-and** convince opposing players of the plausibility of their **alibi**. We also manage lesser known **accounts as** well.

After: We manage some of the highest profile advertising accounts in the company, including Hotintot cereal, Wanna-Go-Faster toy cars, and the Blocks-a-Plenty construction set. We also manage the game, *Take the Stand*, in which individual players brief their cases and convince opposing players of the plausibility of their alibis. We manage lesser-known accounts, as well.

Analysis: Awkward wording: *Most high profile* is better stated, *highest.*

Incorrect punctuation: *Company including* needs a comma separating those words.

Incorrect preposition: *Game . . . where individual players* should read *game . . . in which* because *game* is a thing, not a place.

Sloppy wording: *Players pitch their case* is more correctly stated as *brief their case.* In court, a case is *briefed. Pitch* prepares the recipient to *catch* something.

Mistake: *Players pitch their case* should be plural, *cases.*

Mistake: *Case-and* should not be hyphenated.

Mistake: *Alibi* should be plural, *alibis.*

Mistake: *Accounts as well* needs a comma following *accounts.*

Exercise #92

Before: Responsible for **best practice identification**, designing patterns for infrastructure & cloud solutions, and creating global strategies to **evolve the infrastructure from its current orientation** to a global multi-national and Federally acceptable architecture and design **that insures** alignment and usage of Technology to achieve business strategies and **by improving** the overall **value chain** of the organization.

After: Responsible for identifying best practices, designing patterns for infrastructure and cloud solutions, and creating global strategies to reorient the infrastructure to a global, multi-national, and federally acceptable architecture and design. This approach aligns use of technology to achieve business strategies and improves the overall value of the organization.

Analysis: This example is plagued with strings of nouns used as adjectives, lack of parallel construction, hidden verbs, excessive length, gibberish, missing commas, an incorrect word, and an open garden gate. To begin, correct the parallel construction, resulting in *Responsible for identifying . . . , designing . . . , and creating.* Replace the ampersand symbol (&) with the word *and.* Next, identify the actual verb . . . we use the infinitive *to reorient* instead of *to evolve.* Add the missing commas to *global, multi-national, and federally acceptable.* Note that we did not capitalize *federal.* Break the long sentence, finishing the thought with a second sentence. The author's use of *that* is ill defined in the lengthy original, so we clarify by stating *This approach.* The verb should be *ensures,* not *insures.* However, the real action is not to *ensure,* it is *aligns.* As the penultimate correction, the final words of the original are broken: *by improving* does not make sense. The author probably means to state *and improves.* Finally, the author leaves open the garden gate by prompting the reader to wonder, "What is an organization's value chain?" We eliminate *chain* in the rewrite.

Exercise #93

Before: **Conducted meetings/presentations/seminars to** the county's first responders **on how other units were succeeding throughout the state providing issue papers, guided technical discussions,** leading to **a** decrease **in** response times and increase in the number of calls answered..

After: Gave presentations to and led meetings and seminars with the county's first responders on best practices employed throughout the state. Subsequently provided them issue papers and guided additional technical discussions, leading to decreased response times and an increase in the number of calls answered.

Analysis: This contains a badly broken tether. First, did the author select the proper verb as the base for each of the three associated nouns? Test it and see. *Conduct meetings* works. *Conduct presentations* is awkward. One usually *gives presentations* or *presents material, a briefing, etc. Conduct seminars* works. The next step is to examine the preposition paired with the verb *conduct* and each of the three nouns. *Conduct meetings to responders* does not work. *Conduct presentations to responders* does not work. *Conduct seminars to responders* does not work, either. Note, the problem with broken tethers frequently lies with the associated preposition linking the base to the tethered items. Eliminating words that hog space, we replace *on how other units were succeeding* with *best practices employed.* The *Before* version connects *providing issue papers, guided technical discussions* to *conducted meetings/presentations/seminars,* which does not make sense. Also, it's not appropriate to use slashes (/) in this way in professional writing. Moreover, how can one *provide guided technical discussions*? We change this to *and guided.* We save a bit of space by modifying *a decrease in* to *decreased.* Finally, we corrected the typo of the double period.

Exercise #94

Before: Successfully **collaborating** with other **technology** leaders, including globally dispersed **leaders**, on multiple enterprise-wide initiatives **simultaneously,** in a highly matrixed environment.

After: Successfully collaborated with other technological leaders, including those globally dispersed, on multiple enterprise-wide initiatives in a highly matrixed environment.

Analysis: This contains a redundancy, misplaced adverb, and a misplaced comma. Modify *collaborating* to *collaborated* to provide the sentence a verb. Avoid duplicate mention of *leaders* by replacing the second instance with *those*. *Simultaneously* seems misplaced and orphaned in its original location. We consider moving it to *Successfully collaborated simultaneously* but that, too, is awkward. Deciding it conveys no particular relevance, we delete it. We also eliminate the erroneously placed comma, . . . *simultaneously, in a highly matrixed environment.*

Exercise #95

Before: **Assist** the Office of Computer Defense **with** technical and programmatic **support of** the portfolio **with over $400 Million in annual budget.** Develop **numerous highly** technical proposals and presentations through **substantial research and analysis of data from multiple sources** to inform **Senior Computer Officials** and gain further support in **delivering improvements** to existing **technology** and the development of new **technology aimed at keeping corporate computer networks ahead of the adversary.**

After: Develop technical proposals and presentations for senior officials to improve current and future technology for defending computer networks from attacks by state and non-state adversaries. Support a portfolio valued at $400 million annually.

Analysis: This entry does not say much. *Assist with ... support of* is a boring, unfocused opening that also begs the question, "Assists how?" *With over $400 Million in annual budget* is better stated, *valued at $400 million annually. Numerous* adds nothing to the story, nor does

highly or substantial. Million and *Senior Computer Officers* should not
be capitalized. *Substantial research and analysis of data from multiple
sources* are expected as foundational for proposals and presentations;
therefore, these steps should not be mentioned. *Deliver improvements*
has a hidden verb; state *to improve* instead. No need to repeat
technology. Keeping . . . ahead of the adversary is too colloquial and
unprofessional for this context. We expand the concept of *"adversary"*
and do so using more professional terms. Note, the item does not
stipulate that the senior officers actually received these proposals and
presentations.

Exercise #96

Before: **I think that because I come from a charitable organization
background I tend to look at all sides** of a situation and **do not feel that
I am in a position to make judgments on anyone, but logical thinking,
instead of emotional response are the only way we are going to get
the most effective results.**

After: Because my background is with charitable organizations, I
consider all facets of the situation and am disinclined to judge people.
Logic, rather than emotion, produces the most effective results.

Analysis: We deleted most of the bolded words. We revise *charitable
organization* to *my background with charitable organizations* to focus
on the writer's experience and not the organization. Replace *tend
to look at all sides* with the more professionally worded, *consider all
facets.* Replace *do not feel that I am in a position to make judgments
on anyone* with *disinclined to judge people. But logical thinking, instead
of emotional response are the only way we are going to get the most
effective results* is replaced with, *Logic, rather than emotion, produces
the most effective results.* The revision is thus reduced from 297 to
195 spaces. Did you catch the grammatical mistake? In the phrase *But
logical thinking instead of . . . are,* the *are* should be replaced with *is.*

Exercise #97

Before: First **off, thanks** for the **article suggestion. Second, for many of us who have not experienced or are unfamiliar** with ghetto crime I would **definitely try to state the facts first. Known facts, not conjecture or speculation into what could be or could have been the motivation if this is unknown or unclear. Secondly, I was watching a** CNN report **that went into neighborhoods and interviewed people who had been victimized, those who had been** stopped by the police **as possible suspects, based on their appearance** and those who knew people who were gang members.

After: First, thank you for suggesting the article. Second, I would begin a report by stating facts for readers unfamiliar with the topic of ghetto crime. Third, a CNN reporter interviewed victims, people who knew gang members, and those whom police stopped based solely on personal appearance.

Analysis: Do not write as you speak; *First off* and thanks are prime examples of how not to write. Next, proofread! *Second . . . Secondly* is an obvious error. *For many of us who have not experienced or are* is replaced with, *readers unfamiliar*. The second sentence makes no sense and is impossible to improve. Then, a *report* can't *go into a neighborhood and interview* but a reporter can. Finally, we reorder the sequence of people interviewed, logically beginning with victims, those who knew gang members, and then those stopped for a lesser reason. We reduce the paragraph from 563 to 340 spaces.

Exercise #98

Before: The program that I was watched was with Anderson Cooper

After: I watched the program hosted by Anderson Cooper.

Analysis: Proofread! The *Before* version uses *was* twice and is missing a period at the end. Rewriting with *hosted by* makes it much clearer.

Exercise #99

Before: **I will say that** the most reliable books are **the ones that features** reputable experts **in the field of financial management, The one expert that I think is phenomenal at keeping drama at bay** in general is John Smith.

After: The most reliable books are those authored by reputable experts. John Smith is an expert who excels in financial analysis.

Analysis: Delete unnecessary words: *I will say that.* Replace *the ones that* with *those.* Note the grammatical mistakes: *books . . . that features* and a run-on sentence because the writer used a comma instead of a period in *management, The.* In professional writing, don't write as you speak, as in *keeping drama at bay.* Delete as wasted words *I think.* Replace *phenomenal at keeping drama at bay* with *excels in financial analysis.*

Exercise #100

Before: The **guest** included John Smith, financial analyst, Mary Jones, financial reporter and Harry Peters, Securities Broker. They **conversation was on the speculation** about the impact that the housing market **was going to have** on the stock market, **which was suggested** by the Chairman of the Federal Reserve.

After: Guests included John Smith, financial analyst; Mary Jones, financial reporter; and Harry Peters, securities broker. They speculated on the housing market's possible impact on the stock market, as the Chairman of the Federal Reserve suggested.

Analysis: Proofread! *Guest* should be plural. Punctuate correctly. *The* and not *they* should open the second sentence. Use the verb *speculate.* *Was going to have* are wasted words. Finally, replace *which was suggested* with *as . . . suggested.*

24. Graduation Exercise

Background scenario for this exercise: You, dear reader, are now a member of an awards board and must judge this package. This is a theoretical, or notional, submission to a notional award competition. The notional individual works in a notional facility. Got it? The background information below is "For Your Eyes Only," so to speak, provided to facilitate teaching points of this exercise. Members of the award board will in all likelihood *not* have access to the background information. Remember, write for an unfamiliar reader; the submission must stand on its own.

Background information: Randy works in the notional tri-state Regional Integrated Security Operations Facility (RISOF). The RISOF is a 1,000-person emergency response center that coordinates with hospitals, police stations, and other emergency response organizations at the local, state, and federal government levels. It has a watch center that functions around-the-clock, operated by 240 people divided into 4 watch teams of 60 people each.

This exercise has three tasks:

- First, identify questions you, as a board member, have about the content of this submission. What questions does it raise and leave unanswered? Or asked another way, "Which garden gates does it open?"

- Second, by applying *Word Sculpting Tools,* identify information that should be deleted as useless, redundant, or expected in the normal course of performing his responsibilities. This type of information is unnecessary and dulls the competitive edge of the submission.

- Third, add to or augment the submission by elaborating on Randy's specific skills and accomplishments—those that would matter to the awards board. What sets him apart from the other competitors? What statistics can you add that would better display his successes and results?

Sample solutions to these tasks are provided in Chapter 25, including the fully sculpted nomination. Amplifying—or augmenting—information that more fully develops and adds richness in detail to the final version is *italicized* for your convenience.

Award Submission—The *Before* Version

- Randy is a Watch Chief and one of the best junior officers assigned to the RISOF.

- He is always facility's top pick to lead distinguished visitors on tours of the facility.

  - He gave a tour to Governor Smith.

  - He gave a tour to Police Chief Warner.

  - He gave a tour to U.S. Senator James.

  - He gave a tour to the U.S. Attorney General.

- He is responsible for training his subordinates and ensuring their effective job performance.

- He ensures his personnel are cross-trained and takes a hands-on approach to this important task.

- He stays abreast of current technical and procedural developments and shares knowledge with all who require it.

- He ensures all regulations within his team's resource library are current and up-to-date and all outdated files are removed.

- Randy has great leadership skills; he is concerned equally with both mission and his people.

- He recently completed a thirteen-week Master's degree course, *Interagency Communication & Management*.

- Very active in physical fitness programs, he goes to the local gym every day after work.

- He issued sixty percent more reports than the previous quarter, ensuring counterparts in other states were apprised of developing situations and enabling them to quickly respond to support local communities.
- His team excelled in their duties when the tornadoes hit.

25. Solution to Graduation Exercise

Task 1: List questions raised by the *Before* example.

- What are the responsibilities of a *Watch Chief*?
- What makes him *one of the best*?
- He's *one of the best* out of how many *junior officers*?
- What does *RISOF* mean?
- A *facility* is a building and can't choose a *top pick*. So, whose *top pick* is he?
- What exactly did he do to *train his subordinates*?
- For how many *subordinates* is he responsible?
- What is his *hands-on approach* to training?
- What are some examples of his *leadership skills*?
- Do we care about a *thirteen-week course* he took and participation in the *gym*?
- Is *sixty percent* a big deal? How many *reports* were actually disseminated?
- How exactly did his team *excel in response to the tornadoes*?

Task 2: Identify information to delete. Indicate in bold text.

- Randy is a Watch Chief and one of the best junior officers assigned **to the RISOF.**
- He is always facility's top pick to lead distinguished visitors on tours of the facility.
  - **He gave a tour to** Governor Smith.
  - **He gave a tour to** Police Chief Warner.

- - **He gave a tour to** U.S. Senator James.
  - **He gave a tour to** the U.S. Attorney General.
- **He is responsible for training his subordinates and ensuring their effective job performance.**
- He ensures his personnel are cross-trained and takes a hands-on approach to this important task.
- **He stays abreast of current technical and procedural developments and shares knowledge with all who require it.**
- **He ensures all regulations within his team's resource library are current and up-to-date and all outdated files are removed.**
- **Randy has great leadership skills;** he is concerned equally with both mission and his people.
- **He recently completed a thirteen-week Master's degree course, Interagency Communication & Management.**
- **Very active in physical fitness programs, he goes to the local gym every day after work.**
- He issued sixty percent more reports than the previous quarter, ensuring counterparts in other states were apprised of developing situations and enabling them to quickly respond to support local communities.
- His team excelled in their duties when the tornadoes hit.

Task 3: Sculpted submission with new, augmenting data italicized.

- Randy is the Watch Chief of a *60-person team, selected in a highly competitive process.*
- He is the *Facility Director's #1 pick out of 56 junior officers* to lead distinguished visitors (DVs) on tours of the *1,000-person regional emergency response center.*
  - *Randy's thorough grasp of the mission, honed briefing skills, and self-assurance make him the perfect choice to represent the facility and its people.*

- *He briefed 3 governors, 2 U.S. senators, the U.S. Attorney General, and 8 Chiefs of Police, fielding their questions with ease; the Chief, Facility Operations commended his professionalism.*

- His concise presentations *ensured DVs understood the facility's valuable contributions* to the safety and security of citizens in the region; *DVs' advocacy is critical to continued funding of the operation.*

- *The team to beat!* He has *the best internal training program of the 4 watch teams—his people consistently score higher than their counterparts on all areas of required quarterly skill assessment evaluations.*

- His leadership and the team's training paid dividends! *When the tornadoes hit, they jumped into action, contacting all local, state, and federal authorities, without missing a beat.*

  - *His team marshaled rescue resources (91 ambulance trips, 32 fire alerts) and saved many lives.*

  - The team *issued 250 flawless alert notices, more than doubling that from the previous quarter.*

- He *implemented a new program; personally counsels each of his assigned individuals quarterly to ensure job satisfaction and career progression. Rave reviews and high morale speak to its success.*

- He is concerned with mission and people! *He developed and implemented a program to ensure supervisors capture the significance of subordinates' specific job accomplishments for inclusion in annual appraisals and awards.*

  - *Huge success is reflected by promotion statistics and the number of awards won by his team.*

- *He developed innovative training materials that made data both interesting and easy to assimilate.*

  - *Ensured his people are cross-trained, enabling them to operate with maximum flexibility. This gave his team a critical advantage when responding to real-world emergencies, such as a recent outbreak of tornadoes.*

- *Took initiative, sharing new tools and techniques with other teams because, "Knowledge saves lives."*

- *His mentorship is directly responsible for his deputy winning the award of Emergency Response Officer of the Year at both the facility and regional levels from a field of 300 talented colleagues.*

Summary Observations

- Don't waste four lines listing the distinguished visitors; this is much more effectively expressed as a single item.

- Don't confuse a job description with actual accomplishments; reviewers know the difference, so focus on actual accomplishments.

- Take care with words like *stays abreast* and *shares knowledge.* Not only do these fail to separate the individual from competitors, they also identify activities probably expected as part of normal duty performance.

- Expunge irrelevant or ancillary information to open space for more critical, competitive data.

- Don't spell out RISOF as it is too lengthy. State what the facility is as an alternative.

Part 5

Appendices

Appendix A

Answers to Chapters 6–15 Exercises

CHAPTER 6 ANSWERS

Exercise #1

Before: Scientific research **is continuing the process of** documenting the recovery of endangered species.

After: Scientific research continues to document the recovery of endangered species.

Analysis: Use the simple present tense *continues. The process of* is a wasted phrase.

Exercise #2

Before: The agency decided not to **continue** the service contract **in light of** the **continual** cost overruns.

After: The agency decided to discontinue the service contract, given the continual cost overruns.

Analysis: One word replaces three: *given* instead of *in light of. Discontinue* can replace *not to continue.*

Exercise #3

Before: This critical step **is necessary to** preclude cost overruns.

After: This critical step will preclude cost overruns.

Analysis: Eliminating these useless words saves considerable space. The author might want to use *could* or *should* if *will* is too definitive.

Exercise #4

Before: The **intent of the** article **is to** educate the reader on the stock market.

After: The article educates the reader on the stock market.

Analysis: Discarding useless words results in a crisper sentence. The central verb is *educates.* Note: There might be a nuance in this instance. *The intent of* might be appropriate if the author is critiquing the article, observing that it failed in its "intended" goal.

Exercise #5

Before: **The purpose of** the regulation is **to ensure** the hiring process **is the same** across the corporation.

After: The regulation standardizes the hiring process across the corporation.

Analysis: Discard the useless words *The purpose of* and *to ensure.* The verb *standardizes* replaces *is the same.*

Exercise #6

Before: **There are** many people **that have** vacationed at the beach this summer because it provided **them with** an opportunity to relax.

After: Many people vacationed at the beach this summer to relax.

Analysis: You can—and should—almost always restructure a sentence to avoid *there is/there are* by finding the true subject, in this case *people.* When referring to people, use *who,* not *that.* Simplify the verb by stating *vacationed* and eliminate *have.* Delete *because it provided them with* because it is understood and, therefore, redundant.

Exercise #7

Before: We **are continuing the process of** printing, copying, and sorting applications for the vacant job positions.

After: We continue to print, copy, and sort applications for the vacant job positions.

Analysis: Delete *are continuing* (the *is* form of the verb) and other useless words, such as *the process of* to tighten this sentence.

Exercise #8

Before: We **will have to** check the records to ensure **they are** accurate.

After: We must check the records to ensure their accuracy.

Analysis: Replace *will have to* with *must,* and condense *they are* to *their.*

Exercise #9

Before: I examined four books but didn't buy any **of them**.

After: I examined four books but didn't buy any.

Analysis: *Of them* refers to *books* and is unnecessary.

Exercise #10

Before: Thank you for **your** participation. We will **be** solicit**ing** your comments **in the near future**.

After: Thank you for participating. We will solicit your comments soon.

Analysis: *Your* is unnecessary, so delete it. We use a simpler verb form, *will solicit*. Finally, *in the near future* is reduced to *soon.*

CHAPTER 7 ANSWERS

Exercise #1

Before: She **inquired as to whether** she could bring a colleague to the meeting.

After: She asked if she could bring a colleague to the meeting.

Analysis: *Asked if* is shorter and more focused.

Exercise #2

Before: Jim **keeps track of** incoming requirements.

After: Jack tracks incoming requirements.

Analysis: *Tracks* is the core verb.

Exercise #3

Before: After lengthy study **of the** plan, they are **moving directly to the implementation phase.**

After: They are implementing the plan after lengthy study.

Analysis: Instead of *moving directly to the implementation phase,* simply say *implementing.* We begin directly with the subject and verb, and move the phrase *after lengthy study* to the end of the sentence. Delete *of the* as extraneous words.

Exercise #4

Before: They **were grateful for** the demonstration of support.

After: They appreciated the demonstration of support.

or

They appreciated the support.

Analysis: One word, *appreciated,* replaces *were grateful for.* Eliminate *demonstration of* if the focus is on the support rather than on the demonstration of it.

Exercise #5

Before: He **responded back** to the inquiry **in a timely manner**.

After: He replied promptly to the inquiry.

Analysis: *Replied* replaces *responded back. Back* is redundant, as it is understood in the verb *responded. Promptly* replaces four words, *in a timely manner.*

Exercise #6

Before: **It is essential that** submissions meet the deadline.

After: Submissions must meet the deadline.

Analysis: This requires a simple substitution that saves a great deal of space! *It is essential that* equates to *must.*

Exercise #7

Before: This old alarm system could **provide a gateway that may** allow **for** an unauthorized individual **to** access the facility.

After: This old alarm system could let an unauthorized individual access the facility.

Analysis: *Provide a gateway that may allow . . . to* is replaced with three letters *let.*

Exercise #8

Before: I maintained all documents **in accordance with** the Administrative Instruction **in accordance with** the office policy for all correspondence and maintained the office library for all reference materials.

After: Maintained all documents per the Administrative Instruction and office policy, and maintained the office's reference library.

Analysis: This is based on a resume; therefore, *I* is unnecessary. We eliminate the repeated *in accordance with* and shorten the text further by using the word *per*. Next, we use *reference* as an adjective modifying *library*, discarding several words as a result.

Exercise #9

Before: **We know for a fact that** this design **is similar to** one we reviewed last week.

After: This design definitely resembles one we reviewed last week.

Analysis: *We know for a fact* is redundant. That the author makes this statement is, in itself, a fact. The simple and direct verb *resembles* replaces *is similar to*. The author can add emphasis, if necessary, with the word *definitely.*

Exercise #10

Before: This reorganization will ultimately **help to drive down** costs while **delivering** improved mission services.

After: This reorganization will ultimately reduce costs while improving mission services.

Analysis: Replace *help to drive down* with *reduce* and delete *delivering* by using *improving.*

CHAPTER 8 ANSWERS

Exercise #1

Before: This is an updated **version** of the draft **previously** sent on Jan. 5.

After: This is an update to the Jan. 5 draft.

Analysis: The word *version* is inferred in *updated draft*. *Previously* is redundant because the sentence already states the draft was sent earlier, *on Jan.* 5.

Exercise #2

Before: **Two** reports are due: **one** on Sept. 30 and **the other on** Dec. 31.

After: A report is due on Sept. 30 and Dec. 31.

Analysis: The initial mention of *two* is redundant because two dates are listed. Several words can be eliminated.

Exercise #3

Before: The **annual** report titled *The County Financial Report for 2019* covered the **2019 calendar year**. This was another highlight **from 2019**.

After: Another annual highlight was the publication of *The County Financial Report for 2019.*

Analysis: How often does this example mention *annual* or similar words? Once will suffice. The first use of this word is redundant to the title of the document. We eliminate *titled* because that is indicated through use of italics or quotation marks, depending on the type of title. Eliminate *2019 calendar year* because that is conveyed in the title. Beware of a nuance—sometimes it is necessary to differentiate between *calendar* and *fiscal* year. Depending on the context, *calendar* might be appropriately included in a rewrite.

Exercise #4

Before: The director approved the script **for use in support of** the movie.

After: The director approved the script for the movie.

Analysis: The redundancy lies with *approved* and *for use*. If the director *approved* the script for the movie, it would be *used for* the movie. We also discard *in support of* as useless words.

Exercise #5

Before: **There are** thirty **individuals currently** employed by our company.

After: Our company has thirty employees.

Analysis: We shorten the sentence by transforming *employed* to *employees,* thereby negating the need for *individuals.* We resolve the redundancy of *are* and *currently.* Finally, we discard *There are* as useless words.

Exercise #6

Before: The event demonstrated that businesses could collectively **come together and** respond to a community need.

After: The event demonstrated that businesses could collectively respond to a community need.

Analysis: The redundancy lies in *collectively* and *come together.*

Exercise #7

Before: The Marketing Director **is the single management official who will be the focal point for ensuring** the success of the outreach campaign.

After: The Marketing Director is responsible for the success of the outreach campaign.

Analysis: This contains two examples of redundancy. First, the *Management Director* is by definition a *management official.* Second, *single official* equates to *focal point.*

Exercise #8

Before: **Special attention has been paid in** the design **of the** floor plan to avoid **the occurrence of** stairs.

After: The floor plan is designed to avoid stairs.

Analysis: The redundancy lies in *special attention* and *designed.* We delete many useless words: *has been paid to, of the,* and *the occurrence of.*

Exercise #9

Before: The maintenance shop **is aware of** the broken air conditioner **and is working towards a resolution**.

After: The maintenance shop is repairing the broken air conditioner.

Analysis: This contains an example of a "no-duh" redundancy. The maintenance shop must *be aware of* the broken air conditioner or it couldn't *work towards a resolution.* We replace *working towards a resolution* with a simple verb, *is repairing.*

Exercise #10

Before: The conference **is over** following the keynote speaker**'s address.**

After: The conference concludes following the keynote speaker.

Analysis: Replace *is over* with *concludes* even though the singular word is longer. The redundancy is found in *speaker* and *address.*

CHAPTER 9 ANSWERS

Exercise #1

Before: To quantify the costs and expected benefits of transitioning end-to-end IT services, and to help IT leaders build the business case, **we created a detailed economic model**.

After: We created a detailed economic model to quantify the costs and benefits of transitioning end-to-end IT services, and to help IT leaders build the business case.

Analysis: This is a simple case of putting the horse before the cart.

Exercise #2

Before: **Where possible, (i.e.,** they can be predetermined by the FY calendar or program plans) these functions and critical interfaces **should be captured in Appendix H**.

After: Identify these functions and critical interfaces in Appendix H if they can be predetermined by the FY calendar or program plans.

Analysis: The reader must trudge through thirteen words before reaching the subject—OUCH! Start with the horse, (in this case, the verb) and follow with the direct objects. Let's consider the verb in the *Before* version. *Capture* evokes an image of *functions and critical interfaces* standing in terror at gunpoint! Perhaps another verb *identify, reflect,* or *address* might be more appropriate. Finally, we delete *where possible* as useless words and replace *i.e.,* with the simpler *if.*

Exercise #3

Before: A principal member from each of the twelve counties, designated by the head of each Board of Supervisors, **comprise the Transportation Commission**.

After: The Transportation Commission consists of a principal member from each of the twelve counties, designated by the head of the respective Board of Supervisors.

Analysis: This was a simple matter of beginning with subject and verb, followed by the remaining information.

Exercise #4

Before: As the Hospital Liaison Program evolves and the director makes decisions that affect operational requirements and existing policy, updated **versions** of the Fact Sheet **containing this new information**, will be available online. **In addition, any new** questions **that are** raised based on community feedback, will be included in **updated** Fact **Sheets**.

After: The Fact Sheet will be available online, updated as the Hospital Liaison Program evolves and the director makes decisions that affect operational requirements and existing policy. The Fact Sheet will also respond to questions generated by community feedback.

Analysis: Begin with the subject *the Fact Sheet* (taken here to be the formal title of the product and correctly capitalized). Delete as redundant *containing this new information* because the sentence already states *updated.* We delete the incorrect comma that followed *information.* We delete as unnecessary *In addition, any new, that are,* and *updated.* As originally written, it sounds as though the questions, themselves, will be included in the Fact Sheet, as opposed to the responses thereto. Finally, does this entry involve a single Fact Sheet or several? If space is an issue, the revision reduces the text from 52 to 39 words and from 342 to 221 spaces.

Exercise #5

Before: **A strategic shift from multiple decentralized commercial outlets spread throughout the state to a centralized location near the capital that employs unified business strategies, common business practices, and standardized IT protocols has begun.**

After: The company has begun a strategic shift, centralizing outlets throughout the state into a single campus near the capital. Management at this new site will apply unified business strategies, common business practices, and standardized IT protocols.

or

The company is centralizing outlets throughout the state into a single campus near the capital. Management at this new site will apply unified business strategies, common business practices, and standardized IT protocols.

Analysis: Count them—thirty-one words precede the verb! You know the formula now—subject, verb, object. Lead with the main storyline then provide additional details. Don't be afraid to break snarled writing into more sentences to convey the message clearly. Also note that the wording in the *Before* version suggests that the *capital employs unified business strategies, common business practices, and standardized IT protocols,* obviously not the case. I offer one final thought, as reflected in the alternate *After* version. Depending on the larger context of this document, we can delete *has begun a strategic shift* if the main point is *centralizing,* with little interest as to preliminary steps taken in the process.

Exercise #6

Before: In early 2019, while supporting the American Federation of Organic Horticulturalists and the Virginia Organization of Master Gardeners, **he wrote a feature article on gardening.**

After: He wrote a feature article on gardening in early 2019 while supporting the American Federation of Organic Horticulturalists and the Virginia Organization of Master Gardeners.

Analysis: Simply place the horse before the cart and the rest falls neatly into place.

Exercise #7:

Before: Ensured all official documents meet the quality standards (grammar, completeness, timeliness, technical accuracy) to best represent the corporation to **all of** its clients **through superior writing and editorial skills.**

After: Through superior writing and editorial skills, ensured all official documents meet the quality standards (grammar, completeness, timeliness, and technical accuracy) to best represent the corporation to its clients.

Analysis: This example is based on a resume and does not need to be a complete sentence. The author wants to stress his skill set *superior writing and editorial skills.* Therefore, we place that as the opening volley; the rest falls neatly into place. We delete *all of* as useless words.

Exercise #8

Before: While assigned to the Metropolitan Bureau of Community Development and liaison to the Future Highway Architecture program Office **Mr. Jones drafted a benchmark concept paper**.

After: Mr. Jones drafted a benchmark concept paper while assigned to the Metropolitan Bureau of Community Development and liaison to the Future Highway Architecture Program Office.

Analysis: This is a simple matter of placing the horse first. Begin the sentence with who did what. Do note, however, that the original lacks a comma following *Office*. Additionally, *Program* should be capitalized, presuming it is part of the official title.

Exercise #9

Before: **For a corporate management** team **tasked with deciding among a number of possible options** on fielding a **major** system **worth** 5 **million dollars** to manage product dissemination across the U.S., facilitated a team **to a decision** in four half-day sessions **using FacilitateSystems to solicit opinions about the options; DPX, a marginal benefit-cost decision tool to combine probabilities; DPK, a decision analysis tool combining influence diagrams and decision trees for building technology area roadmaps; and SoundDecisions to evaluate options and present results of the discussion.**

After: Facilitated a twenty-person team, helping it make several decisions about fielding a $5M system to manage product dissemination across the U.S. Did so in four half-day sessions, effectively employing three state-of-the-art IT facilitation tools.

Analysis: This example is based on a resume and does not need complete sentences. First, place the horse before the cart by beginning with the action accomplished, *facilitated a team*. Next, explain what the team did, *reach several key decisions*. About what? We revise the original text to *fielding a $5M system to manage product dissemination across the U.S.* and eliminate *corporate management, tasked with, deciding among a number of possible options, major,* and *worth.* We also use *$5M* to save much space. After clearly stating the accomplishment, the author can amplify on the specifics of how it was achieved; however, the author should determine the need to burden the reader with the specifics of the IT tools. Can that data be placed elsewhere in the product (list of IT skills, perhaps)? Can it simply be deleted? Finally, the author misses a significant data point—the number of people he facilitated. Point of fact, facilitating a group of twenty people is far more complex than a group of five!

Exercise #10

Before: **Network Operation Center (NOC) Expands Operational Capability. As part of the organization's leadership in strengthening existing and building new partnerships with state and local government entities, and with assisting private sector enterprise in protecting critical elements of our infrastructure, the NOC has moved to improve its ability to rapidly communicate, analyze and respond to network threats. The NOC was able to increase existing staff to enable extending its hours to 24 hours/day, 7 days/week. The NOC also has been providing training, conducting micro exercises as staff began to increase to ensure newly assigned personnel were completely proficient in their assigned tasks.**

After: Network Operation Center (NOC) Expands Capability. The NOC extended its operating hours to 24 hours/day, 7 days/week, improving its ability to rapidly communicate, analyze, and respond to network threats. NOC increased its staff to accommodate the expanded hours. It also conducted several training exercises to ensure new personnel were proficient in their assigned tasks. This effort supports the organization's strategic goal of strengthening existing and building new partnerships with offices in state and local governments. It also furthers another strategic goal of assisting private sector enterprises to protect critical elements of the state's infrastructure.

Analysis: The opening line is horrendous with thirty-two words preceding the subject, *the NOC*. It is also four lines in length and constitutes half of the original paragraph. The revision opens with the key to this paragraph *extending operating hours*. Next, the author explains the "so what" resulting from *the extended hours.* Following this, the author explains what the NOC did to achieve this new capability. Finally, this accomplishment is placed in the context of the organization's overall strategic goals.

Here's the evolution. The storyline is: We did 1) which resulted in . . . 2) To attain this we did . . . 3) and . . . 4). The significance and why the reader should care are explained in . . . 5) and . . . 6).

Interim: <u>Network Operation Center (NOC) Expands Operational Capability</u>. As part of the organization's leadership in **5)** strengthening existing and building new partnerships with state and local government entities, and with **6)** assisting private sector enterprise in protecting critical elements of our infrastructure, the NOC has moved to **2)** improve its ability to rapidly communicate, analyze and respond to network threats. The NOC was able to **3)** increase existing staff to enable **1)** extending its hours to 24 hours/day, 7 days/week. The NOC also has been providing **4)** training, conducting micro exercises as staff began to increase to ensure newly assigned personnel were completely proficient in their assigned tasks.

CHAPTER 10 ANSWERS

Exercise # 1

Before: Harry **provided demonstrations** of the new software at the convention.

After: Harry demonstrated the new software at the convention.

<u>Analysis:</u> Skip the word *provided* and explain what Harry actually did— he *demonstrated.*

Exercise #2

Before: Mary **had a meeting** with her partners to **ensure** the schedule **was** coordinated.

After: Mary coordinated the schedule with her partners.

Analysis: Cut to the chase, what did Mary do? She *coordinated the schedule with her partners.* We chose to skip the interim step of *had a meeting with.* If this is necessary, then find the hidden verb and simply say *met.* Finally, using the active voice, we eliminate *was.*

Exercise #3

Before: The boss **was agreeable** to chang**ing** the date **of the** meeting.

After: The boss agreed to change the meeting's date.

Analysis: Instead of *was agreeable to,* simply say, *agreed.* The possessive form of *meeting* allows you to delete *of the.*

Exercise #4

Before: Reporters were **provided with training on the process by which** to conduct interviews with dignitaries.

After: Reporters were trained to interview dignitaries.

Analysis: Use the verb *trained,* and delete several useless words.

Exercise #5

Before: The Memorandum of Agreement **establishes** clearly **defined** responsibilities for managing the program.

After: The Memorandum of Agreement clearly defines responsibilities for managing the program.

Analysis: The core verb is *defines. Establishes* is unnecessary.

Exercise #6

Before: She **demonstrated the ability to** work well under pressure.

After: She works well under pressure.

Analysis: Cut to the chase by eliminating *demonstrated the ability to.*

Exercise #7

Before: The court's interpretation of the law **runs counter to** its intended purpose.

After: The court's interpretation of the law counters its intended purpose.

Analysis: The hidden verb is *counters.*

Exercise #8

Before: He **generated a draft** briefing on the county's quarterly budget.

After: He drafted a briefing on the county's quarterly budget.

Analysis: The hidden verb *is drafted.*

Exercise #9

Before: The corporate representative **was in attendance at** the meeting and will report results **back** to the division chief.

After: The corporate representative attended the meeting and will report results to the division chief.

Analysis: Use the direct verb, *attended.* Delete the useless word *back.*

Exercise #10

Before: Our office **is the lead for** this effort.

After: Our office leads this effort.

Analysis: Exchange three extraneous words for one direct verb, *leads.*

CHAPTER 11 ANSWERS

Exercise #1

Before: Regular staff meetings help to **provide shared operational visibility** on end-of-the-year financial transactions.

After: Regular staff meetings help to share information on end-of-the-year financial transactions.

Analysis: *Provide shared operational visibility* equates to *share information.*

Exercise #2

Before: **Currently, there is a multiplicity of non-interoperable** collaboration IT tools **in use across the** corporation. **This not only** limits **corporate** information sharing **potential**, but also **generates increased** costs.

After: Corporate agencies employ many incompatible IT tools for collaboration, a costly practice that actually impedes sharing information.

Analysis: We delete *Currently* as redundant with the present tense of the sentence. Replace the useless words *there is* with a solid subject and verb, *Corporate agencies employ*. We can now eliminate *in use across the corporation*. Because it hogs space, replace *multiplicity* with *many*. Similarly, *non-interoperable* is replaced with the shorter *incompatible*. Discard the useless words *This not only* and *potential*. Finally, *generates increased costs* is replaced with *costly practice.*

Exercise #3

Before: Users should **be advised up front what to expect that will be** new IT capabilities, **what will no longer be available**, and the major **differences they will see**.

After: Project managers should inform users about impending new IT capabilities, those that will be deleted, and other major functional differences.

Analysis: Begin with the true subject instead of using the passive voice. In this instance, we presume the subject is *project managers.* We replace *be advised up front* with *inform . . . about impending.* Delete the useless words *what to expect that will be.* Deleting words that hog space, we replace *what will no longer be available* with *that will be deleted.* Finally, we delete the useless words *they will see.*

Exercise #4

Before: She **provides** office staff **thought leadership** to projects and process improvement **activities**.

After: She advises office staff on improvements to projects and processes.

Analysis: *Thought leadership* is a recent bureaucratic term that really means *advises.* We choose to shorten and simplify the nouns used as adjectives in *projects and process improvement activities* to *improvements to projects and processes.* Finally, we delete the useless word *activities.*

Exercise #5

Before: I **gathered information** regarding financial management vendors' software and provided a summary of the products.

After: Developed summaries of software designed to facilitate financial management. Division leadership used this information to determine the product and vendor best suited to its mission needs.

Analysis: Exercises 5–10 are based on resume items, so the word *I* and complete sentences are not necessary. Spare the reader the unnecessary information of *I gathered information* because someone can't *provide summaries* without *gathering information.* We conclude with a "so what" sentence, lacking in the original.

Exercise #6

Before: Conduct technical market analysis, concept idea development, design and functional development of new product ideas to ensure the **organizations continued growth**, development of white papers **from resulting research**, software and hardware testing, and **maintaining the organization's competitive position in the marketplace.**

After: Helped ensure the organization's continued growth and competitive position in the marketplace. Did so by conducting technical market research and analysis, developing white papers based on information learned through these efforts, generating new ideas and designs for products, and testing hardware and software.

Analysis: In addition to exemplifying convoluted writing, this item also demonstrates the mistake of burying the golden nugget. The principal bell ringer is the overall contribution to the organization, so that is the new opening line. Then, we place a pause, *Did so by,* to let the reader know that the specifics now follow. Then, we group similar items, such as *market analysis, concept idea development,* and *resulting research* with *new ideas and designs for products.*

Exercise #7

Before: Demonstrated instructional techniques while conducting quarterly training for directorates in accordance with regulations **ABCD-5400.12; EFGH-334.5; XHRZ-4300.2; and Corporate Policy 1002,** *Mandatory Annual Training Requirements.*

After: Demonstrated instructional techniques while conducting quarterly training for directorates in accordance with various corporate regulations and policies.

Analysis: The author does not need to specify governing directives. Identifying the collective group, *various corporate regulations and policies* is more effective and appreciated. Note, this could be shortened more by deleting *various.*

Exercise #8

Before: **Ability to** synthesize data **and prepared**, **designed**, budgetary analysis, manpower data, procurement cost and presented the proposal for a supply depot with cost estimate of **250K** to senior level executives.

After: Prepared and presented to senior-level executives a proposal for a supply depot with a cost estimate of $250K. To do so, synthesized various data to include budgetary analysis, manpower data, and procurement costs.

Analysis: This is a confusing mix of nouns and verbs, further exacerbated by incorrect punctuation. The first step in unraveling this is to find the key point. *Synthesize data* is a means to the end. *Prepared . . . and presented* is the beginning. Presented to whom? Now, presented what? Items to note in the *Before* version: Lack of parallel structure in *ability to . . . and prepared,* lack of hyphen in the adjective *senior level,* and lack of *$* with *250K*. This now has the potential for a good story. Might this be even better with the addition of a line explaining what happened as a result of briefing the senior-level executives?

Exercise #9

Before: Successfully automated inventory control through implementation **of Inventory Access Control System (IACS), Automated Property Supply (APS), Property Accounting System (PAS), Logistics and Infrastructure System (LIS), and the Inventory and Supply Requirements System (ISRS).**

After: Successfully automated control of an inventory valued at $2.5M through creative implementation of five IT systems.

Analysis: The reader probably doesn't need to wade through the list of system names and accompanying acronyms. Skip the names and state what they are, *IT systems.* We also improve this by including the monetary value of the inventory, thus scoping the significance of the accomplishment. With the single word *creative,* we impart a sense of initiative and forward thinking.

Exercise #10

Before: Managed the security program for a **CJTF in Operation Enduring Freedom**.

After: Managed the security program for a 500-person military unit deployed in combat operations in Afghanistan.

Analysis: Many readers will respond to this item with a bewildered, "Huh?" You might attempt to avoid gibberish by translating the unfamiliar acronym *CJTF,* which stands for *Combined Joint Task Force.* However, that might still confuse readers. Instead of using any form of *CJTF,* we state what it is—in this instance, *a 500-person military unit.* I add the statistic to convey the size of the unit and the individual's responsibility in supporting it. Similarly, many readers will not understand *Operation Enduring Freedom.* We avoid that by stating, *combat operations in Afghanistan.* The lesson? Tell the reader what these terms mean instead of using the military jargon.

CHAPTER 12 ANSWERS

Exercise #1

Before: **Manages, conducts research, analysis,** and **provides guidance** on responses to public inquiries.

After: Researches, analyzes, provides guidance on, and manages responses to public inquiries.

Analysis: This is quite a hodgepodge! Let's first identify the base, *responses.* Now, verify the tethers. **Manages** *responses* works but is out of chronological sequence. **Conducts research** *responses* is broken; we simplify to *researches* and it works. **Analysis** *responses* is also broken; moreover, this is a noun and breaks the parallelism. Finally, **provides guidance on** *responses* is functional. We fix them and now validate. *Researches responses, analyzes responses, provides guidance on responses,* and *manages responses* all work. Note, we arrange the actions sequentially.

Exercise #2

Before: **Plans, organizes,** and **exercises control over** all Security Administration processes, procedures and manages staff within the corporate security office.

After: Plans, organizes, and directs all Security Administration processes and procedures and manages staff within the corporate security office.

Analysis: This is based on a resume, so complete sentences are not necessary. The broken element here is the indication that *processes, procedures and manages* is a set. For this tether to work, break the pattern between *procedures* and *manages.* We accomplish this by inserting *and* as shown here, *processes and procedures. Plans, directs, organizes, and exercises control over . . . processes and procedures* is a functional tether. We also find a hidden verb and replace *exercises control over* with *directs*.

Exercise #3

Before: She **reserved the room for, sent invitations,** and **arranged catering of** the annual awards dinner.

After: She reserved the room, sent invitations, and arranged catering for the annual awards dinner.

Analysis: The base is *the annual awards dinner*. Now, check the tethers. *Reserved the room for . . . the annual awards dinner* is a functioning tether. *Sent invitations . . . the annual awards dinner* doesn't work. *Arranged catering of . . . the annual awards dinner* works but could be improved. As so often occurs with tethers, the fix lies with the prepositions. Delete the first instance of *for* and replace *of* with *for* to solve the problem.

Exercise #4

Before: The plan focuses on enabling **integration of** design teams, greater company-wide **communication**, and **on reducing operating** costs through implementation of new software capabilities.

After: The plan focuses on integrating design teams, enhancing company-wide communications, and implementing new software to reduce operating costs.

Analysis: The author intends to convey that the *plan focuses on A, B, and C.* This sentence contains a broken tether with the base, *enabling. The plan focuses on enabling . . . integration of . . . communication . . . on reducing operating costs.* The third tether is broken. Fix it by deleting *enabling,* which leaves *The plan focuses on.* Then identify each of the three elements: *integrating, enhancing,* and *implementing.* Finally, we delete *capabilities* as a useless word.

Exercise #5

Before: This role caused him to **organize**, **shepherd**, and **facilitate** three Senior Executive "Security Pow Wows" for corporate personnel.

After: He organized and facilitated three security meetings for senior executive corporate personnel.

Analysis: First, let's replace *Security Pow Wows* with *security meetings. Pow Wows* is certainly a term unexpected in a resume or any other professional writing. Next, let's check the tether. The base is *meetings.* Examining the *Before* example, the first and third tethers are functional. One can certainly *organize . . . and facilitate* a meeting. But, can one *shepherd* a meeting? Not exactly. So, we delete that term. Another consideration is that a *role* doesn't *cause* anyone to do anything. A boss, however, might be the cause! Alternatively, these words can also be eliminated as presumed, leaving the sentence to begin with "who did what." Another correction is to lowercase *Senior Executive.*

Exercise #6

Before: He demonstrated strong **writing skills** and **communications skills** with audiences of varying backgrounds and authorities.

After: Skilled in both speaking and writing; equally comfortable briefing audiences ranging from interns to senior corporate executives.

Analysis: This item is based on a resume, so we delete *He*. It also exemplifies a broken tether. The base is *with audiences*. The tethers are *writing skills* and *communication skills*. The first fails: *demonstrated . . . writing skills . . . with audiences*; however, the second tether works: *demonstrated . . . communication skills with audiences*.

Exercise #7

Before: He **worked** to identify program requirements that met tactical, operational, and strategic needs information needs; **guided** development of roles, missions, and functions; information requirements; products and services; information sources; IT architecture; **drafted** the Operation's Plan.

After: Assigned as a founding member to a new organization, he identified program requirements that met operational needs, both tactical and strategic; guided the development of roles, missions, and functions, and the resulting requirements for information and sources thereof; delineated products and services that the unit would provide; helped write the supporting IT architecture; and drafted the unit's operations plan.

Analysis: We add a thought to set the context for this individual's actions. *He* is the base. The author tries to state that *He did A, B, C . . .* but does so ineffectively. In the revision, we delete *worked to* and begin with specific actions. We modify the sequence of *tactical, operational, and strategic* to *operational needs, both tactical and strategic* because *tactical* and *strategic* are both part of *operational*. We include *requirements for information and sources* as part of the thought that begins with *guided*. We provide the verb *delineated* to accompany *products and services* and similarly add *helped write* to accompany *IT architecture.* Finally, we add the word *unit's* to specify which *operations plan.* By the way, *Operation's Plan* should neither be capitalized nor in the possessive form. Let's verify the tethers: *He identified . . . guided . . . delineated . . . helped write . . . and drafted.* Yep, they all work!

Exercise #8

Before: **Ensured** and **executed** with professionalism numerous administrative actions in a fast-paced environment. These actions are medical screening, passports/visas, procurement of mission-related clothing and equipment, and more.

Interim Revision: Effectively executed many administrative actions (e.g., medical screening, passports/visas, procurement of mission-related clothing and equipment), expediting the transfer of corporate personnel to overseas assignments.

After: Expedited the transfer of corporate personnel to overseas assignments by effectively executing key administrative actions (e.g., medical screening, passports/visas, and procurement of mission-related clothing and equipment).

Analysis: Let's first examine the two tethers. *Ensured . . . actions* doesn't work. One can "ensure actions are taken" but that is not the text here. The second tether, *execute . . . actions,* works. Now, delete useless words. *Ensured* contributes nothing, so cut it. *With professionalism . . . fast-paced environment* are expected, so delete. *These actions are* is redundant. The first sentence of the interim revision reflects the essence of the *Before* version; we expand it to provide a "so what" statement, *expediting the transfer.* That addition then becomes the buried lead and also reflects the cart before horse, so we flip it for the *Final* version, beginning with *Expedited the transfer . . . by.*

Exercise #9

Before: Conducted **interviews**, employee **evaluations**, and problem **resolution**.

After: Conducted interviews and employee evaluations and resolved problems.

Analysis: The first two tethers are functional: someone can *conduct interviews* and *conduct evaluations.* The third tether, however, is not. You cannot *conduct . . . resolution.* We change *resolution* into a separate verb, *resolved* to be parallel with the verb *conducted.*

Exercise #10

Before: Facilitated meetings in the **design, development, testing, and training** of reporting tools and database architectures.

After: Facilitated meetings in the design, development, and testing of reporting tools and database architectures and on the associated training.

Analysis: Test the tethers. See if these make sense: *design . . . of tools and architectures, development . . . of tools and architectures, testing . . . of tools and architectures.* Yes. How about, *training . . . of tools and architectures*? No, this tether breaks. So, we separate the functional tethers and complete the sentence with *and on the associated training.*

CHAPTER 13 ANSWERS

Exercise #1

Before: The inspector noted several annual financial report **recordkeeping inconsistencies.**

After: The inspector noted several recordkeeping inconsistencies in the annual financial report.

Analysis: This is another example of multiple nouns used as adjectives.

Exercise #2

Before: **To point out to the** employees the many successes of the company this past year, the CEO **presented a briefing** that addressed the overall goals and objectives at both corporate and regional levels, successful marketing strategies, new product lines **developed**, customer feedback, and **wrapped it up** by recognizing **those individuals with the highest sales statistics**.

After: The CEO briefed employees on the company's successful performance this past year. She placed accomplishments in the context of goals and objectives at both the regional and corporate levels. The briefing highlighted successful marketing strategies, new product lines, and customer feedback. She concluded on a high note by recognizing stellar performers in the sales department.

Analysis: This is a mouthful! Let's make it more manageable and give the reader some well-deserved breathers. First, we resolve the cart-and-horse syndrome caused by the excessively long preamble. What is the subject and what did that subject do? Next, use a more direct verb, *briefed* instead of *presented a briefing.* Did you find the redundancy, *new product lines* were, by definition, being *developed.* We select a more professional verb *concluded* to replace the more colloquial *wrapped it up.* Finally, *those individuals with the highest sales statistics* is replaced with *stellar performers in the sales department.* Breaking the original four-line, run-on sentence into four sentences presents a more digestible message.

Exercise #3

Before: **Substantial efforts were applied to make certain the corporate leaders were fully informed and engaged.**

After: Division chiefs regularly updated their directors on the status of the merger. Senior leaders were pleased with the progress.

Analysis: We rewrite this completely! Who is doing what here? What does *substantial efforts were applied to* mean? *Fully informed and engaged* in what? First, identify a clear subject. None is provided, so we invent one. Next, use the active voice and add a solid verb. None is provided, so we invent one here, as well. We now have *Division chiefs regularly updated* in lieu of *substantial efforts were applied to make certain . . . informed.* Let's add more clarity to *corporate leaders* by identifying them as *their directors.* Finally, we add a "so what" statement.

Exercise #4

Before: **The purpose of** the regulation **is to** require agencies **throughout the** corporation to adhere to **standardized** security standards.

After: The regulation requires corporate agencies to adhere to security standards.

Analysis: Begin with the subject *regulation* and delete useless words, *the purpose of, is to,* and *throughout the.* Use a clear verb form *requires.* Resolve the redundancy of *standardized* and *standards.*

Exercise #5

Before: This is no small challenge; **it will take the support of** all corporate partners to implement this program.

After: This is no small challenge; all corporate partners must support implementation of this program.

Analysis: *It* is an extremely vague subject. The key emphasis here is involvement of *corporate partners.* Say that and delete the rest.

Exercise #6

Before: She held her first staff meeting **with the decision agreed upon** to **continue on a monthly basis.**

After: She held her first staff meeting; participants agreed to meet monthly.

Analysis: What verb replaces *with the decision agreed upon*? *Agreed,* of course. Who agreed? Presumably, *participants agreed,* so we add *participants.* What replaces *on a monthly basis*? Simple, *monthly.*

Exercise #7

Before: The policy directs **that** each agency **have a successful implementation of** procedures to train employees.

After: The policy directs each agency to implement procedures to train new employees.

or

The policy directs each agency to train new employees.

Analysis: *That* in this case is a useless word. *Have . . . implementation* equates to the verb *implement.* We delete *successful* because it is presumed and, therefore, redundant. The difference between the two *After* versions lies in the importance of *procedures.* If the author focuses on *procedures* to train, then retain the word. If, on the other hand, the emphasis is on *training,* delete it.

Exercise #8

Before: He was hired to oversee the Information Security Services **capability integration and implementation.**

After: He was hired to oversee the integration and implementation of the Information Security Services.

Analysis: This example uses too many nouns as adjectives in a row. *Information Security Services capability*, a noun-upon-noun within itself, is intended to modify *integration and implementation.* Ask, "He was hired to oversee what?" Answer, "integration and implementation." Then ask, "Integration and implementation of what?" Answer, "the Information Security Services." The word *capability* is useless, so delete it.

Exercise #9

Before: To make an informed decision, comparison of **cloud computing implementation plans** is essential.

After: Comparing plans to implement cloud computing is essential to making an informed decision.

Analysis: This cart before the horse example is not so egregious as others presented so far. However, we prefer to help the reader by beginning with the subject. Therefore, move the phrase *to make an informed decision* to the end of the sentence and begin with the subject, *comparing*, which is simpler than *comparison of.* To avoid employing too many nouns as adjectives, separate *plans* as the simple direct object of *compare.* The rest falls into place.

Exercise #10

Before: **Performed billet management** reporting for the **Division Chief** and provided contact and recall management for **division senior leadership**.

After: Managed the division's twenty-two personnel billets and updated contact data on the recall roster. Regularly briefed the division's leaders.

Analysis: *Performed billet management reporting* equates to *Managed . . . billets.* We add the clarifying detail of *twenty-two personnel.* We eliminate the redundancy of *Division Chief*, which should not be capitalized, and *division senior leadership* by simply stating *Regularly briefed the division's leaders.*

CHAPTER 14 ANSWERS

Exercise #1

Before: Ensured medical records were **updated** and **prepared** for surgery and specialist appointments.

After: Ensured medical records were updated in advance of a patient's surgery and appointments with specialists.

Analysis: This is based on a resume. As originally written, the sentence sounds as though the records themselves were going under the scalpel. So, we clarify. This also leaves the garden gate open because the potential employer probably enjoyed a good laugh, distracting from the very serious effort the individual was making to gain employment.

Exercise #2

Before: **Conducted** weekly **presentations and briefings weekly to** corporate seniors **as well as outside entities with skill and ease. As well as other warehouse and Central Issue Facilities.**

After: Each week, skillfully briefed corporate seniors and leaders from other associated organizations.

Analysis: This example, also based on a resume, exemplifies six *Word Sculpting Tools. Conducted briefings* is better stated as *briefed* (from Chapter 10, "Verbs Are Your Friends: Rely on Them"). Delete the second *weekly,* as it is redundant. Another example of redundancy is the use of two synonyms *presentations* and *briefings.* Select one (from Chapter 8, "Redundancy: Once Will Suffice"). Replace *as well as* with *and* to save space (from Chapter 7, "Shorter Is Better: Don't Hog Space"). *Entities* is too vague, leaving readers to wonder who or what these *entities* are; this causes the reader's attention to drift from the author's intended message (from Chapter 14, "Keep the Focus: Shut the Gates"). *Skillfully* replaces *with skill and ease* (from Chapter 6, "Useless Words: Find, Chisel, Discard"). Finally, the concluding words constitute a sentence fragment that doesn't follow the substance of the previous sentence. Proofreading (from Chapter 15, "Final Steps: Revise, Edit, and Proofread") is the crowning touch, critical to delivering a convincing message.

Exercise #3

Before: The plan provides programs a specific methodology to document **their** architectures.

After: The plan provides program managers a specific methodology to document program architectures.

Analysis: As originally written, the author opens the garden gate; the reader is bewildered. *Programs* do not *document* their [own] *architectures.* By way of clarification, we add *program managers* as the recipient of what the plan provides. Finally, we delete *their,* as its meaning is unclear.

Exercise #4

Before: **Delivered administrative application training**.

After: Trained the office staff on new automated tools that facilitate administrative functions, such as scheduling conference rooms and managing the plethora of tasks assigned to the organization.

Analysis: This is also based on a resume. What does it mean? As originally written, the reader has no idea and wanders through the gate. To unravel this, first identify the verb. In the *Before* version, it is "delivered." What did she deliver? She delivered "training." A more effective way to express "deliver training" is "trained." Another alternative, however, is that she actually "delivered training." I envision an employee pushing down a lengthy, narrow corridor a cart laden with boxes of training manuals destined for some unsuspecting recipient. See how the writer's lack of clarity raised additional questions? Finally, with a little imagination (and presumably a conversation with the author to determine what was actually intended), we add details to more rigorously convey what the individual might have accomplished.

Exercise #5

Before: She **is seasoned with** Executive Order 12543.

After: Fully versed in requirements levied by Executive Order (EO) 12543; helped develop the plan to implement the EO.

Analysis: This is based on a resume in which *she* wouldn't be used. The reader's first reaction is "Seasoned with what? Salt, pepper, perhaps a touch of basil?" What the author intends to say is specified above. We add a bit to amplify what the individual did relative to the EO.

Exercise #6

Before: Mary **executes Protocol as well as orchestrates** the seating of all **Senior Staff Members.**

After: Mary ensures proper protocol is followed to include designated seating of senior staff members.

Analysis: Poor verb selection opens the garden gate! I envision poor old *Protocol* standing blindfolded in front of a firing squad awaiting execution. After discharging her weapon, I see Mary with her arms uplifted, holding a conductor's baton, preparing to *orchestrate* proper seating! *Protocol* and *Senior Staff Members* should not be capitalized, as they are not proper nouns. Always check the use of *as well as,* which can often be replaced with *and.* Those who understand protocol realize that *designated seating* is a subset of *protocol,* which is why we replace *as well as* with *to include.*

Exercise #7

Before: **I am the on-site Project Manager for a project at a major corporation. The project helps the finance department by identifies department-wide files that can be destroyed immediately, can be destroyed in the near future, maintained on site or can be sent to offsite storage. Files that are eligible for immediate destruction are listed on an Excel spreadsheet. The spreadsheet is then submitted to departmental management for review. If the files are approved for destruction, they will be placed in bins and sent for shredding. Files marked for offsite storage are placed in boxes and a box content**

report is prepared electronically. This work is done by a team of eight members which I manage.

After: As Project Manager, I supervise 8 people who determine and then manage the disposition (destroy, maintain on-site, or archive) of 15,000 files belonging to elements throughout the 7,000-person organization.

Analysis: This can benefit from several *Word Sculpting Tools*: redundancy, garden gate, avoid gibberish, and useless words. We remedy two egregious flaws: 1) The author completely loses focus (i.e., the garden gate) and spends most of the space describing the function and only a fraction of the space highlighting his own professional strengths, and 2) The leading line—golden nugget—is buried at the end. The author also misses the opportunity to scope the size of the files and the size of the organization he supports, so we add those additional details to complete the context. With sculpting, we sharpen the story and shave the length from 695 to 212 spaces. Additional errors include *helps . . . by identifies, offsite storage, members which I manage.*

Exercise #8

Before: **Responsible for** scheduling staff meetings for **Senior Government Staff via Lotus Notes.**

Responsible for coordinating **multiple Senior Government Calendars via Lotus Notes.**

After: Scheduled meetings and coordinated calendars for five Senior Executive Service-3 officials.

Analysis: These two sentences are based on sequential items in a resume. They are easily combined to save space and spare the reader excessive, extraneous text. The job applicant opens the gate by leaving the reader to wonder whom did the individual support or at least, at what organizational level. We, therefore, specify the number of officials the individual supported and specify the rank, as well. After all*, senior* exists in widely varying degrees, is subjective, and is open to interpretation. We delete as unnecessary the word *staff* and move *Lotus*

Notes to the Skill Section of the resume. Finally, *Senior Government Staff* and *Senior Government Calendars* are incorrectly capitalized.

Exercise #9

Before: Clear **and** well-defined requirements **up front** would have minimized the **scope creeps**, modifications, and project delays.

After: Clear, well-defined requirements in the beginning would have minimized the project's expanding scope, modifications, and delays.

Analysis: What is the garden gate that diverts the reader's attention? Replace *scope creeps* with *expanding scope* so it doesn't sound so much like Halloween! Further improving this example, we use two adjectives sequentially to delete the word *and.* Replace *up front* with the more professional *in the beginning.* Finally, *scope, modifications,* and *delays* all refer to *project,* so we relocate it accordingly.

Exercise #10

Before: Participated in **Operation NOBLE STEED** in charge of briefing more than sixty pilots and Weapon System Operators on air threats in the African **Theater**.

After: Supervised a five-person team that briefed approximately sixty pilots and Weapon System Operators daily on air threats in the African area of military operations.

Analysis: The opening is awkward in the *Before* example: *Participated in . . . in charge of . . . .* Furthermore, the author misses the opportunity to explain *in charge of*, which opens the garden gate, leaving the reader wondering, "What did she actually do?" So, we open with that critical data point, *Supervised a five-person team*. The author opens a second gate with the words *more than sixty,* which we close by stating *approximately sixty.* We also quantify the accomplishment with the addition of the word *daily*. The author can choose to name the operation and explain what it is or not, but it doesn't contribute to the significance of the sentence. When making this determination, the author should consider how important that data point will be to the reader. If the title is a bell ringer, by all means include it. For the civilian readers of this book, *theater* is a military term, meaning "area of operations."

CHAPTER 15 ANSWERS

Exercise #1

Before: **Reviewed signature** documents **of completeness** prior to dispatch.

After: Proofread all signed documents prior to dispatch.

Analysis: First, what is a *signature document*? Replace this with *signed documents. Review . . . of completeness* should be *reviewed for completeness.* Even this can be improved; we replace those words with *proofread.* Finally, consider this. Wouldn't someone proofread the document before it is signed? Perhaps the author intended to say, *Proofread signed packages for completeness prior to dispatch.* We'll never know.

Exercise #2

Before: We **still need to** document **all of the** steps **we completed to in regards to** preparing the documents for scanning and shipping.

After: We must document steps taken to prepare documents for scanning and shipping.

Analysis: First, correct the errors: *to in regards to* and the extra space preceding the period. Second, delete the useless words *all of the, in regards to,* and the duplicate use of *we.* Third, use more effective verbs: *must* in lieu of *still need to* and *taken* in lieu of *completed.* We reduced the original from 23 words and 124 spaces to 12 words and 78 spaces!

Exercise #3

Before: This memorandum provides guidance for each office that **generate**, maintains, transmits, stores, or **access** information on the

Information Technology (IT) infrastructure. After confirming that **an** a breach has occurred, immediately notify the appropriate security officer. To gain better visibility into**, and understanding of, how** employees **currently** report possible IT incidents**, a study is required.**

After: This memorandum provides guidance for each office that generates, maintains, transmits, stores, or accesses information on the information technology (IT) infrastructure. After confirming that a breach has occurred, immediately notify the appropriate security officer. A study is required to gain better visibility into and understanding of the process by which employees report possible IT incidents.

Analysis: The subjects and verbs don't agree. The text is corrected to *generates . . . accesses.* The original included improper use of capitals because *information technology* is not a proper noun and should not be capitalized. Delete the mistake *an.* Cart before the horse is found in the last line. Begin the third sentence with the subject *A study is required.* Delete commas following *into* and *of.* Replace *how* with *the process by which* because this is more professional terminology.

Exercise #4

Before: A joint working group was formed and **subsequently conducted a two month study** that developed the Funding and Cost Recovery Plan for FY 2013–2016 Staff Paper. The plan includes an anticipated progression in cost recovery from **FY2013** through **FY 2016** for several **mutually-operated systems**. Based on input from the working group, a **variance** of services and best practices **was established. Each** participating agency identified a budget for **their** IT resources.

After: A joint working group was formed and, over two months, developed the staff paper, *Funding and Cost Recovery Plan for FY 2013–2016.* The plan includes an anticipated progression in cost recovery from FY 2013–FY 2016 for several mutually operated systems. Based on input from the working group, agencies established a variance of services and best practices. Each participating agency identified a budget for its IT resources.

Analysis: Delete *subsequently* as redundant. Obviously, it could accomplish nothing prior to being formed. If we had retained it, *two-month* would be hyphenated. We modify this piece because *a study* cannot *develop* a plan. *Staff Paper* is not part of the title, so we revise this to *developed the staff paper* and italicize the title of that document. We standardize the use of FY in two ways: First, by adding a space between *FY* and *2013* and second, by using *FY 2013–FY 2016* and deleting *through.* Adverbs ending in -*ly* should not be hyphenated, thus *mutually operated* systems. We correct the passive voice in *a variance . . . was established* by rewriting in active voice. The possessive pronoun for *each agency* is *its* and not *their.* Note: If the actual formation of the working group is not key to the discussion, eliminate that fact and begin with *Over a two-month period, the joint working group. . . .*

Exercise #5

Before: The goal was to **move** the Hospital Liaison **Program, to** a point of consistent, operational, sustainability. In that context, a **set** of monthly milestones **were** established. One action was to implement a working **group, to** support the governance framework and, along with the Human Resources **department** oversee the assignment process (**e.g,** personnel, shift schedules, **duties)** as well.

After: The goal was to advance the Hospital Liaison Program to a point of consistent, operational sustainability. In that context, a set of monthly milestones was established. One action was to implement a working group to support the governance framework and, along with the Human Resources department, oversee the assignment process (e.g., personnel, shift schedules, and duties), as well.

Analysis: We replace *move* with *advance* only because the latter connotes *forward movement.* Delete the commas following *Program* and *operational.* Change *a set of monthly milestones were* to *a set . . . was.* Remove the comma following *group.* Add a comma following *department* and *duties).* With *e.g,* add a period before the comma.

Exercise #6

Before: Has excellent reading and **comprehensive** skills.

After: Has excellent reading and comprehension skills.

Analysis: The author obviously intends *comprehension.* This is an excellent example of why an author should not rely solely on computer verification of grammar and spelling.

Exercise #7

Before: Analyzed and **effectively** summarized information **and date** in both written and **geographic** format.

After: Analyzed and summarized information in written and graphic format.

Analysis: We delete *and date* because it makes no sense. The author might have meant *data,* but we have no idea. *Geographic* is probably intended to be *graphic.* We delete *effectively* because that is expected and, therefore, unnecessary to state.

Exercise #8

Before: The rescue team complied with all requirements identified in the Community Emergency **actions** and Response Handbook (CEARH) which **services** as the go-to standard for rescue teams across the state. This document can be **accesed** online.

After: The rescue team complied with all requirements identified in the *Community Emergency Actions and Response Handbook* (CEARH), which serves as the go-to standard for rescue teams across the state. This document can be accessed online.

Analysis: This is a simple case of proofreading to catch the mistakes. *Actions* is capitalized as part of a title, and, because it is a book, the title should be in italics. We need to add a comma between *(CEARH)* and *which*. The author uses an incorrect verb *services* instead of *serves.* We correct a misspelling of *accesed* to *accessed.*

Exercise #9

Before: His team **has perform some** significant **results oriented collaborations** with other parts of the organization by **reaching out to all** the teams **working with them to give them** information on the program, **doing boot camps to get them talking on the same page.** The team set up a collaboration **fourm** provide **interface. and** working to provide mission products like BIMP. Through our new **softward,** which has allowed the team to **really** bring mission focus this year through **some really great** interfaces **that the mugs have been very happy to see themselves in the project** and help provide a way towards functional integration. It has been a complete **Team** effort, all helping the others and the groups within the organization and beyond

After: None is possible without interviewing someone.

Analysis: This example is so rife with errors that it must be analyzed functionally, as opposed to sequentially, differing from our usual pattern.

First, correct the errors found by proofreading: *has performed, results-oriented, forum, to provide interface and, software, team (lowercase),* and add a concluding period.

Second, correct the broken tether: *perform . . . collaborations.*

Third, use precise verbs: *Perform . . . collaborations* equates to *collaborate.*

Fourth, get rid of the useless words: There are two instances of *some* that can be deleted.

Fifth, don't hog space: *Reaching out to all* equates to *contacting, working with them* could equate to *partnering, to give them* equates to *provide, to get them talking on the same page* equates to *synchronize efforts.* In most business communications, try to avoid words that imply an author's personal feelings, such as *really, really great,* and *very happy.*

Sixth, close the garden gate: *Boot camp* is distracting and colloquial. This next bit makes no sense and also throws a complete curve with the word *mugs: that the mugs have been very happy to see themselves in the project.* The unfamiliar reader might not know that *mug* refers to *Multiple User Group.* Instead, that reader might mistakenly think the author refers in a slightly derogatory—or perhaps affectionate—term to an individual, *you mug!*

Seventh, avoid gibberish: BIMP is neither spelled out nor explained.

Exercise #10

Before: **With more than ten** major IT **fielding** initiatives in a **dessert** environment, **never had** a security **beach**, never **impacting** a major training operation and never impacted installation operations more than two hours..

After: Oversaw the fielding of fourteen major IT initiatives in a desert environment and did so without a single security breach. Fielding did not impede a major training operation nor did it impact daily operations at the installation for more than two hours.

Analysis: This item lacks a verb explaining what the individual did relative to the IT initiatives. We add *oversaw.* Next, we answer "What did he oversee?" He oversaw the *fielding* because we choose not to use the noun as an adjective as in *fielding initiatives.* We close the garden gate opened by *more than ten* as it begged the question, "Just how many?" Revise *dessert* to *desert* and revise *beach* to *breach.* We add the word *single* to *security breach* to emphasize the strength of this accomplishment. We use *impede* in lieu of *impacting* because the former implies negativity in this case. Did you notice the lack of parallelism in *never impacting* and *never impacted*? We clarify with *daily operations at the installation* as an improvement over installation operations. Finally, we delete the second period at the end of the sentence.

Appendix B

The Dirty Dozen: Most Common Errors in Professional Writing

1. **Failure to proofread.** This includes over-reliance on automated tools or worse, relying on the boss as the initial proofreader. HINT: That's not his or her job! Fail here and you lose your reader. Strive for an error-free product.

2. **Failure to outline and plan your message**. This entails writing from a stream of consciousness, using whatever crosses the computer screen and looks nifty at the time, and results in the following: a) disjointed, poorly organized message, b) inclusion of distracting, tangential information, and c) possible failure to achieve your goals.

3. **Lack of precision.** Run-on sentences, comma splices, sentence fragments, inability to use transition words and phrases between paragraphs, overly long paragraphs, and bureaucratic blather.

4. **Poor word choice.** Excessive redundancy or repetition, lack of variety in vocabulary, and boring prose; use of jargon inappropriate to the audience and acronyms without explanation; and a presumption that the reader understands your message.

5. **Incorrect punctuation.** Especially ubiquitous is misuse of commas and semicolons, failure to employ the Oxford comma (optional, but it helps!) or to employ it consistently, and erroneous application of *e.g., i.e.,* and *etc.*

6. **Excessive use of demonstrative pronouns.** Examples of these include *that, this,* and *they.* A related malady is starting a sentence with *There is* or *There are.*

7. **Excessive use of passive voice.** Use the actual subject and verb. Identify who or what is taking the action and go from there.

8. **Improper subject, verb, and pronoun agreement.** This is simple but requires attention to detail (see #1 above).

9. **Mixed use of first, second, and third person subjects.** Consistency and attention to detail remedy this, too.

10. **Nouns upon nouns upon nouns modifying . . . a noun.** Please don't!

11. **Lack of standardized words to open listed items.** Again, resolved by consistency and attention to detail. Read aloud and listen to the rhythm.

12. **Writing as you speak.** Avoid sloppy, colloquial language in professional products. Pay special attention to this and expunge as you revise your drafts.

Appendix C

Baker's Dozen:
13 Tips to Compose . . .

Grant Submissions

1. **Know your audience.** Tailor your package to the grantmaker's missions, vision, goals, and objectives.

2. **Establish your credibility.** Describe your organization's skills, experience, and resources. Provide similar information about your partners. Make the case that answers, "Why select *you* over others?"

3. **Define the problem.** Explain why the problem your project intends to resolve is sufficiently acute to justify the grantmaker's intervention. Identify the background of the situation, who it affects, and previous attempts to resolve it.

4. **Write a summary statement.** Describe in one paragraph your organization, the project, beneficiaries, and the amount and purpose of requested funds.

5. **Outline the package and then request a vector check.** Follow the terms and sequence of requested information in the Request for Proposal (RFP) . . . precisely. Ask the grantmaker to review the outline.

6. **Hook the reader.** Use a catchy title and clear, precise, focused, and intriguing text. Exude energy, excitement, and commitment throughout the document. Convince the reviewer that you—not someone else—deserve this grant.

7. **Make a puissant case.** Draw as many parallels as possible between your organization, your proposal, and the grantmaker. *Write to Influence!* strategies and *Word Sculpting Tools* are critical to making a captivating argument.

8. **Describe the project's activities.** Describe steps to implement your program and partners' roles, measures of success, and objectives. Remember, detail adds depth, dimension, and impact to your writing.

9. **Develop a budget and spending plan.** Make these detailed, accurate, and line-item specific. Identify matching funds or other funding sources. Demonstrate your calculations.

10. **Address sustainability, longevity, and scalability.** Explain what happens when grant funds have been spent. How will the project continue? How do you envision its future?

11. **Adhere to the application's guidelines.** Mistakes in margins, spacing, type size, and word count can be disqualifying technical errors. Are attachments required or prohibited? Note: Some organizations prefer a letter of inquiry.

12. **Request a review.** Ask someone experienced in this process to review your package for substance and technicalities.

13. **Follow-up with the grantmaker.** Call to ensure the grantmaker received your submission. During the review process, tell the grantmaker if you had a major success or received media coverage in a related area. Provide a copy of the article or video URL. Good news might help sway the decision!

Input to Your Performance Appraisal

I told my troops, "Learn to write powerfully. When your boss requests input for your appraisal, provide facts—clear, concise, and compelling."

1. **Investigate!** – Like the reporter, dig for facts about your performance. What did you achieve? Did you supervise others? Launch any initiatives?

2. **Emphasize the "so what"** – What was your value added? How did you contribute to the mission?

3. **Triage the information** – Decide what NOT to include. Base this on scope of impact and available space.

4. **Grab the reader's attention** – Open with a hook. Conclude on a strong note. Leave the reader wanting more.

5. **Frame the story** – At what level did you work? Whom did you support? Details help readers grasp context and impact.

6. **Highlight accolades** – Cite the bonuses, awards, and kudos from your boss or clients.

7. **Stand out from the crowd** – Use words to connote "selection" and demonstrate breadth, e.g., "agency-wide."

8. **Highlight the golden nugget** – Place prominently facts you want noticed. Don't bury them in less important text.

9. **Find and discard useless words** – Space is precious. Each word counts.

10. **Avoid gibberish** – It loses the reader (e.g., excessive detail and job-related jargon readers won't understand).

11. **Shorter is better** – Don't use words that hog space.

12. **Verbs are your friends** – Use hard-hitting, action-oriented verbs. Avoid verbs such as *supported, contributed to, assisted*; these prompt questions, and do not explain your contributions.

13. **Revise . . . Edit . . . Proofread!**

Your Resume

This resembles the Baker's Dozen *Input for Your Appraisal*, for good reason. The strategies and *Word Sculpting Tools* apply to both!

1. **Investigate!** – Like the reporter, dig for facts about your performance. What did you achieve? Did you supervise others? Launch any initiatives?

2. **Emphasize the "so what"** – What was your value added? How did you contribute to the mission?

3. **Triage the information** – Decide what NOT to include. Base it on scope of impact and available space.

4. **Grab the reader's attention** – Open with a hook. Conclude on a strong note. Leave the reader wanting more.

5. **Frame the story** – At what level did you work? Whom did you support? Details help readers grasp context and impact.

6. **Highlight accolades** – Cite the bonuses, awards, and kudos from your boss or client.

7. **Stand out from the crowd** – Use words to connote "selection" and demonstrate breadth, e.g., "agency-wide."

8. **Find and discard useless words** – Space is precious. Each word counts.

9. **Avoid gibberish** – It loses the reader (e.g., excessive detail and job-related jargon readers won't understand).

10. **Shorter is better** – Don't use words that hog space.

11. **Verbs are your friends** – Use hard-hitting, action-oriented verbs. Avoid verbs such as *supported, contributed to, assisted*; these prompt questions do not explain your contributions.

12. **Keep the Focus – Shut the Garden Gate** – Don't let readers wander from your message. Tell the right stories.

13. **Revise . . . Edit . . . Proofread!**

Email

1. **Triage the information** – Lead with the most important.

2. **Read the entire email** – 'Nuf said.

3. **Tailor the title** – Ensure it reflects the content; adjust if information addressed shifted from the original email.

4. **Make the connection** – Responding to a question? Referencing an earlier email? Cite it in the opening text.

5. **Sequence attachments** – Append in the sequence they appear in the email; identify in the text, e.g., "Attach. 1 is . . . ."

6. **Edit thyself** – This, too, is a professional correspondence.

7. **Be brief in substance** – This is not a lengthy report.

8. **Be concise in text** – Write telegraphically.

9. **Toooooo much info!** – Exclude overly personal information.

10. **To whom are you speaking?** – Differentiate between action and information addressees (i.e., "To" and "cc").

11. **Be selective with "Send"** – "Reply All" only when necessary.

12. **Watch your language** – Subtle meanings don't convey.

13. **Who Are You?** – Include your signature block!

A Report

The previous Baker's Dozens consist of suggested actions. This, however, is a checklist to develop a report.

1. Did you begin with an outline?

2. Does the draft address all points in the outline?

3. Does the draft include information **not** in the outline? Do these points contribute to or distract from the message?

4. Does your opening "hook" the reader?

5. Does each paragraph support your thesis?

6. Do paragraphs flow smoothly and build on each other?

7. Do you use transitions and strong topic sentences?

8. Does each sentence correlate to its respective topic sentence?

9. Is your product thorough, balanced, and objective?

10. Are all points sufficiently supported, especially opposing positions?

11. Do the conclusion and opening statement align?

12. Did you apply *Write to Influence!* strategies and *Word Sculpting Tools*?

13. Did you validate your product with Appendix B, "The Dirty Dozen: Most Common Errors in Professional Writing"?

Appendix D

Grammar Highlights: Commas, Semicolons, and Capitalization

Commas, semicolons, and capitalization, although miniscule in size, are significant factors as the reader evaluates your competency as an author, the grammatical quality of your work, and your writing skills. These also constitute the most common errors in professional writing. I, therefore, include a section to vanquish confusion about these troublesome elements.

Commas & Semicolons

1. Commas and the Clause. To correctly use the comma, writers must understand the rudimentary building block of a sentence—the clause. This unit consists of a subject and a verb, referred to here as "a couple." A subject paired with a verb equals one couple, for example, *I travel*. Clauses can be independent, meaning they can stand alone, as in the example just presented.

Clauses can also be dependent, meaning they provide additional information about the core subject of the sentence. This type cannot stand alone; that's why it's called "dependent." Here are some examples with the subject and verb underlined:

- *If they study hard*
- *Because they take detailed notes*
- *Because they attend class regularly*

The dependent clause can either precede or follow the independent clause. The independent clause used in this case is *They will receive a good grade.*

RULE: If the dependent clause comes *first*, use a comma to separate it from the independent clause. [As shown in the preceding sentence].

- *If they study hard, they will receive a good grade.*

- *Because they take detailed notes, they will receive a good grade.*

- *Because they attend class regularly, they will receive a good grade.*

RULE: Don't use a comma if the dependent clause *follows* the independent clause. [As shown in this preceding sentence. See the difference?]

- *They will receive a good grade if they study hard.*

- *They will receive a good grade because they take detailed notes.*

- *They will receive a good grade because they attend class regularly.*

2. Commas and the Sentence. There are four types of sentences: simple, compound, complex, and complex-compound. Stay with me, it's not as bad as it sounds!

- Simple sentence: One independent clause or couple (a subject and a verb).

  - *I travel.*

  - *They study.*

- Compound sentence: Two or more independent clauses. Think of two couples double dating. The clauses must be joined by a conjunction *(and, but, or, nor, for, so, yet).*

RULE: If the sentence has two independent clauses (couples), place a comma after the first clause (couple) and before the conjunction.

- *I travel often, **and** I have a large travel budget.*

To test this rule, remove the conjunction. If the two pieces form complete sentences and can stand alone, the comma is required.

RULE: If the subject is missing from the second clause (and, therefore, is no longer a clause), do not use a comma.

Watch . . . this is a common error . . .

- *I travel often **and** have a large travel budget.*

- Complex sentence: One independent clause and one or more dependent clauses.

RULE: If the dependent clause comes *first*, use a comma to separate it from the independent clause.

- *Although the* job is *demanding, my sister enjoys it.*

RULE: Don't use a comma if the dependent clause *follows* the independent clause.

- *My sister enjoys the job although it is demanding.*

- Complex-compound sentence: Two or more independent clauses paired with one or more dependent clauses.

RULE: If the dependent clause precedes two independent clauses, separate the dependent clause with a comma but do not separate the independent clauses with a comma.

- *Because I work for a magazine, I travel extensively and I earn many frequent flyer miles.*

- *Because they take detailed notes, they will receive a good grade and I will take them to dinner!*

"But, you just said to separate two independent clauses with a comma!" Yes, I hear you and that's correct. However, grammar rules provide structure and order, and generally hope to preclude complexity and confusion. Don't laugh! In this instance, applying the rule discussed earlier would result in too many commas. Here is how one such sentence would otherwise look:

- *Because they take detailed notes, they will receive a good grade, and I will take them to a celebratory dinner!*

It's definitely best not to include the comma between the two independent clauses, if preceded by its dependent cousin.

3. Commas and Amplifying, Non-essential Information. Additional words often amplify, interrupt, or contrast with the primary thought. In all cases, the sentence can stand alone if such information is deleted.

RULE: Use a comma to separate information non-essential to a sentence's meaning.

- *I travel extensively, usually to Europe, and my sister works at a law firm.*
- *I travel extensively; my sister, on the other hand, works at a law firm.*
- *They study at the library, despite its distance from the dormitory, but they meet in this building for lectures.*
- *There are, of course, other applications of commas beyond that of clauses.*
- *After studying at the library, one student preferred to go to dinner, not a movie.*
- *I prefer to travel on vacation rather than work, don't you?*

4. Commas and Defining Information. Sentences often include information needed to define or specifically identify the topic of the sentence. This is considered "essential."

RULE: Do not use a comma if the information defines the subject and is essential to a sentence's meaning.

- *I visited my granddaughter Felicity. (I have three granddaughters, so the name is essential.)*
- *I vacationed with my sister, Claudia. (I have only one sister, so the name is nonessential.)*

5. Commas and Relative Clauses. Segueing off this discussion about amplifying vs. defining information, we turn now to the relative clause. This critter begins with one of the relative pronouns *who, whom, that, which, whose, where, when* and also either amplifies or defines the subject. Here are some examples of amplifying relative clauses:

RULE: The rule regarding commas for relative clauses is the same as addressed above for amplifying information. If the clause amplifies the main subject—can be removed from the sentence and the sentence still makes sense—use a comma to set it off from the rest of the sentence.

- *My sister, who lives nearby, works at a law firm.*
- *They study at the library with Professor Brown, whom they very much admire.*
- *I will take them to a celebratory dinner, which will be a delightful experience!*

Items underlined below exemplify defining information. Do not separate with commas because the remaining text would not make sense.

RULE: If the clause defines the specific person or thing addressed—and cannot logically be removed—do not set that information off with a comma.

- *The candidate who had the least money lost the election.*
- *The book that I borrowed from you is excellent.*
- *People who cheat only harm themselves.*

6. Commas and Adjectives. Two or more adjectives are often used sequentially in a sentence. To determine if each modifies an associated noun, you should be able to logically place the word *and* between the adjectives. In professional communications, most sequential adjectives modify the noun and, therefore, require a comma.

RULE: Use a comma to separate adjectives that independently modify a noun. If this is not the case, do not separate the adjectives with a comma.

- *This is a logical, fact-based, and well-presented paper.*
- *I admired the deep, blue, and beautiful Pacific Ocean.* (The Pacific Ocean was deep and blue and beautiful.)

  but . . .

- *My car is deep blue and beautiful.* (The color is deep blue – not light blue, orange, or green. *Deep* modifies *blue*, not *car*. Hence, no comma needed between *deep* and *blue*.)

7. Commas and Quotations. Use a comma between the main thought and a quotation shorter than three lines.

- *She declared, "This is the best vacation I've ever taken!"*
- *"This is the best vacation I've ever taken," she declared.*

8. Commas and Personal Titles, Degrees, etc. Use a comma when citing degrees, certifications, titles, and indicating instances of direct address.

- *The signature block read, "Mary Jones, PhD."*
- *Thank you very much for attending the reception, Senator.*
- *Sarah, that was a fabulous dinner!*

9. Commas and a Series. Use commas to separate three or more words written as a series. The comma that precedes the conjunction is called the Oxford or serial comma. While not required, it clarifies information.

- *I love my parents, Barry Manilow and Sting.*
- *I love my parents, **Barry Manilow, and Sting**.*

Do not place a comma after the conjunction.

- *Her hobbies are cooking, reading, and, biking.*

10. Commas and Dates. When stating the day of the week, the month, date of the month, and year, separate each by a comma. Follow the year with a comma, as well, if it's embedded in a sentence.

- *I traveled to Germany on Monday, September 15, 1978, the month of Oktoberfest.*

No comma is needed if only the month and year are used.

- I traveled to Germany in September 1978.

Commas can be avoided by using the sequence of date, month, and year. I prefer this format for its simplicity.

- *I traveled to Germany on 15 September 1978, the month of Oktoberfest.*

11. Commas and Geography. Use commas to separate geographic elements. As seen with the year above, use a concluding comma if this occurs mid-sentence.

- *I traveled to Wiesbaden, Germany.*
- *I traveled to Wiesbaden, Germany, in 1978.*

12. Commas and Numbers. Use a comma after the first numeral of a four-digit numeral. To indicate place value, work from right to left, adding a comma in front of each group of three numerals. Years, page numbers, and street addresses do not follow this rule.

- *They collected 2,458 antique paintings, the most expensive of which sold for $10,222,450.*

13. Commas and *i.e., e.g.,* and *etc.* The first term, *i.e.,* stands for *id est,* which means "that is" and specifically identifies an item or items previously discussed.

- *I have one steadfast rule in traveling, i.e., don't forget the passport!*

The second term, *e.g.,* is the abbreviation for *exempli gratia,* which means "for example" and precedes samples of what was just discussed.

- *I traveled to many wonderful countries, e.g., Germany, Italy, and Spain.*

The third term, *etc.,* is an abbreviation of *et cetera* and means "and other things." It concludes a list of items exemplifying what was just discussed.

- *The vacation package includes plane fare, port taxes, deluxe hotel rooms, etc.*

Do not mix these terms. If you list representative examples, *i.e.,* is incorrect. When using *e.g.,* do not conclude the list with *etc.* Why? Because *e.g.,* indicates a few examples; therefore, adding *etc.* is not only unnecessary, it is incorrect. Regarding punctuation of these items, guidance varies. I prefer to enclose *i.e.,* and *e.g.,* with commas if used internally to a sentence. Whatever style you choose—comma or no comma—be consistent. Oh, yes—please spell *etc.* correctly! It is often written incorrectly as "ect."

14. Commas—How Not to Use. Commas are used erroneously as often as they are erroneously omitted. Case in point is comma splicing, the incorrect application of a comma to join two independent thoughts (i.e., each can stand alone), as exemplified below. This error results in a run-on sentence:

Incorrect:

- *My sister worked a 70-hour week, she had to complete the project.*

Each of the three options below is correct:

Option 1: *My sister worked a 70-hour week; she had to complete the project.*

Option 2: *My sister worked a 70-hour week. She had to complete the project.*

Option 3: *My sister worked a 70-hour week, but she had to complete the project.*

15. Commas and Semicolons. A semicolon performs two basic functions. First, it joins two closely related, complete thoughts. To reinforce the concept of semicolons used in this capacity, repeated below is the example showing how to use the semicolon to avoid comma splicing.

- *My sister worked a 70-hour week; she had to remain and complete the project.*

Second, and as they relate to commas, semicolons are used to separate three or more elements in a series when one of those elements, itself, contains commas:

- *To prepare for the trip, she had to **pack** slacks, sweaters, shoes, and jewelry; **reserve** a hotel; and **find** someone to watch her pets.*

The items in this series above that need to be separated are *pack, reserve, and find.* Because several items were included in *pack,* so the semicolon separates *pack . . . reserve . . . and find.* Were we to delete *slacks, sweaters, shoes, and jewelry,* commas would have been the correct punctuation instead of the semicolons. The sentence would have read *To prepare for the trip, she had to pack, reserve a hotel, and find someone to watch her pets.*

Capitalization

Improper capitalization ranks second to commas as the most common grammatical mistake in professional writing. Most authors correctly capitalize the first word in a sentence. Beyond that, correct capitalization becomes sporadic. Addressed below are aspects that seem to be most problematic. I encourage you to explore the books in the "List of References" in Appendix F for a more comprehensive discussion on all aspects of capitalization.

1. Capitalizing Titles of Works. Capitalize the first and last words of titles of publications such as books, newspapers, and magazines; movies, plays, and television and radio programs; and songs and musical collections. Within the titles, capitalize nouns, pronouns, adjectives, verbs, adverbs, and subordinating conjunctions (*as, that, if, because,* etc.) Do not capitalize articles *(a, an, the),* or coordinating conjunctions *(and, but, or, for, nor).* Capitalizing prepositions (*on, through, beside*) is a matter of personal preference or house style; for example many people and organizations decide to use uppercase for all prepositions of more than 4 or 5 letters.

- *The Day of the Jackal*
- *A Tale of Two Cities*
- *What Color Is Your Parachute?*

2. Capitalizing Points of the Compass. Capitalize points of the compass when referring to specific regions, but not otherwise.

- *We had three visitors from the South.*
- But do not capitalize it in this case:
- *Go south three blocks and turn left.*

3. Capitalizing Levels of Government. Capitalize *federal* or *state* as part of an official agency name. If they are used as general terms, don't capitalize.

- *The state has evidence to the contrary.*
- *The State Board of Equalization collects state taxes.*
- *We will visit three states during our vacation.*
- *The Federal Bureau of Investigation is located in Washington, D.C.*
- *Her company must comply with all county, state, and federal laws.*

Rules are similar relating to the capitalization of words relating to *Congress.* If referring to the body of government, *Congress* is a proper noun and should be capitalized. However, used as an adjective, *congressional* should not be capitalized.

- *Many individuals have testified before Congress on health-related issues.*

- *Foreign trade is a topic addressed by many congressional delegations.*

4. Capitalization and Hyphens. Do not capitalize the second word of a hyphenated set in sentences. However, in titles of works, the second word of a hyphenated set is usually capitalized. In these cases, follow the rules for capitalizing titles of works.

- Incorrect: *Government-Level spending surged.*

- Correct: *Government-level spending surged.*

- Incorrect: *The Self-reliant Child (book title)*

- Correct: *The Self-Reliant Child (book title)*

5. Capitalization and Acronyms. Do not capitalize words when spelling out an acronym unless they constitute a proper noun, such as the Federal Bureau of Investigation (FBI). As a reminder, do not use the abbreviated acronym unless the term will be repeated elsewhere in the document.

- Incorrect: *The contract included a section on Terms Of Reference (TOR).*

- Correct: *The contract included a section on terms of reference (TOR).*

- Incorrect: *Receiving Authority To Operate (ATO) is a key milestone.*

- Correct: *Receiving authority to operate (ATO) is a key milestone.*

Appendix E

Editor's Challenge: Don't Tread on My Writing

The Gadsden Flag ("Don't Tread on Me") reflects the contentious relationship that can exist between editors and authors, who resent having their work edited. The author usually enjoys complete leeway in arranging thoughts, rewording, adding and deleting material, and so on. The editor is sometimes limited to superficial polishing, such as correcting errors in grammar and punctuation.

As an editor, how do you respond when presented an ineffective draft replete with writing that resembles *Before* examples in this book? How do you engage when a product requires major surgery, not a minor facelift? The challenge intensifies when the editor is paired with a defensive author, intransigent to all but minor edits.

The answer lies in your approach. Contain your enthusiasm, don't overtly rejoice at the prospect of editing someone's work. Because I'm passionate about writing, this was a difficult lesson. I have inadvertently offended authors; their enthusiasm for my participation didn't match my own, given the opportunity to "improve" their work.

I once edited—actually rewrote—someone's report, transforming it from that proverbial "sow's ear into a silk purse" and was shocked when confronted by the incensed author. The fact that the revision was imminently more effective than the original did not diffuse his resentment.

I exacerbated the situation by doggedly standing my ground, insisting he incorporate my modifications. Why? First, I was confident in the improvements. Second, vanity and pride—if *my* name was associated with the product, I wanted it to reflect *my* standards of composition. Third, I'm bullheaded. Hint: Wrong approach!

The answer—**push back gently but remember, it is not your product.** To avoid alienating the author, I take a more subdued, collegial approach by determining the desired level of editorial assistance. We then collaborate, blending my ability to write with the author's subject matter expertise. My approach is now, "Help me to help you." This really works!

I've also learned to pick my battles by categorizing suggested modifications as either grammatical or substantive. Most authors readily agree to edits such as spelling and punctuation, so I begin with these to establish a positive rapport and demonstrate my value. Substantive modifications, however, can be tricky. I categorize these as follows:

- Must have (fundamental to the credibility or effectiveness of the document) and determine how to "fall on the sword" judiciously and painlessly to attain them;

- Nice to have (still important to the product's smooth delivery and effectiveness); and

- Nice-to-have, professional polish (bonus items).

Bottom line: Help as much as you are allowed, always remembering the author makes the final determination.

Appendix F

Write to Influence! in a Nutshell

1. **Know your audience.** Provide needed information in language the audience understands.

2. **Use an outline.** This helps maintain focus as you write.

3. **Present your message logically.** Base it on the inverted triangle (big picture down to fine detail) or the upright triangle (fine detail building to the big picture), or another determined strategy that works for you.

4. **Underpin the message with substance.** Facts, figures, and detail give it focus, dimension, and impact.

5. **Write clear, succinct sentences.** Apply the formula, "Who-does-what-to-whom?" Avoid bureaucratic gibberish.

6. **Be consistent in presenting terms, dates, and acronyms.**

7. **Punctuate correctly!** Pay special attention to commas, semicolons, and abbreviations such as *i.e., e.g.,* and *etc.*

8. **Revise, Edit, and Proofread!** Check for every single item listed above. Note: I specifically state, "every single" for emphasis . . . like a drumbeat . . . every single item . . . boom, boom, boom . . . one by one!

9. **Validate against the Dirty Dozen!** Review your final draft in the context of Appendix B, *The Dirty Dozen: Most Common Errors in Professional Writing.*

Appendix G

List of References

1. *The Best Grammar Workbook Ever! Grammar, Punctuation, and Word Usage for Ages 10 Through 110* by Arlene Miller. bigwords 101: 2015.

2. *The Best Punctuation Book, Period: A Comprehensive Guide for Every Writer, Editor, Student, and Businessperson* by June Casagrande. Ten Speed Press: 2014.

3. *Between You and Me: Confessions of a Comma Queen* by Mary Norris. W.W. Norton and Company: 2016.

4. *The Chicago Manual of Style*, Sixteenth Edition. University of Chicago Press: 2010.

5. *Disciplined Writing and Career Development* by Mortimer D. Goldstein. Foreign Service Institute: 1986.

6. *Eats, Shoots and Leaves* by Lynne Truss. Gotham Books: 2003

7. *Elements of Style* by William Strunk Jr. and E.B. White. Longman: 1999.

8. *Essentials of English Grammar: The Quick Guide to Good English,* Third Edition, by L. Sue Baugh. McGraw-Hill: 2005.

9. *Everybody Writes: Your Go-To Guide to Creating Ridiculously Good Content* by Ann Handley. Wiley & Sons: 2014.

10. *Grammar Girl Presents the Ultimate Writing Guide for Students* by Mignon Fogarty. St. Martin's Griffin: 2011.

11. *Grammar Girl's Quick and Dirty Tips for Better Writing* by Mignon Fogarty. Henry Holt and Company: 2008.

12. *Grammatically Correct: The Essential Guide to Spelling, Style, Usage, Grammar, and Punctuation,* Second Edition, by Anne Stilman. Writer's Digest Books: 2010.

13. *The New York Times Manual of Style and Usage,* Fifth Edition, by Allan M. Siegal and William G. Connolly. The New York Times Company: 2015.

14. *Nitty-Gritty Grammar: A Not-So-Serious Guide to Clear Communication* by Edith H. Fine and Judith P. Josephson. Ten Speed Press: 1998.

15. *On Writing Well: 30th Anniversary Edition*: *The Classic Guide to Writing Nonfiction* by William Zinsser. HarperCollins Publishers: 2006.

16. *Painless Grammar* by Rebecca Elliott, Ph.D. Barron's Educational Series, Inc.: 2011.

17. *Speaking and Writing Well* by Kathy Alba, Ph.D. Thatch Tree Publications: 2001.

18. *Writing with Style: Conversations on the Art of Writing,* Third Edition, by John R. Trimble. Longman: 2010.

About the Artist

Tim Newlin is a freelance graphic artist, communications consultant, and owner of Tim's Features (timtim.com). Over his 40-year career, he edited scientific grant proposals worth millions of euros for research groups in Scandinavia. He also applied his info-graphic skills for clients in government, private business (e.g., manufacturers of scientific equipment), research laboratories, and universities. Tim's niche—helping professionals in technical fields explain complicated projects to non-technical boards that fund research. On the lighter side, Tim contributed dozens of drawings featured in Denmark's five leading family publications and is a Disney-certified illustrator.

About the Author

Carla D. Bass, Colonel, USAF (Ret), an award-winning author and speaker, served 30 years in the Air Force and 12 more with a federal agency. She is also an adjunct instructor with the National Intelligence University.

Carla shares her expertise through workshops for wide-ranging audiences—governmental, corporate, and NGO staffs through high school students. Her battle cry is "Powerful writing changes lives!" Why? Because, it does!

Throughout her career, Carla wrote hundreds of performance reviews, award nominations, and other competitive packages; talking points; elevator speeches; letters for executive signature; and products sent to the White House and Congress. She worked directly with generals, ambassadors, foreign dignitaries, and other senior leaders for whom five minutes was significant.

Carla developed her writing methodology and taught professional writing to thousands of Air Force personnel for fifteen years—to rave reviews.

Air University published her dissertation, "Building Castles on Sand—Ignoring the Riptide of Information Operations," and the *Air Power Journal* published an updated version the next year.

Her assignments included Washington, D.C.; Hawaii; Germany; Korea; and Bulgaria. Carla and her husband, Lynn Reeves, live in Virginia. They have two adult children, Sarah and Eric, happily enjoying their own life's adventures.

Contact the Author

Thank you for purchasing *Write to Influence!* I welcome feedback via online reviews or the links below. May *Write to Influence!* help open those doors to opportunity!

Carla D. Bass

Email: Carla@writetoinfluence.net

Website: https://www.writetoinfluence.net

LinkedIn: https://www.LinkedIn.com/in/carladbass

Become a fan of *Write to Influence!* and follow me on Facebook: www.facebook.com/WritetoInfluence.01

Index

A

accolade(s), iii, 24, 29, 158, 252, 325, 326

accomplishment(s), 3, 16, 17, 18, 24, 25, 28, 29, 32, 35, 36, 45, 83, 94, 95, 97, 122, 126, 127, 130, 131, 132, 153, 154, 155, 158, 159, 189, 213, 214, 216, 254, 255, 256, 258, 260, 269, 275, 276, 292, 293, 299, 306, 314, 320

acronym(s), 1, 90, 91, 92, 93, 95, 97, 99, 101, 126, 143, 161, 193, 227, 233, 238, 239, 299, 300, 321, 339, 343

active voice, 76, 85, 119, 121, 223, 228, 244, 245, 294, 307, 317

adjective(s), 53, 73, 75, 76, 89, 95, 103, 112, 113, 118, 120, 121, 122, 132, 143, 226, 238, 243, 244, 245, 262, 284, 297, 299, 305, 308, 309, 314, 320, 333, 334, 338, 339

adverb(s), 53, 75, 86, 120, 264, 317, 338

article(s)

    as parts of speech, 338

    as publications, xi, xv, 15, 29, 30, 49, 78, 174, 218, 257, 266, 280, 290, 324

audience(s), iii, ix, xi, xiii, 1, 3, 4, 5, 6, 9, 11–13, 15, 19, 20, 23, 28, 37, 39, 62, 65, 72, 73, 89, 90, 91, 92, 95, 99, 103, 114, 126, 128, 136, 151, 167, 169, 178, 185, 189, 190, 191, 192, 193, 194, 200, 227, 228, 303, 321, 323, 343, 349. *See also* reader(s)

author biography, 349

award(s), v, ix, xiv, 3, 16, 18, 25, 26, 51, 62, 63, 85, 90, 91, 93, 113, 114, 129, 130, 156, 157, 158, 159, 166, 269, 270, 275, 276, 301, 325, 349

B

Baker's Dozen, xiii, 323–328

"bottom line up front" (BLUF), 72

briefing(s), 17, 18, 28, 35, 51, 62, 87, 112, 113, 123, 130, 133, 134, 141, 143, 144, 155, 157, 166, 176, 177, 189–194, 207, 240, 255, 263, 274, 295, 299, 303, 306, 310, 314

bullet(s), xiii, 29, 64, 91, 109, 113, 140, 154, 155, 159, 162, 165, 177, 191, 192, 193, 228, 229, 238, 240, 246, 246, 248, 251, 255

C

capitalization, xiii, 125, 138, 139, 142, 144, 162, 164, 192, 193, 242, 250, 329, 337–339

"cart before the horse" (periodic sentences), 71–79, 118, 121, 132, 226, 232, 233, 234, 241, 290, 291, 304, 309, 316

clarity. *See* writing, clarity

clichés, 45

college application(s), iii, iv, xi, xii, 12, 13, 19, 23, 14–152

college scholarship(s), 23, 51, 187

colloquial language, 45, 119, 244, 265, 306, 320, 322

comma(s), xiii, 47, 99, 103, 138, 139, 140, 216, 231, 235, 242, 243, 251, 259, 261, 262, 264, 267, 289, 291, 316, 317, 318, 321, 329–337, 343, 345. *See also* punctuation

common errors, xiii, 45, 92, 95, 192, 321–322

conclusion(s), ii, 8, 9, 31, 33, 72, 100, 137, 152, 158, 174, 178, 190, 258, 328

consistency, 126, 234, 322

context, xiii, 11, 12, 22, 26, 27, 28, 36, 37, 61, 63, 90, 94, 98, 109, 127, 130, 138, 145, 150, 179, 180, 182, 190, 212, 229, 241, 242, 252, 265, 285, 290, 293, 303, 306, 313, 317, 325, 326, 343

contract(s), 5, 7, 12, 13, 32, 49, 141, 161, 163, 164, 167, 279, 339

credibility, 36, 38, 136, 169, 170, 174, 194, 323, 342

D

dates, 24, 98, 101, 102, 111, 145, 176, 177, 182, 274, 285, 294, 318, 335, 343

Dirty Dozen, xiii, 45, 95, 321–322, 328, 343. *See also* common errors

distract(ing). *See* writing, distracting

E

edit(ing), iv, xii, xiii, 1, 2, 10, 29, 45, 78, 109, 135, 137, 179, 213, 247, 253, 254, 290, 310, 325, 326, 327, 341, 342, 343

elevator speech, xii, 64, 185–188, 349

email, xii, xiii, 24, 45, 72, 96, 120, 139, 175–184, 201, 213, 214, 228, 253, 254, 255, 327, 350

essay(s), xi, xii, 13, 16, 19, 149–152

F

fact(s), 16, 18, 23, 24, 25, 31, 32, 33, 36, 38, 72, 157, 169, 177, 218, 266, 325, 326, 343

fellowship(s), 51

focus, v, x, xiv, 2, 4, 7, 12, 26, 27, 37, 46, 47, 51, 62, 81, 84, 92, 112, 113, 114, 117, 125–134, 138, 146, 150, 160, 161, 185, 186, 190, 191, 264, 265, 276, 282, 283, 302, 308, 310, 313, 319, 324, 326, 343

format(s), 1, 12, 17, 145, 174, 176, 177, 335

framework, *See* outline(ing)

G

gibberish, xii, 10, 13, 89–106, 174, 237, 238, 239, 240, 241, 262, 300, 313, 320, 325, 326, 343. *See also* jargon

grammar, ix, xiii, xiv, 78, 122, 137, 290, 318, 329–339, 341, 345

grant(s), xi, xii, xiii, 5, 7, 12, 13, 51, 94, 167–174, 187, 233, 323–324

Index

H

hook(s), xi, 13, 15–22, 189, 227, 243, 324, 325, 326, 328. *See* opening

hyphen(s), 144, 163, 164, 227, 250, 251, 262, 299, 317, 339

I

impact(s), 3, 11, 16, 24, 25, 30, 31, 32, 33, 38, 45, 51, 53, 84, 85, 86, 91, 97, 127, 146, 149, 153, 155, 157, 174, 203, 219, 231, 232, 267, 320, 324, 325, 326, 343

inconsistency, 234

information. *See* facts

Internet, 94, 232

internship(s), 23, 28, 35

J

jargon, 1, 12, 13, 28, 89, 90, 99, 126, 300, 321, 325, 326. *See also* gibberish

job(s), xi, xiii, xiv, , 2, 12, 13, 17, 26, 27, 29, 50, 72, 89, 90, 91, 94, 129, 130, 131, 150, 154, 158, 160, 162, 165, 178, 186, 241, 242, 270, 274, 275, 276, 281, 313, 321, 325, 326, 331

M

market(ing), ix, 5, 12, 32, 49, 69, 105, 108, 123, 131, 153, 185, 186, 210, 213, 219, 248, 253, 267, 280, 286, 298, 306

metaphor(s), 128

N

noun(s), 64, 73, 75, 89, 95, 97, 103, 112, 113, 118, 120, 121, 122, 139, 142, 143, 155, 156, 161, 178, 193, 226, 238, 243, 244, 245, 253, 254, 262, 263, 297, 300, 305, 308, 309, 312, 316, 317, 320, 322, 333, 334, 338, 339

as adjectives, 73, 75, 89, 103, 112,118, 120, 121, 122, 143, 226, 238, 243, 244, 262, 297, 305, 308, 309

parallel (gerunds), 46, 76, 112, 113, 141, 163, 242, 262, 299, 300, 320

O

objectivity, xi, 36, 37, 136

opening ("hook"), xi, xiii, 8, 15–22, 27, 34, 72, 98, 137, 151, 152, 155, 172, 179, 194, 227, 232, 241, 243, 246, 251, 256, 264, 290, 292, 298, 314, 327, 328

organizing material, xi, 4, 5, 6, 23–30, 37–39, 136, 137. *See also* outline(ing).

outline(ing), 7–10, 31, 32, 136, 150, 151, 171, 190, 194, 321, 324, 328, 343

P

passive voice, 54, 67, 85, 90, 97, 103, 118, 223, 226, 245, 297, 317, 322

performance appraisal(s), xi, 3, 24, 29, 30, 35, 62, 127, 129, 130, 153, 158, 166, 213, 253, 325, 326, 349

period(s) 139, 164, 193, 222, 263, 266, 267, 315, 317, 319, 320. *See also* punctuation personnel appraisal(s), xi, 3, 24, 29, 30, 35, 62, 127, 129, 130, 153, 158, 166, 213, 253, 325, 326, 349

persuasive writing, xiii, xiv, 4, 6, 37, 90

preposition(s), 112, 113, 261, 263, 301, 338

presentation(s), xii, 5, 37, 62, 63, 75, 90, 98, 103, 133, 140, 159, 162, 189–194, 207, 209, 217, 218, 236, 238, 240, 246, 255, 263, 264, 265, 275, 310

pronoun(s), 64, 65, 161, 228, 234, 250, 317, 322, 333, 338

proofread(ing), xii, 1, 2, 10, 135–146, 161, 162, 175, 180, 266, 267, 310, 315, 318, 319, 321, 325, 326, 343

proposal(s), xii, xiv, 24, 32, 34, 51, 52, 84, 98, 105, 161, 168, 169, 170, 171, 173, 174, 187, 209, 218, 246, 264, 265, 299, 324, 347

punctuation, 75, 125, 138, 140, 162, 192, 193, 231, 246, 261, 299, 321, 336, 337, 341, 342, 345. *See also* comma(s); hyphen(s); period(s); semicolon(s)

R

reader(s), v, 1, 2, 4, 7, 8, 9, 12, 15, 16, 17, 19, 20, 21, 26, 27, 28, 29, 30, 31, 32, 33, 34, 36, 37, 38, 45, 47, 52, 53, 63, 71, 72, 83, 86, 89, 91, 92, 93, 94, 95, 96, 97, 98, 99, 100, 101, 103, 117, 118, 120, 122, 125, 126, 127, 128, 129, 131, 135, 136, 142, 143, 144, 149, 150, 156, 160, 161, 162, 163, 165, 170, 172, 237, 238, 239, 240, 241, 246,

248, 249, 252, 253, 258, 260, 263, 266, 269, 280, 288, 292, 293, 297, 298, 299, 300, 306, 309, 310, 311, 312, 313, 314, 315, 321, 324, 325, 326, 328, 329. *See also* audience(s)

redundancy, xii, 2, 10, 54, 61–69, 111, 118, 130, 131, 141, 142, 155, 164, 200, 223, 224, 226, 227, 228, 229, 230, 232, 234, 235, 236, 238, 241, 242, 244, 247, 251, 256, 257, 258, 264, 269, 280, 283, 284, 285, 286, 287, 289, 296, 304, 306, 307, 308, 309, 310, 313, 317, 321

repetition. *See* redundancy

report(s), vi, xiii, 7, 15, 18, 24, 25, 45, 54, 62, 64, 68, 72, 88, 92, 97, 98, 100, 108, 112, 117, 118, 123, 130, 131, 134, 141, 144, 150, 155, 157, 158, 169, 174, 204, 207, 208, 209, 218, 234, 240, 244, 246, 260, 266, 271, 273, 285, 295, 305, 313, 316, 327, 328, 342

resume(s), xi, xii, xiii, 17, 29, 64, 93, 94, 95, 98, 99, 100, 113, 126, 129, 130, 131, 138, 153–166, 167, 169, 185, 228, 229, 238, 240, 246, 248, 250, 284, 290, 291, 297, 301, 302, 303, 310, 311, 312, 313, 314, 326

revise (revising, revision), xii, 1, 2, 10, 34, 45, 54, 56, 61, 62, 64, 82, 85, 91, 97, 103, 110, 112, 118, 119, 120, 121, 122, 130, 132, 135–146, 164, 176, 228, 233, 241, 242, 246, 250, 251, 265, 289, 291, 292, 303, 304, 310, 317, 320, 322, 325, 326, 342, 343

Index

S

scholarship(s), 23, 51, 187

sculpting, word. *See* word sculpting

semicolon(s), xiii, 75, 222, 231, 243, 250, 321, 329–337, 343. *See also* punctuation

sentence(s). *See also* opening; tether(s)

  complex, 303, 331

  complex-compound, 330, 331

  compound, 330

  fragment(s), xii, 310, 321

  periodic, 71–79, 118, 121, 132, 226, 232, 233, 234, 241, 290, 291, 304, 309, 316. *See also* "cart before the horse"

  simple, 330

signposts, 34

similes, 128

spelling, 92, 103, 125, 138, 139, 192, 193, 233, 318, 339, 342, 345

statistics, xi, 26, 27, 28, 95, 123, 127, 130, 166, 176, 177, 190, 214, 254, 255, 256, 270, 275, 300, 306

subject, xii, xiii, xiv, 11, 20, 36, 37, 43, 44, 46, 48, 54, 66, 71, 73, 74, 75, 76, 83, 85, 86, 117, 120, 121, 127, 132, 137, 160, 163, 176, 177, 178, 179, 190, 221, 226, 231, 244, 245, 246, 256, 280, 282, 288, 289, 292, 296, 297, 306, 307, 309, 316, 322, 329, 330, 331, 332, 333

  and verb agreement, 163, 226, 245

T

tether(s) (sentence construction), xii, 10, 107–115, 130, 141, 164, 242, 259, 261, 263, 300, 301, 302, 303, 304, 305

there is/there are, 43, 83 280

titles

  of people, 24, 101, 184, 237, 334

  of works, xi, 19, 20, 21, 22, 68, 137, 152, 172, 179, 192, 193, 221, 241, 285, 289, 291, 315, 317, 318, 324, 327, 338, 339

U

useless words. *See* words, useless

V

verbs

  hidden, 43, 61, 82, 85, 112, 222, 224, 225, 226, 231, 235, 262, 265, 294, 295, 301

  subject-verb agreement, 163, 226, 245

  tense, 67, 137, 141, 155, 156, 228, 230, 250, 251, 253, 279, 296

  vague, 83, 142, 161

W

web pages, 5, 51, 72, 169, 178, 184, 198, 203, 209, 211, 224, 232, 245, 249, 350

word sculpting, ix, xi, xii, 1, 2, 5, 6, 9, 10, 13, 21, 41–146, 150, 152, 153, 170, 180, 187, 191, 193, 229, 247, 269, 270, 274, 310, 313, 324, 326, 328 words

    inferred, 61, 285

    powerful, iii, iv, xiii, 3, 11, 41, 42, 109, 187, 325, 349

    precise, 53, 82–83, 172, 186, 250, 251, 256, 319, 324

    short. *See* writing, concise

    useless, xii, 2, 10, 43–50, 55, 56, 73, 75, 76, 83, 84, 85, 98, 118, 144, 221, 222, 224, 226, 227, 228, 235, 236, 237, 241, 243, 244, 257, 269, 280, 281, 285, 286, 287, 288, 290, 294, 295, 296, 297, 302, 304, 307, 308, 310, 313, 315, 319, 325, 326

writing

    bureaucratic, 9, 81, 82, 95, 112, 117, 120, 137, 174, 226, 227, 243, 245, 297, 321, 343

    clarity, iv, 76, 97, 142, 174, 307, 311

    concise, v, vi, xi, 41, 98, 173, 180, 182, 186, 187, 275, 325, 327

    distract(ing), 27, 97, 125, 126, 127, 135, 138, 140, 156, 193, 194, 248, 250, 253, 310, 320, 321, 328

focus, v, x, xiv, 2, 4, 7, 12, 26, 27, 37, 46, 47, 51, 62, 81, 84, 92, 112, 113, 114, 117, 125–134, 138, 146, 150, 160, 161, 185, 186, 190, 191, 264, 265, 276, 282, 283, 302, 308, 310, 313, 319, 324, 326, 343

lengthy, 6, 34, 71, 73, 75, 91, 92, 137, 149, 152, 154, 165, 182, 223, 226, 234, 239, 250, 262, 276, 282, 292, 313, 327

objectively, 36–37, 136

persuasive, xiii, xiv, 4, 6, 37, 90

powerful, iii, iv, xiii, 3, 11, 41, 42, 109, 187, 325, 349

precise, 53, 82–83, 172, 186, 250, 251, 256, 319, 324

strategies, v, xi, xii, 1, 3, 4, 5–39, 109, 153, 170, 180, 187, 189, 191, 326, 328, 343

vague, 6, 25, 83, 98, 103, 137, 142, 161, 307, 310